CRATER'S EDGE

CRATER'S EDGE

Michał Giedroyć

with a preface by Norman Davies

Bene Factum Publishing
LONDON

Crater's Edge
A family's epic journey through wartime Russia

First published in 2010 by
Bene Factum Publishing Ltd
P O Box 58122
London sw8 5wz

Email: inquiries@bene-factum.co.uk
www.bene-factum.co.uk

ISBN: 978-1-903071-24-3

Text © Michał Giedroyć
Maps © John Gilkes

Design and typesetting by Simon Rendall
Cover design by Fielding Design Ltd
Printed and bound by Clays Ltd
St Ives plc, Suffolk UK

For my Parents

Contents

[vii]

Preface

Seventy years after the Second World War numerous wartime memoirs
are being published. Many of them are written by people who saw only
a tiny corner of events; others by people who are unable to place their
experiences in the wider context, or who at the time were too young or
too isolated to understand what was happening. A large category of these
publications is the work of sons and daughters of veterans, who seek to
preserve the memory of their parents' or grandparents' ordeals, but who
do not themselves possess the authenticity of an eye-witness.

This memoir by Michał Giedroyć, therefore, is something rather
special. Though still a boy during the war years, he was old enough to
comprehend the brutal maltreatment of his family and to remember it
vividly. He embarked on an involuntary odyssey which took him far
beyond the Eastern Marches of Poland to the Middle East and the
Mediterranean, and eventually to Britain. And, as an accomplished historian, he is able to combine the concerns of a teenager with the reflec-
tions of a mature analyst. There are very few survivors of the War who
can match his breadth of knowledge, or produce an account of such
class.

Born into an aristocratic family in the district of Nowogródek, in
today's Belarus', Michał Giedroyć has been steeped all his life in the
affairs of the former Grand Duchy of Lithuania. His forbears were
princes. The late Jerzy Giedroyć, editor of the Parisian journal *Kultura*,
was his cousin and both were brought up in a lost pre-war world of
landed wealth and intellectual sophistication. Yet Michał shared the fate
of hundreds of thousands of deportees and refugees – penniless, homeless, underfed, half-frozen, and dumped in the wildernesses of various
foreign countries. His family were doubly discriminated against – as
Poles (whom Stalin (rightly) suspected of being less than enthusiastic
about the Soviet Union), and as landowners whom Communist theory
(unjustly) condemned as parasites and exploiters. First, they were
thrown off their land. Then, when the father was arrested, the family

was separated and finally pushed into wagons heading eastwards into the unknown. Michał, fortunately, was with his mother, a woman of great resource and courage. As the train chugged beneath the walls of the castle of Minsk they knew that their father and husband was imprisoned inside those walls and they could only hope that he would emerge alive.

The Polish Odyssey to Siberia in 1940-41, and thence to Persia, Iraq and Palestine, has been described several times in recent years. In itself, it is no longer one of the "sensations of history", which can be presented as a total revelation. Yet all readers will benefit greatly from Michał Giedroyć's approach. Britons and Americans, who have always been taught about one great wartime evil – the German Nazis – will learn that the western accounts of the war are extremely one-sided. Readers from Eastern Europe, and from Poland in particular, who were raised in the post-war era, will learn just how far the historical facts differ from the falsified version of history that was officially promoted before 1989.

Much of the book's charm and value however, is in the details. Michał Giedroyć has the skill to evoke the feelings of a watching child as his home is plundered, or to appreciate the ruses whereby his mother copes with hostile and predatory officials. One of the most fascinating episodes takes place in Persia where the children who could read and write were told to sit down and to compose their own biographies and those of their friends. Thousands of Polish children, many of them orphans, were evacuated from Siberia, all of them malnourished and deprived of proper schooling. The author has had the extraordinary good fortune to obtain that report written by and about himself in 1943, (preserved in the archives of the Hoover Institution), and to evaluate it with the eyes of a mature adult and scholar.

What the memoir omits of course is the sequel. It ends when Southampton harbour heaves into sight. Yet readers will be interested to know that the young Michał Giedroyć made good. He drew strength from the knowledge that he was lucky to be alive. He adapted well to his adopted country, learned the language very exactly, thrived in business, and settled down with his English wife to a model family life with four admirable children. He has also found time after early retirement to study the origins of mediaeval Lithuania (for which he has an obvious affinity), to publish books and articles, and to open his home generously to friends and colleagues. Nowadays an heir to mores long past, he and Rosy his wife can look back with pride and contentment at a long life built against the odds from such inauspicious beginnings. Theirs is a fireside, round which friends from all over the world can congregate with pleasure, soaking up the lessons of *savoir vivre* and *savoir survivre*.

Norman Davies

A guide to Polish pronunciation

ą – similar to French *on* as in *bon*

c – *ts* as in *its*

ć, ci, cz – *ch* as in *cheap*

dź, dż – *g* as in *gin*

ę – similar to French *in* as in *fin*

g – as in *go*

j – *y* as in *young*

Ł, ł – *w* as in *wet*; traditionally pronounced *ll* as in *ill*

ń – *n* as in *new*

ó – *oo* as in *tool*

rz – like *s* in *measure*

ś, sz – *sh* as in *she*

w – *v* as in *vest*

ź, ż - like *s* in *measure*

With thanks to Gerald Stone, whose *Introduction to Polish* (Bristol Classical Press, 1992) provides a much more thorough guide.

CHAPTER 1

Peril

August of 1939 ran its course. City guests were gone; the harvest was brought in. After a busy summer, my mother returned to what she loved best, her orchards and beehives, bravely enduring stings and swollen eyes. My father was well again after his summer holiday, sunburnt and lean. He shaved off his beard, and tried to restore a passable growth of hair to his shorn head.

My elder sister Anuśka was banished to the furthest guest-room, known as *norka* (little burrow), to study away from distractions. She had to retake her first-year university exams, which she had failed two months earlier in the wake of the Warsaw season. Anuśka kept the window wide open onto the park, and through that window, one morning, an owl flew in looking for a quiet corner after a night's hunting. My sister welcomed company, and the owl took up residence on a tall stove. *Norka* thus became a shared refuge, and my father, ever an optimist, saw in this an omen: the owl, symbol of lofty thought, encouraging a frivolous student. In fact, my elder sister seemed not to apply herself all that strenuously. Her relaxed routine matched the unhurried lifestyle of the owl. The atmosphere of *norka* was in harmony with the hot summer outside.

My sister Tereska had just passed her *matura* (baccalaureate) examination. At the age of seventeen this was something of an achievement, which my parents decided to reward by letting her enter the Warsaw Higher School of Journalism. That dream was to be fulfilled in September, which she awaited in a state of euphoria. In the meantime she spent every spare moment in the saddle, as if to reassure her temperamental gelding, Breeze, that parting would be temporary. The atmosphere in the stables was emotional.

I too was about to enter the World. My father decreed that for one year I was to attend 'the best' private day school in Warsaw, called, somewhat pretentiously, 'The Future'. That was to be followed by the First Cadet Corps at Lwów. My father formed a view that I was in need of discipline dispensed by men; and for this the Lwów military school was renowned. I welcomed these plans. The glamour of the capital, and the prospect of military glory (the First Corps was the school of my dreams) outweighed any doubts I may have had regarding army discipline.

The manor and its two home farms – the small world around me – continued its peaceful and self-centred existence. There was talk of war, of course, and we knew that our local cavalry brigade, commanded by a young major-general called Władysław Anders, had already been deployed near the East Prussian border. We had caught glimpses of his mounted squadrons during recent manoeuvres; we believed them invincible. Twenty years earlier, in the Polish-Soviet War, men like Anders had defeated Lenin's Red Army. I failed to notice how concerned my father (an experienced staff officer) was becoming. The large map of Europe – a new addition to his office – was peppered with pins and arrows pointing towards Warsaw from the north, west and south. Soon after, our German governess, Fräulein Marie Schmidt, was sent back to Berlin. The fruit contractors – also German – quietly disappeared. Mlle Félicité, the French governess, left for home. In the dying days of that August, mounted messengers began making frequent trips to the local post office: my father was anxiously awaiting instructions from Warsaw.

And I, surrounded by all these events, remained casually oblivious to their significance. Instead, I was absorbed by my new role as my father's companion on his rounds of inspection. This was a rite of passage: the shedding of women and nursery in favour of a public presence alongside my father. In the parlance of the home farms and the villages, I was assuming the position of 'Young Master' (*Panicz* in Polish) at the elbow of my father. I remember how carefully he watched me during these outings. At the time I assumed that he was checking my horsemanship. It occurs to me now that on the eve of the storm he suddenly became concerned for my capacity to grow up unaided.

On 1st September, in glorious late summer weather, German Panzers rolled into Poland. The wireless reported indiscriminate bombing of civilian targets. Even before the violation of the Polish frontier, General

Werner von Richthofen of the Luftwaffe ordered his dive-bombers to strike at Wieluń, a small border town of no importance. For the general on the other hand, the foray itself was of the greatest importance: he had just launched the definitive test-flight, with a live target, for his latest Stukas. The Luftwaffe flattened the town's school and cottage hospital, and virtually everything else. On that September morning Wieluń assumed its place in history alongside Guernica. The Polish regular army was denied its reserves because in the dying days of peace Poland's Western Allies repeatedly asked the Polish Government to delay general mobilisation – until it was too late. My father's summons did not reach him either: Łobzów, in the depth of the Eastern Marches, was beyond the reach of a communication system stretched to the limit.

1st September began in an orderly fashion. Early in the morning a police constable cycled over from Dereczyn to inquire about the whereabouts of Łobzów's Germans, the governess and the orchard contractors. Satisfied that they were no longer with us, he moved on. Later in the morning my mother decided to visit Dereczyn. I noted that the trip was unscheduled because it was a Friday, and my mother's weekly visit always took place on Tuesdays – market day. I asked permission to accompany her and we set off together in the *wolant* (our four-wheeled everyday carriage), with the coachman Kosowicc on the box wearing his summer *pudermantel* and peaked cap. We arrived at Mr Wieniacki's store to confront the familiar ritual: the owner stepping out to offer his guests chocolates on a silver salver. The only difference was that the store was unusually crowded. My mother swept in, chatted to friends and acquaintances, and then, quite deliberately, bought just two kilos of sugar. The crowd began to disperse, reassured that there was no need for panic buying. It was an impressive example of public relations, although perhaps it would have been more prudent not to discourage the housewives of Dereczyn from stocking their larders.

My father's increasingly desperate attempts to contact the Parliament offices in Wiejska Street remained fruitless. Over a tense luncheon he spoke of going off to his regiment. It was a pipe dream: he knew very well that senators were debarred from active service. What he could not have known was that this law was to be relaxed two days later, on 3rd September. So he did what the best of Napolcon's marshals would have done in the circumstances: he decided to 'march towards the sound of the guns'. On that same 3rd September the coachman Kosowiec took him, this time in the shining victoria (our formal carriage), to the railway station. At Zelwa my father began his race against German armour towards Warsaw.

My mother, quietly resolute, was left behind in charge of Łobzów. The news from the front was bad, but I for one remained unaffected, since there were no dramatic symptoms of conflict around me. My mother, ever sanguine, insisted that intervention by France and England was imminent. Her confidence was reassuring to our agent Mr Dąbrowski and his staff. The manor and its home farms, away from the battlefield and major highways or railroads, continued its uninterrupted routine.

There was, in fact, an early meeting with the enemy, but it turned out to be innocent. My mother was doing the rounds of her beehives and orchards when she heard the sound of a low-flying aeroplane. As it swept past her, she – quite certain that it was one of ours – waved at the pilot, and he waved back. Then my mother saw on the fuselage a black cross. Marteczka, my nanny, was furious, and for the first time I heard her scold her mistress: 'You really should try to be more careful!'

It must have been a reconnaissance aircraft, because soon afterwards we heard the sound of distant bombs. Later we were told that the bridge on the river Niemen, some 30 kilometres away, was destroyed. On that cloudless afternoon people looked to the sky; and, sure enough, a flight droned overhead at high altitude, dropping one single bomb on Dereczyn. Our church spire was the marker, obviously, because the bomb exploded nearby. A largish crater marked the spot. Mercifully there were no casualties.

The war had arrived on our doorstep. Yet still there was no news from Warsaw. My mother placed the victoria at the railway station on permanent stand-by, and, as we waited, tension began to mount.

One morning – it was, I think, 12th September – I was told that my father had returned in the early hours, and that we should be quiet because he was resting. When eventually he emerged, he still looked tired. And, surprisingly, the great raconteur was silent. My mother did manage to winkle out of him a few details and these I now put together to reconstruct what had happened. At Zelwa (our railway station) he was told that the direct line to Warsaw had already been disrupted. He was advised to take a roundabout route via Brest (Brześć), a good 150 kilometres due south-west. When he eventually arrived there, he noticed long anonymous trains in the sidings. He was told (in whispers) that this was the first wave of evacuation, involving the senior echelons of government. My father should perhaps have turned round at Brest, but he did not; he decided to go against the current, hopeful that instructions might still be awaiting him in the capital.

He reached Warsaw on the 6th and found the Senate chamber, corridors, and offices deserted; Parliament had left the capital the day before. The city under air bombardment was blacked out, public transport was overcrowded, telephones more often than not dead, and all the railway stations besieged by refugees. The next day my father decided to turn around and go eastwards: the state administration was already there – and also his wife and children. Going against the current was hard enough; joining the exodus became a nightmare. Roads and railways were virtually grid-locked, and along these my father picked his way, first by car and later – when there was no more petrol – by train, cart, and on foot. He did not want to talk about this part of his journey. All he said was that he was surrounded by 'fire and blood'. The Luftwaffe saw to that. German armour took up its positions on the approaches to Warsaw on the 8th.

During the next five days a strange, tense silence descended on Łobzów. Except, that is, for one interruption, which happened soon after my father's return. At lunch – still an orderly affair with servants and restrained conversation – we were disturbed by the sound of an aeroplane. By then there were few, if any, Polish aircraft flying, and my father's instinctive reaction was to order all of us to gather tightly around the doorway between the dining room and the big drawing room. Which was all that he could do. The sound became a roar – and then it faded away. No violence was done on this occasion. We all returned to the table. Life went back to 'normal': the farming routines continued and the sky remained cloudless.

My father stayed glued to the wireless, and when the batteries went dead he began taking frequent walks to the village to listen to the wireless of Mr Stećko, the school-teacher. I went with him, and I soon discovered that the two men were now listening to Moscow, not Warsaw or Berlin. The Russian word *neitralitet* (neutrality) came over the airwaves more than once. On 17th September the Soviet radio announced that the Red Army had crossed the border of the Polish Republic. A second invasion of our country had begun.

Łobzów manor, an outpost of the old order, now found itself in no-man's-land between two enemies: in the west the Germans, and in the east the Red Army. Law and order, in force as long as the Polish Army fought its defensive campaign against the Wehrmacht, suddenly collapsed. All now depended on the reaction of the local communities: our two Belarus'ian villages of Łobzów and Kotczyn, and the ethnically mixed township of Dereczyn. My father looked to them for signals.

Word came almost immediately from the local 'committees' that they would be willing to discuss interim arrangements with the 'Master-Heir'. The committees were a spontaneous response to danger. They were concerned with immediate security, but they also sensed opportunities for land redistribution.

These early contacts between the manor and the committees were not hostile, or even tense. Our villages remembered my father as a useful neighbour and, perhaps even more importantly, as a just and sympathetic local magistrate. The members of the committees, at this stage all of them village elders, were well known to my parents, and some of them were on friendly terms with the manor. Through them arrangements were made for a meeting in Dereczyn, to which my father intended to take the whole family in case it was decided to stay in Dereczyn, or even move to Słonim, a town some thirty-five kilometres to the east.

On this same 17th day of September, quite early in the morning, a yellow cabriolet, pulled by a handsome pair of greys, came up the front drive. In it sat a mustachioed old gentleman accompanied by two young women and a large, *soigné*-looking bulldog. In an automatic reaction reminiscent of the Conciergerie under the Terror, my parents formally received their guests in the porch – with the committee members at a discreet distance. The guests were the Staszewskis, a gentleman and his two nieces, Zosia and Margot, from the Hniezna estate near Wołkowysk, about forty kilometres to the west. My parents did not know them, but knew of them. The girls looked extremely sophisticated and my younger sister Tereska – aged seventeen and still under wraps – eyed them with some envy. They were escaping from the approaching Germans – straight into the open arms of the Soviets…. The committee received our guests with reservation, and – since there was a danger that criminal gangs might approach from further afield – they asked my father to take the Staszewskis with us to Dereczyn.

The meeting with the committees began in the early afternoon of the 18th, across the table in the mayor's office. I remember it well because we were all present. The meeting was long, and to me boring. I did not know that around that table arrangements were being made for the next two or three days; those two or three days, that today seem to me the most dangerous days of our lives. The committees told my father that within our commune of Dereczyn he and his family were safe. They could not however guarantee our safety further afield, and for that reason they advised against the journey to Słonim. The decision was taken that the Giedroyćes (and their guests) return to the manor. My father closed the meeting with a statement that a new order was about to arrive, and that 'our' two villages should immediately assume the role of stewards of the manor's assets, in this way asserting their claim to the home farms in the face of the Soviet authorities. It was a calm and pragmatic acceptance of the inevitable, and at the same time a hint of what a post-Soviet future might ultimately hold for the smallholders of Łobzów and Kotczyn. The priceless gift of safety, however brittle and short-lived, was repaid with far-sighted advice.

Staszewski was asked to surrender his gun, but my father was allowed to keep his. Late at night we arrived back at the manor, where the children were put to bed fully dressed, and the adults – my parents, Staszewski and our 'minders' sent by the village of Łobzów – began their vigil. The night was not peaceful. A small detachment of the Polish Army, a dozen or so hungry and disoriented men with an officer, arrived on the doorstep. They had to be fed and comforted; and our Łobzów minders had to be reassured that no plans were being hatched behind their backs towards restoration of the old social order. Eventually the soldiers took to the road, having been told by my father that the enclave they were leaving behind was at peace with itself, for the time being at least.

Tuesday the 19th was quiet. The presence of the committee was reassuring, and a feeling of shared danger strengthened the bond between the minders and the minded. There were even some laughs, as when my mother suggested that in anticipation of the arrival of the Soviet authorities she should make up some red armbands for the committee members. The offer was readily accepted. And it proved timely, because late that night a Soviet reconnaissance patrol knocked on our front door.

It was obviously an elite detachment, led by a polite and very professional officer. At supper, to which he was invited, he showed me his heavy *nagan* (Russian-style revolver), and to my father he revealed his detailed map with instructions how to find the home of Senator Giedroyć. The patrol departed quietly, and then my sister Tereska and I hatched the stupidest plot imaginable. We decided to bury several bottles of our favourite cherry syrup at the far corner of the park, because we did not wish the newcomers to steal this treasured delicacy. The deed was done as the sky darkened, the wind rose, and the trees of the park became agitated. This silly piece of conspiracy was almost certainly noticed by the minders; they kept their counsel, but would not have been amused.

Another tense night followed. During that night – my last at Łobzów, on a sofa, fully dressed – the committee was suddenly alerted that a criminal gang from further afield was approaching the manor to take revenge on the 'enemies of the people'. The villagers of Łobzów immediately came over in force, confronted the intruders at the back entrance to the park, and chased them away. The lives of the Giedroyćes (and of the Staszewskis) – the Polish-speaking representatives of the old order – were saved by the Łobzów villagers in the name of friendship, which had taken root over the preceding thirteen years.

As the dawn of Wednesday 20th September broke, the winds subsided. In the early hours of a wet and still morning Soviet armoured vehicles violated our front lawn. On it, opposite my window, a small silver fir had been planted by the gardener 'in better times', in my honour I suppose. That morning I watched a Soviet tank maliciously drive straight over it. From behind the tanks emerged a carload of officers in blue caps, accompanied by one or two young local activists unknown to my parents. Huddled together in the small drawing room, we watched a contingent of NKVD (the Soviet security police, forerunners of the KGB) come up to the front door. In the entrance hall the Staszewski bulldog growled at the intruders. This was followed by a single shot. The hall obviously had good acoustics, because the report was deafening. The dog died instantly. The party then came through the door to confront my father, who moved to the centre of the room; as if to draw their fire. One of the men said, in an aside, that in the Soviet Union lead was plentiful. It was an in-joke which created some NKVD-style merriment. Its sinister undertone was lost on me. The senior man in an ankle-length *burka* then squared up to my father and said, '*Fadei Ivanovich Gedroits – ruki vverkh!*' (Hands up). He knew the patronymic, and this impressed me. My father was disarmed, searched, and then closely questioned, with some prompting from local informers, about the Łobzów arms cache. There was none, of course, and he said so. He was backed in this by the Łobzów committee, who joined my father in inviting the NKVD to search the house and grounds. And then the penny dropped: the fleeting visit of the Polish Army detachment was obviously linked in the mind of an informer with the nocturnal disposal of the cherry syrup.

The beginning of the search coincided with the formal arrest of my father. The procedure was coldly correct. No charge was made, and he was handed over to a Red Army – not NKVD – officer, who conducted him to a waiting motor with an armed escort. My mother waved from the porch and I noticed that she was trembling, but not crying. She did not know where they were taking him.

In the meantime the search was pursued. I noticed the soldiers taking away all the photograph albums; there were many of them. The whole experience was entirely new to me, and I observed it with fascination.

My sisters and I became objects of unconcealed interest to the intruders. We sat on a sofa in my sisters' quarters like prize exhibits, stared at by a succession of armed men smelling of leather and cheap eau-de-cologne. I noticed in the audience one or two women in uniform. The observers were coldly curious. Only one smiled, displaying several steel teeth.

After a while I ventured away from the sofa and mingled with the searchers. I noticed two or three women – wives of our farm-hands – sneaking out through a back door with bundles of bed linen. These were the only cases of plunder by our own employees; the minders saw to that. And the villagers of Łobzów behaved impeccably. The only concession to the new order was a red flag which I noticed on one of the outbuildings. I would like to think that it was hoisted in a spirit that matched the issue of the red arm-bands.

We were told later of one inexplicable act of vandalism which took place during that morning. The coachman Kosowiec, my father's favourite, went berserk and began hacking at a beloved avenue of hornbeams with an axe. He was restrained by the minders before any serious damage was done. Whether it was an act of hate or of despair, I shall never know. I hope that it was despair.

Meanwhile the home farm was systematically plundered by the Red Army. The pig farm was subjected to wholesale slaughter, conducted by amateurs because the noise of wounded animals was shrill and continuous – an aural background to the 'requisition' of our best horses. These were paraded before the senior officers standing in the porch. Lalka (Dolly), the beautiful and ill-tempered matriarch of all our half-bloods, was included among those to be taken away. We knew that she was too old to be of any use to the Red Army, and Tereska expressed a whispered hope that before her inevitable early demise Lalka would still manage a few of her famous bites and kicks. The greys from Hniezna were included in the haul. Soon after that we said good-bye to the Staszewskis, who – unmolested – were allowed to begin their homeward trek on foot.

Less than an hour after my father's arrest, the Red Army officer who had taken him away returned. My mother rushed towards him and he handed her a scrap of paper. On it, in pencil, was a handwritten message from her husband. This small bluish-grey piece of paper I have here beside me:

> *Dearest Anuleczko!*
> *Please give to the bearer of this message your wrist watch.*

*He is asking for this, and he will pay twenty zlotys. The bearer
is a kind man. I embrace you most tenderly.
Your Tadeusz
20/9/39, Dereczyn*

I noticed that the man bearing the message had kind eyes; he looked
at my mother with concern. Twenty zlotys was a token sum. The
message was a confirmation of my father's safe arrival in Dereczyn, and
the 'watch transaction' a means of saying thank you to the escort for his
life thus far. It was also a formula which took note of the *amour propre*
of this decent soldier.

At this point my mother panicked. Torn between the conflicting
claims of children and husband, she saw the children effectively ignored
in the chaos of a house search, but her husband, alone in Dereczyn,
facing danger – perhaps death? – at the hands of the enemy secret police.
She said that she would go to Dereczyn. 'Going' meant walking across
wet fields for over three kilometres. The enterprise was extremely
dangerous because our friendly committees controlled the villages, but
not the stretches between them. Nanny Marteczka without hesitation
volunteered to go with her. After moving us three to the agent's quarters
in the annexe, the two women set out along the causeway towards the
fields.

In the annexe I noticed that Mr Dąbrowski, the agent, was no longer
to be seen. Later we learned that he had managed to get away to his own
house in Dereczyn. Mrs Dąbrowska stayed behind with her children,
and she now took charge of the three Giedroyćes. Almost immediately
a Soviet officer – an NKVD man? – burst in. Finding us there he pulled
out his revolver, pointed it at me and began yelling, *'Ya etogo shchenka
ub'yu'* (I will kill this puppy). I do not recall any sensation of terror. And,
presumably for that reason, I remember exactly what the man looked
like. Out of a dark face a pair of burning eyes stared straight at me. They
belonged to a tall man in regulation leather. And I, unaware of danger,
looked placidly into the barrel of his gun. To this day, as a delayed
reaction I suppose, I cannot stand black leather coats; or even black
leather jackets.

Mrs Dąbrowska bravely intervened in an attempt to calm the man down. Eventually he put the gun away, and summoned an armed escort. An order was issued that we were to be taken to the furthest outbuilding of the estate. We were now in the hands of the enemy, represented by the hysterical *komandir* and his three men, bayonets at the ready. In a dark and empty room, at the furthest corner of the home farm, the escort robbed us of our wrist watches. It was a neat coincidence: three watches and three of them. I will never know what further instructions the trigger-happy officer had given to the soldiers, because immediately afterwards a new threesome of armed men arrived on the scene. This time they were civilians equipped with my father's hunting guns, and sporting my mother's red armbands. We recognised our minders. They told the Soviet escort that they were ordered to deliver the young Giedroyćes to Dereczyn gaol. And under the protection of what I am now convinced was a rescue party, we set off on foot towards our next destination.

It was late afternoon. On the little white bridge down the causeway, we met my mother and Marteczka rushing back from Dereczyn to rejoin us. We learned that my father was alive – and 'safe' – in Dereczyn gaol. My mother, having told Nanny to go back to Łobzów, now claimed her right to join her children. And so the four of us set off along the road that led to our father. For my mother it was her third march of the day between the manor and the town. Alongside a potato field I asked to stop for a moment. Permission was granted, and I was able to relieve myself. In this earthy manner the Young Master and his inheritance said farewell to one another.

Later in the afternoon the reunion of the family took place in Dereczyn gaol. To my mother, dead tired and almost joyful, 'a happy end to a long day'. Thus ended Wednesday 20th September 1939. To me, sixty-nine years on, my Longest Day.

CHAPTER 2

Łobzów

The neighbouring estates of Kotczyn and Łobzów had been given to my parents by a pair of maiden aunts, Helena and Marynia Połubiński, in 1926. They had inherited the properties at the end of the 19th century: two manor houses with farms, a total of between 5,000 and 6,000 acres with forest, pasture and arable land, all in a sorry condition. During the First World War the estates had suffered further damage. The manor of Kotczyn was destroyed by fire, leaving only the chapel and one substantial outbuilding. Further decline was accelerated by mismanagement under two corrupt administrators in succession. They devastated the forests and exploited the home farms for their own gain.

In the early 1920s, after the Polish-Soviet war, ruin was imminent: Łobzów manor had been allowed to deteriorate almost beyond economic repair; the farms and outbuildings were dilapidated, the livestock was depleted, and the estate burdened with debts beyond the repayment capacity of the enterprise. In effect, Helena and Marynia Połubiński were facing bankruptcy, unable to honour even the backlog of unpaid wages owed to the two neighbouring villages.

At this critical juncture the sisters turned to my parents with an offer. The Giedroyćes would succeed to Łobzów and Kotczyn as joint heirs on the understanding that they would do their utmost to rescue as much as was practicable.

When my parents' engagement was announced in 1919, Aunts Hela and Marynia had said in unison: 'Tadzio has found a pearl!' *(Tadzio perlę wziął)*. The comment went beyond her personal qualities: the Aunts knew Ania's *curriculum vitae*. They also knew of Tadzio's record as a gifted administrator, a lawyer of quality, but above all else a man capable of calculated risk-taking. Neither did his wide contacts in the nascent Polish administration pass unnoticed. The young couple seemed ideal for the daunting task envisaged for them.

Acceptance of the inheritance was by no means a foregone conclusion. The difficulties were enormous, as were the risks. And yet, after lengthy heart-searching, Tadzio and Ania decided to take it on. My mother often spoke to me about this turning point in their lives, and the reasons for their decision. At the most elementary level, the new owners were securing for themselves and their children a style of life which was then highly valued. At the same time they were well aware of the social and political role which a landed estate could play in an area reduced to subsistence not only by war and the backwardness of Imperial Russia, but also by the earlier irresponsibility of the Polish-Lithuanian landowning class. In economic terms, the role amounted to the contribution that a larger agricultural unit, run efficiently, could make to the regeneration of a backward agriculture based almost entirely on smallholdings. Last but not least came the responsibility towards the historical heritage. Łobzów was a fine manor house of architectural significance; it still held an important archive, a collection of good family portraits, the magnificent Połubiński silver and much besides. In short, the decision to accept Łobzów with all its problems amounted to an intention to play a constructive role.

The estate no longer had forests. I assume that they had not been sold but taken over by the Polish State, because Tadzio soon began preparing the case for reclaiming them. In the meantime this loss relieved the pressure on capital requirements. The entire project depended above all else on Tadzio's personal credit-worthiness, and to a lesser extent on the sale of some farm land. The combined effect of my father's reputation, his personal earning capacity, and the funds realized from the sale ensured the feasibility of the operation. The new stewardship was inaugurated with the repayment of all outstanding wages, which immediately created much goodwill among the manor's neighbours.

Łobzów was chosen as the main residence, and the grounds of Kotczyn manor were sold off; in effect, Kotczyn was reduced to the status of a satellite home farm. The Łobzów home farm was to be the centre of operations, designated for mixed farming best suited to the quality of soil, geography and climate. Horses were chosen as the main source of pulling power, to be matched by the best available farm machinery. Deliberate overcapacity of machinery suggests that the needs of the neighbouring villages, starved of purchasing power, would be taken into account.

A major programme of out-building construction was launched, based on local materials: stone and timber. The layout of the farm buildings was carefully planned, with emphasis on amenities such as paved sidewalks and sanitation. The building programme was accompanied by recruitment of staff and farm labour, a phased introduction of horses and other livestock, and – lastly – the long and demanding restoration of the manor house itself.

When they arrived in 1926, Tadzio and Ania came up against the feudal ways of the backwoods. There was much servile deference about the place, including the kissing of the master's hand, the strict observance of the old modes of address (*Księżna Pani,* or 'Princess Ma'am'), the parish priest to be robed and waiting for the manor contingent before Sunday Mass could begin, and so on. My late friend Jaś Zdański told me that his father – a typical nineteenth century squire – would sit at Mass inside the confessional, from where audible snoring would be heard during the sermon, followed by grunts associated with awakening, and then an imperious 'What?' – at which the preacher would quickly deliver a précis of what he had said so far. As to deference, Jaś reminisced how his own factor would say, 'I beg your pardon,' every time he, Jaś, stumbled on a stone or on uneven ground in the course of their walks of inspection. Jaś was susceptible to frequent stumbling.

I hasten to add that at Łobzów in 1926 the Połubiński ways were less outrageous. And there was a humorous side to these quaint customs, as when a prescription was issued by the Dereczyn chemist to one of my aunts: 'These pills are to be placed on the Serene Tongue, and then swallowed...'

My parents were open-minded liberals, keen to dispense with the old conventions; but they had also to address urgently the atmosphere of mistrust surrounding the manor. This was far more difficult. My parents knew that deeds, not words, would count; and that they would be carefully watched by the villagers for genuine dedication and constancy.

The manor house of Łobzów was a traditional 18th century design, built of timber on stone foundations which had originally supported a castle.

The house was long and low, with a steep roof and an elegant porch at the main entrance. The horizontal design was practical and good-looking, adhering to the principle that the height of the house should be compatible with the height of the surrounding trees. The windows were generous and well proportioned. Mercifully, the manor had escaped attempts at extensions or improvements of the do-it-yourself kind. It came to us in its handsome simplicity.

The roof was covered with pine shingles, and the walls with vertical narrow wooden boards tightly fitted to ensure waterproofing. Brick was employed for fireplaces and chimneys.

Originally there were four large reception rooms, but one of these was put aside in the late 1920s for the use of my two sisters. Of the remaining three, all connecting with the spacious entrance hall, one was the principal drawing room leading through French windows to the terrace, the second was the smaller ('blue') drawing room, and the third the dining room, complete with massive open fireplace. All these rooms had plain parquet flooring.

Adjacent to the dining room was the pantry (also used for informal dining), and beyond it the kitchen with access to larders and cellars. At the other end of the house was the bakery, a room fitted with a brick stove exclusively for bread-making and occupying most of the floor area. The remaining nine rooms were used as bedrooms.

The house was heated by stoves burning peat and timber from the estate. There was no electricity, and its wireless set depended on batteries. The telephone in Dereczyn's post office my father declared as sufficient, although in this respect he found himself in a minority of one.

There were two exotic additional features. One was a complete second set of windows, installed every autumn and taken out every spring – an operation that required much planning and skilled manpower. The other was the water barrel. This was huge and had its own horse-drawn two-wheeled undercarriage. The sole function of this contraption was to supply the big house with all the water it needed.

Łobzów had its own private chapel, contemporary to the main house and built in the same 18th century neoclassical style. It was situated at the far end of the park and did not survive the rescue operation. The cost of its renovation would have been beyond Łobzów's resources. In any case my parents thought it proper to integrate the household into the parish life of Dereczyn. When the chapel was dismantled, its liturgical contents (chalices, vestments, etc.) were donated to the nearby parish of Skrundzie which had historical links with the Kotczyn-Łobzów demesne.

The furniture of the manor, and its book collection, had suffered serious damage during the First World War. My parents began restocking the library soon after 1926, and by the late 1930s it was already useful, although still modest. The restoration of the furniture was pursued with greater vigour. Those pieces that had escaped destruction were used as models by the manor's resident carpenter, who was persuaded to try to reconstruct the sets. Łobzów was in luck: he revealed himself to be an exceptionally gifted cabinet maker. For the upholstery my mother asked local weavers to create traditional patterns known as *radziuszki*, for which the villages around Dereczyn, and particularly the village of Aleksicze, were well known. These tartan-like linen products soon graced the restored manor furniture. The fame of our *radziuszki* was spread far and wide by visitors to Łobzów.

The front porch of the house faced a huge heart-shaped lawn with a sand-and gravel drive around it; my father's strict instruction was that this must be used anticlockwise, to avoid traffic accidents. In view of the easy pace of our existence these seemed unlikely, and my father's bylaw earned him some gentle teasing.

The open space in front of the house had a recent – and controversial – origin. When my parents inherited Łobzów, it came with a dense and unkempt jungle of magnificent trees encroaching onto the porch and scratching at the windows. My mother declared that she could not co-exist with this. In pursuit of air, sunshine and a vista, she ordered the trees to be felled. The deed was done, but the resident Połubiński aunts, who had grown up in this undergrowth, reacted with a peaceful protest: they hung muslin curtains in their windows.

In fact, my mother did make a small concession to the Połubiński susceptibilities by reprieving a splendid old ash near the porch. But the concession concentrated the aunts' attention on the survivor of the massacre, and made matters worse. To the end of their lives Aunt Hela and Aunt Marynia mourned the companions of their childhood.

The park at the back of the house had a handsome double set of avenues, laid out in a broad U-shape at the turn of the 18th-19th centuries in the 'classical Polish-Lithuanian style'. Hornbeam was the favoured tree in those parts, and the Łobzów avenues contained between 150 and 200 of them, planted densely to give a tunnel effect. The hornbeam is a lovable tree, particularly when constrained into a slender form. Its leaves are almost transparent, and the light-green foliage contrasts dramatically with the dark trunk. The leaves tremble in the slightest breeze, making the tree appear vulnerable. The lowest branches of a mature hornbeam are particularly decorative because they seek to lay themselves in a graceful recline near, or even on, the ground.

The Łobzów hornbeams were loved in equal measure by my parents and the gardener Juleczek (Julius). But a difference arose as to how to present them to their best advantage. Juleczek, keen on clean-cut order, decided (during my parents' absence) to cut off all those reclining lowest branches, 'for the sake of tidiness'. And so a hundred years of husbandry was brushed aside. My parents were distressed, but they could not be angry. Juleczek had came to us with Łobzów, and he was a faithful and hard-working gardener. My parents' devotion to the hornbeams became if anything fiercer – the kind of love reserved for beauty enhanced in the eye of the beholder by a shortcoming... And my mother, having taken in this instance the side of the trees, was atoning to some extent for her earlier exploits at the front of the house.

Several kinds of lilac and jasmine were encouraged on the front lawn and on both sides of the house. Banks of standard roses grew along the walls – their pink, yellow and creamy white blooms contrasting with the grey stone; there were long stretches of phlox in front and at the back; and a succession of various flowers, taking their turn around the roses, to fill the borders. Among them I remember snap-dragons and nicotiana, and others which I cannot name. The overall effect was exquisite.

My mother, for whom Łobzów was the antechapel to heaven, claimed that the place was exceptionally peaceful. In a sense it was, but at the same time it was far from quiet. In the background there was the continuous hum of the busy home farm, accompanied for much of the day by birdsong. The house was exposed to an extremely vigorous dawn chorus, repeated at lunch time as an encore, just before the performers retired for their afternoon siesta. By the early evening they were in full voice again.

Inside the house we were subjected to interminable scales, pounded out on the piano by my almost tone-deaf sisters. My father, who was very musical and a lover of opera, suffered this in silence, ever hopeful for future dividends. Relief came from resident crickets, established among the timber beams and frames in the vicinity of stoves. And the ultimate reward was provided by the nightingales, who gave a recital every evening. For me the summer evenings at Łobzów will remain inseparable from the song of a nightingale, and the scent of jasmine.

The manor houses of our region were highly self-sufficient, and Łobzów was no exception. This depended on access to the produce of the home farms and the kitchen gardens, which provided fruit and vegetables, dairy products, honey, meat, flour and so on. Łobzów had several fish ponds, but these still needed a thorough overhaul; their revival was thwarted by World War II. The provision of firewood, and peat discovered under one of the outlying pastures, was an enterprise shared by the manor and the farms. The estate had as yet no electricity, so food preservation depended on the services of the ice-house and the smoke-house.

These were efficient relics of an earlier era. Our ice-house was a semi-submerged cellar surrounded by an earth mound (a God-send to tobogganists), and covered with a well insulated roof. At the height of winter it was packed solid with large slabs of ice harvested from the nearby river. In the 1930s the Łobzów ice-house became the source of delicious ice-cream, created by our cook, Kasia Suprun, with the help of a manually operated rotary machine. The fame of Kasia's ice-cream travelled abroad with the home-bound governesses. The ice-house was large enough to cater for the whole year to both the manor and the home farm.

The smoke-house was more exclusive, serving mainly the manor. It was an unusual edifice in the shape of a stunted cone, placed in the far corner of the grounds. When active, it gave off deliciously aromatic fumes. A pair of storks used to nest on it every summer. These dignified creatures fascinated me and I tried hard to make friends with their young.

The storks kept their distance, but the friendship of a more exotic bird made up for their aloofness. The Łobzów fields had always been a staging post for migrating cranes. These would descend on us in huge numbers twice a year. As a rule they were even more unapproachable than the storks. But then, during one spring transit, a young bird damaged a wing while trying to take off and was left lying injured on the ground. My rescue party picked him up – he was immensely heavy – and the vet was summoned from Dereczyn to set the wing. In the meantime we began feeding the patient with frogs, of which there was an abundance. The crane responded with unquestioning friendship. This feeling he focused on me, guessing perhaps that I had initiated the rescue. Quite soon he began following me like a dog, flapping his good wing and noisily demanding more frogs. Feeding my new friend became a strenuous occupation.

This relationship continued until the flocks returned in the autumn. Żuraś (Polish for 'Craney') was torn between domestication and the urge to return to his kind. On the morning of the mass take-off he walked out on me and took to the air. His earth-bound friend was left behind trying to convince himself that Żuraś had done the right thing.

Animals played an important part in my life, as they did for all on the estate. My earliest memory is of a hot, sunny day, feeding the calves on the home farm. There were many of these, all identical in colour, a deep red. The person in charge of them was a young woman called Adela. She had black shining eyes and a mane of dark hair, and wore a flowery dress.

According to Marteczka I was moved to utter my first Polish sentence, *Adela poi cielęta*, which means 'Adela is feeding the calves'. The grammar of the sentence was correct and for that reason the women present declared it to be a literary sensation.

As I grew up I managed to penetrate the outer regions of the home farm. There I was befriended by several farm-hands, who treated me as an equal. This was a welcome contrast to the fussy attentions of women. My new friends allowed me to observe the ritualised and carefully controlled sex life of our livestock. I was overwhelmed by the vigour of these happenings, and by the sight of the enormous genitals not very far above my head. It was an early introduction to the 'facts of life' of the shock therapy kind, very different to the measured lessons in today's classrooms.

I well remember the arrival of two grey cuddly puppies, destined to become the ancestors of a fearsome pack of guard dogs. There were at least six of them at any one time. Much later it was explained to me that guard dogs were necessary during the twenties, and even the early thirties, in areas close to the Soviet border, across which our eastern neighbour tended to encourage sabotage. Our dogs were a mixture of wolf and shepherd, a fitting cocktail for the job in hand. At night their handler took them out to patrol the perimeter of the park. During the day they led a leisured existence inside a spacious enclosure.

Only three people were on friendly terms with them: the chief gardener (who was also their keeper), my father, and in due course me. Mine was the closest relationship, I think; this was noticed by my father, and encouraged. I remember the happy interludes inside the kennels, where I vied with the puppies for their mother's attention. Marteczka was appalled, but unable to countermand my father. She particularly resented the 'de-fleaing' sessions. I still thrill at the memory of the crowded kennel and the warm presence of my canine friends. With them I felt free of the rigours of civilisation. It was one of my mother's rules that the house was out-of-bounds for the dogs, but during her absences the rule was often relaxed so that my father could enjoy their company, and I could laugh at their discomfort on slippery parquet floors.

I also loved horses, and was allowed to explore the coach-house and the stables. Among my closest friends were the horses serving the 'big house': two matching pairs for the carriages, and three or four others for riding. They were of the handsomest, and their grooming was impeccable. I began my riding instruction at the age of three, on one of these horses: my father did not approve of boys on ponies. My instructor was a former cavalry sergeant who came to us as assistant to Mr Dąbrowski. My mount's name was Thunderbolt, which was a misnomer; he was uncommonly placid. I remember being totally at ease with him, despite his great height.

The Łobzów-Kotczyn agricultural enterprise consisted of three separate elements, in effect three specialised farms: the mixed cereal farm, the dairy, and the pig farm. Rye was grown almost entirely at Kotczyn, and wheat at Łobzów where the soil was more suitable. Towards the end of the 1930s sugar beet was added as a new venture. Natural fertiliser came from the livestock. The volume of straw recovered from the cereal operation and essential for the control of the fertiliser was boosted by the choice of long-stem varieties of wheat and rye. Natural fertiliser was complemented with chemical substitutes where necessary. For its own use Łobzów also produced oats, barley, potatoes, buckwheat and flax.

There were some fifty Polish Red cows. My mother took a close interest in the selection of these gentle creatures, and in their subsequent welfare. The choice of names was a lengthy and at times abrasive procedure. All the names in any one year began with the same letter: this was not controversial because my mother followed the alphabet. But individual names were put forward and then canvassed by factions seldom willing to negotiate. My mother must have been a skilful diplomat because the names finally agreed upon were on the whole charming and imaginative. She was particularly proud of the *curricula vitarum* displayed on blackboards above the stalls allotted to individual animals. The information included a record of daily milk output, and also a schedule of each cow's romantic encounters with the head of this community – a resplendent and terrifying bull. Łobzów's ample cellars were used for the production of cheeses described as 'Swiss', and for the making of butter on a commercial scale. My mother boasted that both products were known as far as Białystok, 120 kilometres away.

The pig farm was the most ambitious of our three ventures. Here too my mother was in charge, taking personal interest in the design of the accommodation to the best standards of the day. Each adult animal was housed in a separate spacious cubicle, fitted with a low bed covered in fresh straw. The cement floors were washed down regularly, and each cubicle had a supply of fresh water. My mother insisted that these five-star conditions would release her pigs' latent inclination to hygiene and tidy appearance. And so it did – to everyone's amazement. The pig-cuisine's standards were also impressive: modern cooking equipment was installed to match the pigs' menus. The majestic boar at the head of this extended family was chosen for his resounding genealogy, because the animals were bred for bacon with export in mind. He came to us with the name of, I think, Caracalla; or was it Caligula? Caracalla's Belarus'ian keeper found the appellation unpronounceable, so he replaced it with the homely Stepa (Stevie).

My mother's interest in bees led to fruit production, the two being interdependent. The old run-down orchards were replaced, and then expanded by 10 to 20 hectares with new varieties of apples and pears. The bee-hives were distributed among the fruit trees, and the ground beneath was sown with grasses and wild flowers particularly appealing to the bee. This produced a distinctive Łobzów honey, processed for sale on newly acquired centrifuges. Fruit collection was handed over to an outside contractor from Germany. During the season he and his helpers moved into open-air accommodation among the fruit trees.

Heavy duty horses were still the best source of pulling power for our corner of Europe. The choice of horses also made the manorial techniques compatible with those employed by the neighbouring villages, which was important to my father. Several pairs of horses, in the care of experienced farm hands, took care of our grain production. At different times Łobzów deployed between five and ten such teams. Motor power was confined to threshing machines. The technology was the best available. Film clips showing farming in England around the First World War illustrate practices quite similar to those at Łobzów c. 1926.

The management of the home farms was in the hands of Mr Kazimierz Dąbrowski. He was occasionally helped by a student trainee from one of the country's agricultural colleges. During my parents' increasingly frequent absences, his wife, Mrs Dąbrowska , was in charge of the house. The most senior member of the domestic staff was the family's nanny: Miss Marcjanna Lewkowicz, the beloved Marteczka. Miss Katarzyna (Kasia) Suprun was our accomplished cook. In the period 1938-9 we had two governesses: French and German.

During my father's term of office as local magistrate (1929-1932) he was served by a valet and a chauffeur who looked after our 1926 Chevrolet. The two horse-drawn carriages, together with the horses serving the manor, were in the care of the coachman, Kosowiec. In the late 1930s the old gardener, Julek ('Juleczek'), was succeeded by Mr Moś, responsible not only for the gardens and the park, but also for the security of the estate. He was helped by casual labour, as were Mrs Dąbrowska and Miss Lewkowicz in the house. The carpenter, Mr Sokołowski, shared by the home farms and the manor, generously allowed me to assist him from time to time and I loved watching him work.

The skilled farm-hands were the backbone of the permanent labour force. They were supported by seasonal workers drawn from the neighbouring villages, mainly Łobzów, at times of maximum effort, such as the harvest.

Łobzów was served by an independent blacksmith based on Kotczyn, who also worked for other villages. Watching him was as exciting as helping Sokołowski. Harness manufacture and maintenance was carried out by a travelling saddler. Both these highly regarded craftsmen were Jews. I used to sit in on the harness sessions, conducted in total silence. The eating habits of our harness man – he was strictly Orthodox – were as fascinating as his skills.

Our local builder, Mr Suprun, lived in Dereczyn. He was in fact the brother of our cook Kasia. Suprun was the regular contractor for such major undertakings as the extension of the cellars, the building of the terrace, the construction of the summer house, etc.

My parents established at Łobzów their own private health service, available at no cost to their employees. Routine medical care was in the hands of our general practitioner in Dereczyn, and serious cases and accidents were referred to the hospital in Słonim. First aid was provided by Ania herself, and in her absence either by Mrs Dąbrowska or Marteczka. First aid service was also made available to the neighbouring villages. This facility was very popular, especially among the women, who enjoyed opportunities for gossip.

The children of our employees began their education at the village school of Łobzów, and then went on to the primary school of Dereczyn. The spiritual needs of the manor were served by the two parishes of Dereczyn, Orthodox and Catholic. Our community was multilingual, which might be illustrated by my own case: I grew up speaking Polish, French, and Belarus'ian concurrently.

Conventional wisdom would have said that the rescue of Łobzów and Kotczyn as conceived and executed by my parents had placed an unbearable burden on the home farms, now made to support a residence originally matched to a larger property. And yet, under my parents, Łobzów not only survived the crisis of the early 1930s, but towards the end of the decade registered modest progress and some useful reinvestments. This great achievement must be attributed to tight control of costs, transfers to Łobzów of some of my father's earnings, and the determination to avoid extravagant consumption.

The restoration of trust between the manor and its Belarus'ian neighbours, the villages of Łobzów and Kotczyn, was the most important priority facing my parents. After the settlement of outstanding debts relations began to develop satisfactorily, both parties seeking ever closer co-operation to mutual advantage. The most ambitious joint venture was the milk cooperative, launched in the late 1930s by Łobzów and the two nearest villages. The manor provided machinery and know-how, and the villages contributed labour and accommodation.

Tadzio also made himself freely accessible as an advisor. The village elders were informed that the manor was ready to lend (at no charge) its farm machinery. My mother remembered long meetings between Tadzio and the village representatives, held round the table in the porch of the manor house, at which these matters were discussed and co-ordinated. Mutual trust and friendly relations between the manor and the villages were cemented by my father's record as the local magistrate, a position he held at Dereczyn from 1929 till 1932. The litigants soon discovered that 'their judge', as the villagers came to call him, preferred to conciliate rather than dispense justice. In due course this particular landowner-cum-magistrate was recognised as a friend of the community.

~

Life at Łobzów was enriched by the presence of the Połubiński aunts who had inherited the shattered estates of Łobzów and Kotczyn, and passed them on to my parents in 1926. Aunt Helena died there a few days after my birth in January 1929, so I never knew her. She was by all accounts sociable, extrovert, and totally incapable of managing their affairs. Aunt Marynia, on the other hand, lived on into the 1930s. She was my best childhood friend.

She was the younger of the two sisters. Tiny and frail, not too good on her legs, she found it difficult to move without her stick, and her hands always trembled. Outwardly, though, she was perfectly made, with clear blue eyes and a sculpted face seemingly immune to the passage of time. Inside her there lurked an eternal teenager, eager to offer friendship to her four-year-old godson.

The source of Aunt Marynia's disability was explained to me later. The sisters were the fruit of a marriage between two first cousins, the heirs respectively to Łobzów and Kotczyn. It seems they were pressed into an alliance, although there was also love between them. Dispensation was secured from the Vatican on the grounds that there was a baby on the way. (My mother was adamant that there was no baby: the Połubiński standards would not have allowed it. But they were apparently flexible enough to permit a touch of blackmail based on a lie.) Aunt Marynia was to bear the consequences of this genetic proximity. I hasten to add that my father was related to the Połubińskis *upstream* of Aunts Hela and Marynia, and my mother was in fact the aunts' first cousin twice removed. The term 'Aunt Marynia' was intended to by-pass the tedium of precision. She was in fact my Great Great Aunt.

Marynia was born in the late 1840s. As I write this, I reflect that she overlapped by several years my dashing kinsman Joseph (Etienne-François-Xavier) Giedroyć, *Adjudant Commandant* at Napoleon's HQ. He was promoted by the Emperor to the rank of brigadier general on the field of Waterloo. The promotion was never gazetted for obvious reasons, and cousin Joseph, in the meantime stripped of his properties in Lithuania by the Russians, was reduced to subsistence in Paris on a mere colonel's pension. He had been born in 1787, thus providing me, via Aunt Marynia, with a span of living memory stretching back into the 18th century.

As a young girl Aunt Marynia became involved in the Polish-Lithuanian insurrection of 1863, encouraged no doubt by her two cousins who took up arms against the Russian Empire. At that time she must have been not just beautiful, but also full of fun. There was a suitor; my mother inherited a time-piece of hers with an inscription: *la rose est pour un jour, mais vous êtes pour toujours* (the rose is for a day but you are for ever). Nothing came of it in the end. One suspects that her condition deterred the suitor's family. She slipped into the role of one of those spinster aunts, much loved and so indispensable to country life before the collapse of the old world. I have a feeling that she enjoyed her special status.

Aunt Marynia, this figurine of porcelain, smoked like a chimney. The habit may not have matched her exterior, or indeed the usage of the day, but it reflected her independent spirit. Indeed, she was no run-of-the-mill addict. A connoisseur of the finest tobaccos, she experimented with blends and created her own mixture. All I know is that it involved various Turkish and Virginia tobaccos; the proportions were never divulged. There was a problem however: the mixture had to be transformed into a cigarette with the help of an intricate Victorian machine. And this was difficult for her poor trembling hands. So she approached me (then aged four or five) with a proposition: she would allow me to play with her machine, and I might perhaps, in time, become proficient enough to make some cigarettes for her. The offer was irresistible. It was a privilege to handle this piece of advanced technology; and there was in the proposition a challenge. Soon I became skilled at cigarette-making and the two of us enjoyed happy interludes during which I applied myself, and she devised amusements. Occasionally her sense of fun would carry her away, as when, one memorable afternoon, she whipped out both her sets of false teeth and proceeded to clatter them in front of me. To this day I find the sight of false teeth disturbing.

My mother was certainly unaware of all these goings-on, which added a frisson to our conspiracy. Marteczka knew about it, of course, but chose not to intervene; she did not wish to spoil Aunt Marynia's fun.

The news that I had access to high quality tobacco soon spread round the home farm. There was, I imagine, some hope that I might help with a little redistribution of wealth. I do not recall becoming totally corrupt, but one or two of my closest friends did enjoy the occasional taste of my aunt's exotic mixture. In the end I could not resist telling my aunt how highly her cigarettes were praised. This I did not regret, seeing how she enjoyed the acclaim.

Aunt Marynia hardly ever talked about her ancestors. She was surrounded by their portraits, and she moved among them with cheerful familiarity. Every night she would 'visit' her parents to say good-night to them. We all knew – and she knew that we knew – that hers was a special role in her family's history: she was the last of her line, destined to place the Połubiński heritage in the hands of her chosen successors, the Giedroyćes.

Part of this heritage was a collection of family anecdotes which she recounted with gusto. One reflected the legendary meanness of a relative, who kept a padlocked lid on her sugar bowl; not satisfied with this, she used to imprison a fly inside the bowl before she locked it. If the fly was gone when she opened it, she knew a theft had occurred. Hygiene, of course, was of secondary importance to this obsessed individual.

Another story concerned two enterprises at Kotczyn: the manufacture of cherry-flavoured liquor for which the manor was famous, and the turkey farm alongside. On one occasion the person in charge of the 'cherry-vodka' carelessly disposed of a mountain of cherries soaked in pure alcohol, which the turkeys discovered and consumed. Soon after, the yard was strewn with stone-drunk birds, which were declared – too hastily – victims of plague. The farmhands proceeded to pluck the unfortunate drunkards, putting the 'carcasses' to one side for disposal. Before this could be done the carcasses woke up and the yard was filled with naked and disorientated turkeys (I can still see Aunt Marynia's laughing eyes as she comes to the climax of the tale). Sadly, the animals had to be put down, and for a long time afterwards the menus of the manor included 'turkey under a thousand guises'.

Aunt Marynia, the laughing conspirator and storyteller, was also a *grande dame*. These two sides of her personality coexisted naturally and gracefully. She never dreamed of pontificating, or wished to be the centre of attention. She hated to be a burden to anyone, especially to those who looked after her. One morning late in 1935 – I remember it vividly – she said that she felt a little tired. She was helped onto her bed, and there she died as she had lived, peacefully and quietly. Her small godson, whose friendship she cultivated with charm and mischief, was left bereft.

$\sim$

Daily life at Łobzów was simple and frugal. Amusements were home-made and consisted of riding, picnic parties, amateur theatricals, and excursions to the river Szczara. Bought-in luxuries were frowned upon. The youngest children cultivated the art of walking on stilts, which were home-made and extremely high. In 1938 a tennis court was installed with the help of local untutored resources. It was just good enough for beginners.

My parents held the view that there was no need for touristy foreign travel. Restaurants were avoided on the grounds that Kasia Suprun's creations were as good as any town chef's. One sweet per day was rationed out under the slogan *quelque chose de bon* (the earlier family motto *pro publico bono* having been abandoned as too intellectual). On the other hand, during visits to Warsaw or Wilno (today's Vilnius), we would usually go to the theatre or the opera – at the instigation of my father.

There was a continuous stream of visits by cousins and friends from Wilno, Warsaw, and the Lithuanian Republic. Aunt Maniusia, my mother's elder sister, came often, armed with nursery rhymes of her own making designed to shock Nanny Marteczka, one of them a classic ditty in praise of nose-picking.

Uncle Henio's visits were landmarks. Children and women adored him. To this day I receive phone calls from a lady in her nineties, who steers our conversations towards 'your Uncle Henio'. He was thoughtful, and therefore very punctual. The household would spot him at the bottom of our kilometre-long causeway, reclining in the shade of a tree under which his car was parked, waiting for the appointed time. Only then would he drive up in triumph. For me he had a special song, in which he cleverly imitated the instruments of an orchestra. And for my friends and relations he created a saga of two Portuguese noblemen, the Marquis Bigolasco and his much younger cousin Count Valgodesco. 'Bigolasco' was an Iberian-sounding derivative of our own Polish *'Bij-go-laską'* which means 'hit him with a stick'. Valgodesco's origin was *'Wal-go-deską'*- 'whack him with a plank'. The high point of Uncle Henio's visits was the unveiling of the latest instalment of our heroes' adventures, spiced with feats of arms and amorous conquests.

We also received more formal visits – from politicians and military officers, from our local priest, the mayor of Dereczyn, Mr Józef Dąbrowski (brother of my father's agent), and the magistrate, Mr Wyszomirski, who particularly impressed my sister Anuśka. He rode over on his powerful motorbike and informed her that he 'flew on it like a canawy' (he had a problem with the letter 'r').

The highlight of the summer season was the feast-day of Ania and Anuśka on 26th July. Amateur theatricals would be performed using the porch as the stage, for the benefit of family, guests, staff and families on the home farm. Tereska riding her horse Breeze was always written into the script, and Breeze – in spite of our fervent hopes – always behaved impeccably. The last such occasion, 26th July 1939, was memorable for the fine weather, and several other reasons. One was the contribution from our German governess, who regimented the younger children into a German playlet, which they, not exactly fluent in that language, strongly resented. But then came the reward: a firework display in honour of the two 'feast-day girls', accompanied by the illumination of all the avenues of the park with home-made Chinese lanterns. Dancing on the terrace to my sisters' gramophone continued deep into the night. Mr Dąbrowski meanwhile circled the perimeter of the grounds with a team of fire-fighters. No damage was done that night to the wheat fields beyond. It was the last such occasion before Łobzów's destruction by Soviet artillery.

CHAPTER 3

Dereczyn to Słonim

On 23rd August 1939, the German and Russian foreign ministers, Ribbentrop and Molotov, signed a secret treaty dividing Poland between them. On 1st September Germany invaded its eastern neighbour, and seventeen days later Germany's Soviet ally fulfilled its obligation by stabbing Poland in the back. It was a timely intervention because by then the momentum of the Blitzkrieg was beginning to falter, the weather was breaking, and Polish resistance was starting to stiffen. The Soviet attack thus ensured that nothing would now stand in the way of the century's most conspicuous act of international gangsterism.

Łobzów manor, our family home, fell prey to the Soviets. On 20th September an armoured detachment of the Red Army entered Łobzów, and with it the NKVD, partner and mirror image of the Gestapo. They came to seek out and take away my father – landowner, jurist and a senator of the Polish Second Republic; in other words, an enemy of the people.

On the night of 20th September 1939, our re-united family huddled in a small corner on the floor of the Dereczyn town gaol. Sharing that space with us were fifty or so male prisoners attempting either to sleep sardine-fashion, or to shuffle towards the window for air. The morning brought some relief, as the men stood up to stretch their legs. And then the routine of the previous day resumed: queuing for air, asking for the lavatory, and waiting. Very late that evening, as the cell was preparing for another night, the door opened and an NKVD man shouted: 'Any women or children?'

My father shouted back: 'Three women and one boy.'

There was little time for farewells. When I came up to my father to receive a hug and a sign of the cross on the forehead – our family routine before departures – I was aware that this goodbye was an extremely public act, watched at close quarters by the fifty men who were to remain. And so I behaved accordingly: no tears, no questions, above all *pas de nerfs*. I was anxious not to disappoint my father, mindful of the good 'public' manners that he expected of us. I was absorbed by the protocol. Today I wish I had given him an uninhibited bear-hug, never mind conventions. I did not know that I would never see him again.

My mother and the three of us were released, as we were, onto the empty and cold main street of Dereczyn. After some hesitation we knocked on the door of Kazimierz Dąbrowski, our agent, who had joined his family in Dereczyn. Marteczka, if my memory is correct, was already there. Mr Dąbrowski let us in, and allowed us to camp in his front room. For the first time in three days I undressed for the night. But we sensed that our presence here was a burden.

At the time my mother was saddened by this apparent lack of welcome. Today I am capable of a more detached view. My father's agent and right-hand man must have felt vulnerable. To shelter the 'enemies of the New System' would have called for total loyalty – in the name of which our most senior employee was not prepared to risk his, and his family's, safety. After another night, on the morning of 23rd September, Dąbrowski asked us to leave.

As we prepared to depart, an incident took place which taught me a great deal about human nature. The Dąbrowskis' younger son, Leonek, three years older than I and up to now my constant companion and protector, came up to me accompanied by his younger siblings. I thought that he was coming to say good bye, but I noticed on his face a smile that I had never seen before. He then struck me in the face. And I burst into tears. It was not fear, or anger; these were tears of mourning for a friendship betrayed. After that I have learned to look for friendships with greater care; and I have never again encountered gratuitous violence of this kind.

Manners were always high on my mother's – and Marteczka's – agenda; and to my father manners and self-control were inseparable. So I quickly composed myself, and we stepped out into the street again. There we stood, in front of Kazimierz Dąbrowski's house, my mother not quite knowing which way to turn. And then Providence intervened. Jan Skibiński, who was aged nineteen in 1939, and lived opposite the Dąbrowskis, recalls what happened: 'That morning my father and I stabled the horses after a morning's work and went in for breakfast. During that breakfast, noticing you all standing on the other side of the street, my parents decided to give you shelter.'

Antoni Skibiński, Janek's father, was a prominent and well-established citizen of Dereczyn – just as suspect to the Soviet regime as our former agent. But the Skibińskis did not hesitate. They gave us sanctuary which was as sumptuous as it was welcoming. Their large front room and a small kitchen were both well appointed; and they soon rearranged things to provide maximum comfort for the homeless ex-prisoners. I will never forget the feeling of joy and almost painful relief: on that morning of Saturday 23rd September 1939, we were again among friends.

The Skibińskis gave us more than accommodation. They gave us a safe home, in the privacy of which the healing and then convalescence after the trauma of the previous week would take its course. For my mother, of course, the drama continued, because every day she would present herself at the prison gate to hand in food and fresh clothes for my father. She was allowed to speak to him quite frequently, and during these brief encounters they tried to comfort one another. My father remained stoic, and to my mother he showed a cheerful front. That cheer she in turn brought back to us. It was all part of the constant care which our parents gave us even in circumstances such as these.

With shelter came a discreet but steady stream of supplies: bread, vegetables, milk, some meat, and so on. Most of it was provided jointly by the Skibińskis and the Józef Dąbrowskis (the latter our agent's older brother and a friend of my father's; his house was next to that of Kazimierz, on the opposite side of the street). Our parish priest, Canon Antoni Dziczkaniec, also offered succour, both moral and material (his sister's beautifully soft white bread). The town's Jewish community sent in some of their delicacies through the ritual of Marteczka's *pokhodka*, a weekly round of social calls undertaken by my nanny and encouraged by the town's notables so that offerings might be presented indirectly.

Soon word came from the Łobzów committee that they would like my mother to come to the manor to reclaim some of our personal possessions. This was an initiative undertaken behind the backs of the Soviet authorities. Transport was provided, and this potentially distressing trip proved in the event to be another moving reassurance that our neighbours remained our friends. The committee insisted that she should take all she wanted, not just the necessities. My mother had to restrain them when they began to load the cart with our family silver. Still, quite a lot of it found its way to us in Dereczyn, becoming something of an embarrassment.

My mother did ask for one special concession: would she be allowed to take with her the plans of the grounds and the home farms? The committee cheerfully obliged – a brave step in the circumstances, since the Soviet authorities were determined to wipe out all traces of ownership. Our own staff also wished to make a gesture. They delegated their senior member, the carpenter Sokołowski, to go to Dereczyn and present my mother with the keys to the manor. It was a symbolic act of reconciliation. My mother had some difficulty in explaining to him that to accept the keys would be dangerous not only to her, but also to him and the people he represented.

She was unable to restrain the ultimate act of support from the village of Łobzów, which bordered on the reckless. Unbeknown to my parents, a smallholder called Tataryn composed a petition to the Soviets asking for the release of my father from prison on the grounds that he – even though a landowner – was an honourable judge. Tataryn collected signatures and submitted the petition. He was arrested shortly afterwards. I do not know his fate, but I wish now to put on record our gratitude to this brave and faithful friend.

The official world beyond this circle of friendship remained hostile. The Dereczyn committee was replaced by a 'Dereczyn Soviet', manned by younger zealots, some of them imported. My mother and her children were known to the townspeople, and for that reason easy to invigilate. We were observed by this Soviet at a distance, and so far without interference. Pressure was applied, however, on our host Antoni Skibiński: 'Why do you shelter these landowners? Watch out!'

Skibiński refused to be intimidated. He and his family escaped persecution, however, because one of the members of the Soviet was their former employee, who more than once succeeded in crossing off the Skibiński family from the list of those destined for deportation or worse.

Our life on the edge began to acquire a routine. Plans for the future were studiously avoided, and each day was received with gratitude. My sisters stayed indoors, and my mother – apart from visiting the prison – ventured out only to attend early Mass. These were clandestine expeditions, which she undertook across the backs of gardens, wrapped up in a shawl which, she claimed, made her less recognisable. This myth was maintained by the locals, who pretended not to recognise her. Our cook Kasia Suprun, back in her family home, also took part in this charade, but she carried it to the extent of never calling on us at the Skibińskis. My mother was saddened by this, and on one occasion ventured out to call on Kasia. She discovered that our former cook, like Kazimierz Dąbrowski, felt vulnerable and anxious to avoid compromising contacts. My mother withdrew; and I, today, understand Kasia's fears.

One concession was made to the new regime: my mother sent me to the local school. The message was to be that the Giedroyćes were ready to accept the so-called 'objective changes'. My mother must have discussed this step with my father, but knowing her I suspect that it was her initiative. Had I understood the purpose of this exercise, I would have done my best. As it was, I was puzzled, even distressed. Twice a day I had to walk the length of town; an empty town of closed shutters and bare shops. Twice a day I had to go past the prison where my father was incarcerated. The school was in disarray, and those teachers still in place were bullied and confused. One of my early experiences of Soviet-style education was a meeting of all the children in the Dereczyn cinema. There a political commissar in uniform gave a long speech with many references to Stalin. Whenever the great man's name was uttered, a verse of the Internationale was relayed over the loudspeaker and we all had to jump to our feet.

The other children left me alone, for which I was grateful. The son of one of our former policemen (in prison, of course) befriended me, perhaps in the name of solidarity among marked men. Unfortunately he suffered from monumentally bad breath. But we stuck together, in spite of this.

One day a fellow pupil brought to school a book from the Łobzów library. We looked together at the ex-libris and the catalogue number. I felt no urge to reclaim it, and I am still puzzled why he should have wished to show this book to me. There was no malice in it; possibly there was a desire to reassure me that the book was looked after...

At the Skibińskis there was talk of the Polish government in France, and of the Polish Army alongside the Western Allies. So, when in the course of a geography lesson the teacher invited us to name any European country, I volunteered Poland. A severe reprimand followed: 'Poland no longer exists!' The voice of Germany's ally was loud and clear.

After the takeover of the school by new teachers imported from the East, and the switch to the Russian language, I took to my bed. It was a lengthy influenza rather than a political gesture, and it took some time to clear. When I finally recovered (it was by then late November) I asked my mother to be allowed to stay at home. Thus began the first 'year off' in my chequered education.

Meanwhile we made one or two tentative social contacts from our safe house at the Skibińskis. The first was with Zbyszek Michalski, a teenager from the nearby estate of Wojniłowce, whom we discovered hiding in one of the Dereczyn cottages. I went to visit him and asked if he was involved in an anti-Soviet conspiracy; towards which I then offered my services. Rather than respond to my offer, Zbyszek told me at length of his recent arrest, during which he was threatened with a firing squad. After his ordeal he was clearly in a state of shock, and my mother told me to leave him be.

The other contact was far less distressing. One day a 'Mrs' (we suspected that she was a 'Miss') Kutkowska appeared on our doorstep, escorted by a young man in a pince-nez. We had heard of her as a rather terrifying amazon who farmed her property near Słonim. The young man was presented to my mother as Mr Ruocco – I do not recall the christian name – her land agent. I was sure that Mr Ruocco was a secret agent. He had a high forehead, a powerful torso, and very short legs. And a twinkle in his eye, which shone promisingly from behind his overbearing employer. They, like Zbyszek Michalski, did not feel safe in their locality, and sought anonymity in Dereczyn.

We saw quite a lot of the Kutkowska-Ruocco duo, and enjoyed the amazon's outrageous eccentricities, seasoned with Ruocco's comments behind her back. My clever sister Tereska and Ruocco became good friends, and they made us all – even my mother – laugh. In my poor mother's absences there were giggles and shrieks. In the course of these visits we discovered that Mrs Kutkowska disliked children intensely. A situation was contrived in which she was made to endure my company long enough to explode: 'But this boy is full of simian malice!' Her stormy departure was followed by yells of delight from Tereska and Ruocco. I, on the other hand, was upset by the verdict, because I was trying to be polite. My reaction added greatly to the general mirth.

Such lighter moments were welcome but hardly sufficient to ease my mother's burden. In need of distraction, she remembered her skills with the needle. She hinted to one or two friends that she would be happy to accept sewing commissions. This created a sensation among the women of Dereczyn: the mistress of the manor offering her services as a seamstress! Orders followed, clients enjoyed extended fitting sessions, and my mother was able to forget her troubles, albeit intermittently. She charged very little, and then in kind; but it was the therapy that mattered.

She also set an example for her children. Janek Skibiński remembers how my two sisters adjusted to the new circumstances. Anuśka particularly, because she always enjoyed the ways of the countryside: at Łobzów she often took part in the milking (by hand in those days), and was acclaimed by other milkmaids as the champion. Janek begins his memoir gallantly: 'Your mother was a beautiful woman.' He then relates how Anuśka and Tereska borrowed two spades from him, so that a path could be cleared of snow around the house each day before their mother's walk to church – well before six o'clock in the morning. He also describes my sisters' determination to learn how to make bread. On this matter they approached the Skibiński grandmother, who provided them with aprons and proceeded to apprentice them to this difficult art. Bread-making evenings became social occasions, enjoyed by participants and onlookers. Anuśka and Tereska also wanted to chop wood for our own use, so that Janek would not be overburdened; he – a true gentleman – would not let them: 'It is a man's job'.

Gatherings of a more serious nature also took place at the Skibińskis every evening, when my mother would listen to Paris or London on the wireless, and then translate the news items. One of them, the assumption of the office of President of Poland by Władysław Raczkiewicz, raised a cheer at the Skibińskis, and then became a whispered Dereczyn sensation. Raczkiewicz was a friend of the family, and the town remembered his visits to Łobzów.

Janek adds that my mother's duties at the evening gatherings were soon extended to include her reminiscences. She was a good storyteller and the audience wished to hear about people my parents knew, and events they had witnessed.

Meanwhile, beyond the Skibiński doorstep, the hostile world was closing in. Late in October the prisoners of Dereczyn were moved to Słonim. They were marched over 30 kilometres, the departure taking place secretly, before dawn, but still noticed. The news filtered back from Słonim that my father's feet were covered with sores. My mother immediately began laying plans for a clandestine journey to Słonim to deliver medicines and food.

At about the same time the charade of voluntary incorporation of the eastern half of the Polish Second Republic into the Soviet Union was staged. An 'election' to the 'People's Assembly of Western Belarus'' was held on 22nd October. All eligible inhabitants of Dereczyn were compelled to take part, including my mother, Marteczka and Anuśka, but not Tereska who was still 17. The Soviet police rounded up the voters into a dwelling liberally adorned with red flags, and there instructed them to put suitably doctored papers into the 'voting urns'. In this way an overwhelming majority was secured in favour of pliant candidates. Soon after, the Assembly petitioned for incorporation into the Soviet Union, which was granted on 2nd November.

Towards the end of October a man unknown to us appeared before my mother and identified himself – to her satisfaction – as an emissary from her sisters, now in comparative safety in Wilno. I say safety, because the Wilno region fleetingly found itself within the Lithuanian Republic – just before its occupation by the Soviets. The emissary came to offer his services as a guide across the Soviet-Lithuanian border. He was a professional smuggler (mainly of people) with an impressive record of success. After a sleepless night my mother told the man, in our presence, that she was unable to accept the offer. This was her first important decision taken without her husband at her side. She explained that her first duty was to be as near to her husband as possible; and her children, naturally, had to remain with her. Soon after, her plan to go to Słonim was put into operation.

This was a risky move because we were under NKVD surveillance. Travel by enemies of the state was anathema. Help came readily from Józef Dąbrowski who, in the name of long friendship, was prepared to defy the authorities. My sisters and I stayed conspicuously behind under the care of Marteczka, which made our mother's absence less noticeable. Travelling by horse-drawn sledge, Dąbrowski successfully avoided road checks and delivered my mother to the prison gate. The parcel with food and medicines was handed in, and a receipt, signed by my father, was brought to her. The date on the slip (I have it here before me) is 30th November 1939.

My mother then began circling the perimeter of Słonim prison, hoping to catch a glimpse of her husband. Suddenly, in one of the prison windows, she saw his silhouette – a chance in a thousand. My father had just enough time to make the sign of the cross in her direction. She was then surrounded by an armed patrol, and taken inside. A lengthy interrogation followed, interspersed with threats. The prospect of both our parents in the clutches of the NKVD came close to being realised. Her straight answers saved her. She knew that her husband would also tell the truth; which he did, because she was eventually released. It was just as well that we children and Marteczka knew nothing of these dangers. The return journey to Dereczyn, perilous enough as it was, seemed to my mother uneventful. Later the news filtered through that my father paid for that glimpse of his wife with solitary confinement. It was to be his last sight of her.

Christmas came and went. We did not even attempt to celebrate it. I vaguely remember a quiet Mass on the morning of Christmas day. My 11th birthday in January passed unnoticed. The winter was exceptionally severe, and in the depth of it – on 10th February 1940 – the first wave of deportations took place. Nearly a quarter of a million Polish citizens were packed into cattle trucks and sent towards the Russian Arctic, or beyond the Urals. Several families from Dereczyn were taken, among them our friends the Zięciaks.

In the aftermath of this event my mother took her second decision:

she would take us to Słonim. Our escape – because that is what it amounted to – would bring us closer to our father, and at the same time perhaps give us some anonymity. Once again Józef Dąbrowski offered his services. His two sons joined in the conspiracy, and two sledges were laid on in strict secrecy. We said good bye to the Skibińskis, our protectors, asking Antoni Skibiński for one last favour: to accept for safe keeping some of the Łobzów silver returned to my mother by the village committee, and the plans of the home farms. Antoni promised to hide these mementos on his premises, and no doubt did so faithfully. Today no one knows where they might be hidden; Janek's father never spoke of it to his son. Perhaps this modest treasure, charged with sentimental value, might one day fire the imagination of one of my grandchildren to go and seek it out.

On a very cold morning in mid-February, before dawn, two sledges slipped out of Dereczyn unnoticed, to take a roundabout route to Słonim. The Dąbrowskis knew the area intimately. All the same, it was a close-run thing. A telegram was sent by the Dereczyn Soviet to Hołynka, an unavoidable point on the route, as soon as our absence was discovered: *'Krupnaya barynya ubezhala – zaderzhat'* (an important lady has escaped – detain her). The message arrived too late, and we safely reached our destination.

Janek Skibiński remembers the questioning and intimidation that followed our disappearance. The police wanted to find out where we were hiding. Antoni Skibiński stood his ground. I do not know whether Józef Dąbrowski and his sons were molested; I hope they managed to avoid the clutches of the Soviet secret police. Antoni Skibiński, his wife Wiktoria, and Józef Dąbrowski with his two gallant sons will be always remembered by the Giedroyćes of Łobzów as their benefactors.

∾

In 1939 the town of Słonim had some 17,000 inhabitants. At the outbreak of the war the population must have increased through the influx of refugees. My mother's search for a hiding place in a crowded town led her to an elderly widow called Mrs Galinajtis (a Lithuanian sounding name) who lived in a small cottage surrounded by an apple orchard, away from the town-centre and close to the famous seventeenth century

Słonim synagogue. Mrs Galinajtis let us have her largest room (it was quite small, actually), into which the four of us and Marteczka moved hugger-mugger. I was singled out by our landlady for special attention: from time to time she would give me some of her home-made jam on a small saucer. I became devoted to her.

My mother's main concern was the welfare of her husband, still in Słonim prison and not in the best of health. This information she obtained from a prison nurse, who looked after my father's feet. I do not know how my mother made contact with her. However, I do remember that the nurse was rewarded with one of the two silver candlesticks salvaged from Łobzów and not deposited at the Skibińskis; one of my candlesticks, because they always lit up my bedroom before I went to sleep. My mother now began paying frequent visits to the prison gate, pleading for her parcels of medicines, food and clean shirts to be passed on to her husband. One or two of them – I do not know how many – got through. I wonder if it occurred to my mother that her attempts at anonymity were not compatible with her conspicuous presence at the prison gate. But of course she had her priorities.

In Słonim we discovered some old acquaintances, also trying to melt away in the crowds of a largish town. These were the Łętowskis and the Bitner-Glindziczes, local landowning families. The wives with the children (the husbands were in prison) had set up a *komuna* (commune) in one of the apartment blocks in the main street of Słonim, and pretended they were anonymous newcomers. On the outskirts of town we found Mrs Rudlicka with her charming daughter Krysia; their disguise was more discreet.

The *komuna* decided to give me their Guinea Pig (I use capitals because it had no name), presumably for reasons of space and hygiene. At Mrs Galinajtis's, space was also at a premium, but my mother noticed how desperately I wanted to adopt the little creature. Somehow, Guinea Pig was fitted into our dormitory, providing joyful distraction to her new keeper.

A gift from heaven was Sister Helena of the local Community of the Immaculate Conception. A widow who had taken the veil, her name had been Wika Kotwiczowa. She was my mother's cousin, and one of the finest horsewomen of her generation. In Vienna people used to line the route of her promenade, on occasions joined by Emperor Franz-Josef himself. Noticing him, she would perform a little impromptu dressage, which he would acknowledge by raising his hat. The wise and serene Sister Helena was older than my mother, and she now came forward with spiritual succour mixed with ready laughter.

She introduced us to the convent's chaplain, Father Adam Sztark SJ. My mother began to attend his daily Mass. She did not send me to school, but instead asked me to accompany her to church. Soon I became Fr Sztark's regular altar-boy, and with my mother in tow we would do the rounds of the three Catholic churches still allowed to function: the church of the Convent, the Bernardines, and the parish church of St Andrew. I distinctly remember being struck, for the first time in my life, with the architecture of these churches. I thought them awe-inspiring.

There were of course other altar-boys on Father Sztark's books, and we had some good times in the Convent's sacristy – behind Sister Sacristan's back. Our favourite game was to hear each other's outrageous mock-confessions in a particularly ornate confessional placed in the sacristy for – I must presume – the most wayward penitents.

Somehow I must have retained a special position in the servers' hierarchy, because on one occasion it was I who was sent by Sister Sacristan to the altar of St Anthony to pray for the recovery of a vestment which she had mislaid. The item was found, and my position was consolidated even further. But how I was teased!

Today my memories of our Słonim interlude are inseparable from the image of my mother in prayer. It was almost as if she went into a private retreat – not an easy matter amongst pressures and dangers. She was calm, busy – and entirely prepared when the news filtered out of the prison that my father had been transferred to the notorious gaol of Minsk. She then began selling off for Soviet roubles those remaining possessions not essential for survival, and also sewing into the hems of our greatcoats the few items of jewellery that remained. In all this there was no hint of resignation. She was getting ready for the next wave of deportations. It seems to me now that with her it was almost a subconscious wish to be sent eastwards in the wake of her husband.

In the early hours of Saturday 13th April 1940 we were woken by a detachment of armed soldiers under the guidance of two young *politruks* (political officers) in plain clothes, members of the Słonim Jewish community now in the service of the Russians. The classic instruction was issued – *'Sobiraites' s veshchami'* (get ready with your things) – followed by a skilfully executed search, during which my mother's trinkets were easily discovered in all those hems. The scene that followed I shall never forget: one of the plain-clothed zealots handing over a fistful of rings, earrings etc. to the senior soldier sitting in a chair; the soldier – a sergeant with grey hair – looking at these things, raising his eyes to meet my mother's, and then quietly returning the cache to its owner. The young activists did not dare to question the soldier's act of charity. This sergeant was the second honourable Soviet soldier that we had the luck to encounter in our hour of need; the first was the officer who safely conducted my father from Łobzów to Dereczyn. I often think of them.

The second wave of deportations – around a third of a million old men, women and children – was aimed at the families of prisoners. Our fate was thus sealed. The only remaining concern was Nanny Marteczka's safety. My mother explained to the officials that she was not a member of the family but a former employee. It was a painful lie because Marteczka to all of us, and especially to me, was a member of the family. However, the class-conscious aparatchiks were more than willing to let her go. Marteczka attempted to reverse the dismissal, and then I heard my mother actually ordering her to leave us. I had never seen my mother ordering Marteczka to do anything. On this one occasion, as the dawn of 13th April 1940 was breaking over Słonim, Marteczka submitted to the will of her mistress and best friend. I realised then that I was about to lose my surrogate mother. It was a sudden shock, about which I find it difficult to speak even today.

As I write all this I reflect that back in Dereczyn my mother could have sent just the three of us to Wilno, where there were still opportunities for travel to Sweden or even Japan. But the thought never crossed her mind. She knew that mother and children must stay together whatever the circumstances. Even into exile…

At one point that morning it occurred to me that I might try to escape. I asked to be excused – permission granted by the sergeant – and went off to the far corner of the large orchard where a privy stood near the fence. All I had to do (I thought) was jump over it. My wish to defy the enemy was strong, as in Dereczyn when I had imagined I could offer my services to the imaginary resistance movement. The thought that I should stay with my family in order to help, or even protect, my mother and sisters, had not yet crossed my mind. Mercifully, the feeling did not last. Wishing to be safely back with my mother, I quietly returned to the house.

Later in the morning a truck arrived, with an armed escort under a young NKVD officer. I had just enough time to say goodbye to Guinea Pig, and to place it under the joint care of Marteczka and Mrs Galinajtis. My mother was calm; we knew that she was silently praying. We scrambled onto the back of the lorry and quietly settled on our bundles, Tereska clutching a bottle of milk which Marteczka had given her. The secret police officer was puzzled: 'Why are you not crying?' he demanded. Tereska looked away and said in Polish: 'I am going to break this bottle on his head.' The officer did not understand, which was fortunate. My mother smiled.

At the station a train was already waiting: innumerable cattle trucks 'adapted' for human cargo, some of them fitted with elevated cabins for armed guards. We were loaded into one of these, and the final headcount was about forty persons: mainly women, some old men, and quite a few children. The four small high windows were barred, there was no heating, and a hole in the floor was to serve as a lavatory. The truck did contain a few bunks, but there was no water supply, and no arrangement for feeding the prisoners.

The doors were locked and the train surrounded by soldiers who attempted to keep away large crowds of townspeople flocking to the station to hand in food and wave goodbye. Food did filter through to the prisoners when the guards were not looking. Most offerings were anonymous, but we noticed our Marteczka desperately trying to locate our truck. She succeeded, and her bread and some smoked pork was successfully passed on to us. Last farewells were exchanged. This time there were tears. With her I noticed Father Sztark. He dashed up to my window, thrust into my hand a small wooden crucifix, and gave a blessing. Much later we learned that on 28th December 1942 Father

Sztark was executed by the Germans for sheltering the Jewish children of Słonim during the liquidation of the local ghetto.

The train did not move for twelve hours. Once during the day we were allowed out to fetch water. At the tap my mother exchanged a few words with one or two members of the Słonim *komuna* – they too were on the train. With them my mother was able to share some of her roubles. Back in the truck the atmosphere was close to despair. My mother noticed in a corner a very corpulent lady clutching a guitar. Her name was Mrs Bazylewska – our paths were to cross again and again. At this our first encounter in that cattle truck, my mother asked her to play for us. She struck some familiar chords, the inmates relaxed, and then began to sing. She played some popular songs, and the recital ended with a hymn, which was picked up by other trucks along the train.

As we prayed, the train began rolling eastwards towards Minsk. My mother whispered to us that for this journey we had been blessed not once but twice: by our father from his prison back in November, and today by Father Sztark through the bars of the truck window.

CHAPTER 4

Into Siberia

The mass deportation of 13th April 1940 was another smoothly executed act of international gangsterism. On the appointed day several hundred cattle trains began moving eastwards in unison, bearing to their fate in the labour camps and collective farms of the Soviet Union a third of a million old men, women and children. Writing this in October of 2001, I find it difficult to avoid comparisons with Manhattan of 11th September. The Soviet variant of 1940 was devised towards the annihilation not of thousands, but hundreds of thousands, of innocent human beings.

The speed of integration of the eastern half of Poland into the Soviet Union was equally impressive. Not more than 50 kilometres east of Słonim we discovered that the railway line had already been adjusted to the Soviet wide gauge, and that a 'wide' cattle-train was ready and waiting for us at the station of Baranowicze. It was identical to ours, except for one refinement: the sanitary holes-in-the-floor were now fitted with chutes pointing outwards. The two trains stood alongside one another and the inmates of each truck were simply herded across the lines. Most of our contingent scrambled for places on the floor of the truck; for contiguous warmth, I presume. My mother thought differently: she claimed a space for the four of us on the upper bunk by the small window. It was cold up there, but the air was better and there was more room. The Naumowicz family of three settled next to us. The father was in prison and his wife, the gentle Pani Nadzia, was included in the round-up with her teenage daughter Zosia. The son Władek, a railwayman, returned home from away-duty the day before the 13th, and for that reason was not 'on the list'. He insisted on submitting himself to the fate of the Naumowicz women – an impressive act of filial and brotherly duty. The only other inmates on the ground floor that I remember were Mrs Bazylewska with her guitar, a very old Rabbi deep in prayer and apparently oblivious to the surroundings, and a Jewish boy persistently but in vain demanding *kogele-mogele mit monchkes* – an egg-nog with sugar.

Within our corner I was allowed the 'window seat' with a view of the outside world. At the little station of Negoreloe – the old Polish-Soviet border – we entered the Motherland of the Proletariat. My first impression was of grinding poverty. By comparison, the modest pre-war Polish Borderlands seemed cheerful and tidy.

On 15th April we approached the main railway station of Minsk, the capital of Soviet Belarus'. Its suburbs were in a state of advanced dilapidation. The station was busy – mainly with other cattle trains full of deportees. The guards called for volunteers to fetch water, and I offered my services on behalf of our truck. This afforded an opportunity for stretching my legs, and for exploring. I knew that my father was incarcerated in Minsk, and I asked the guards for the whereabouts of the prison. They pointed to a vast stronghold overshadowing the station. Someone explained that it was a former Sapieha castle; the Sapiehas of Dereczyn, kinsmen of ours… I realised that my father and I came fleetingly to within a few hundred yards of one another. He was never to know that his wife and children brushed against the walls of his prison.

In the afternoon of 15th April the train moved on eastwards, still within the territories that until 1772 had formed the Polish-Lithuanian Royal Commonwealth. Glued to my observation post, I was able to decipher names familiar to readers of *Trylogia*, a classic of Polish historical romance by Sienkiewicz. We trundled through Borisov on to Orsha where in 1514 the armies of the Grand Duchy of Lithuania had stopped the westward progress of Muscovy. On 17th April we reached the city of Smolensk, but did not stop, which was surprising. Today the reasons for this haste are all too clear.

Before reaching Smolensk we passed through a small station called Katyń, some sixteen miles due west of the city. Immediately afterwards we came to within two kilometres of a forest which the Russians call Kozogory, and the Poles Kozie Góry. On that very day, 17th April 1940, the forest of Kozogory was witness to the mass execution of some 420 Polish officers. This day's work was no isolated outrage. Between 4th

April and 12th May twenty contingents of Polish officers captured by the Red Army in September 1939 – a total of 4,143 men – were transported from the Prisoner of War camp of Kozel'sk near Kaluga to the Kozogory forest. There each victim was overpowered, dragged to the edge of a communal grave, and shot by a skilled NKVD executioner through the base of the skull. To the rest of the world this breathtaking crime is known today as the Katyń Wood Murders. Similar massacres were simultaneously carried out in Kharkov and in Mednoe not far from Tver', accounting for a further ten and a half thousand victims. In this way 'the flower of the Polish nation' was annihilated; in this way the Central Committee of the Soviet Union and its General Secretary, Iosif Dzhugashvili, also known as Stalin, took revenge on the army which in the summer of 1920 had stopped the Soviet march on Western Europe.

Throughout April 1940 Smolensk railway station was busy holding and shunting the carriages containing the doomed Polish officers. No wonder the Soviet authorities thought it prudent to deny the trainloads of Polish deportees direct evidence of this most hideous of crimes.

Beyond Smolensk we entered the lands of historic Muscovy. In the face of geographic names no longer familiar, and of the monotony of dilapidation in the countryside, I began losing interest in the world beyond my barred window. I noticed that the rest of the truck fell silent even before I did. Nervous energy was now spent, and defensive passivity – that well-tried formula for survival – took over.

The journey lasted two weeks. From time to time we were given *kasha* or soup. Once a day cold water was fetched by nominees from each truck under armed guard. Bread was distributed – on just two occasions. People became sick. Medical care amounted to iodine and *waleriana* (a sedative). Someone in despair committed suicide under the wheels of another train – the news, shouted between the wagons, travelled like wildfire. Prayers were sung collectively every morning and night.

The battle for survival amounted to careful rationing of the provisions (bread and smoked pork) that the kind people of Słonim were able to slip into the trucks on 13th April. This called for iron discipline because we did not know how long the journey would take. But we soon discovered that we were actually – even though only transiently – better off than the people outside. In some areas starving women and children

invaded station platforms to beg for food from us. Quite a few deportees (my mother among them) found it in their hearts to hand over to these unfortunates some of our 'Słonim iron rations'.

On 22nd April or thereabouts we crossed the mighty Volga near Kuibyshev. This event rekindled my interest in the outside world. Soon we found ourselves in the land of the Bashkirs, and the exotic-sounding Ufa, Bashkiria's principal city, caught my attention. Our 'transport unit' was kept away from Moscow, and today, with the help of a map of the Soviet rail network c. 1940, I am able to attempt a reconstruction of our route between Smolensk and Ufa. I am fairly certain that we would have passed through Vyaz´ma, Kaluga, Tula and Penza.

The tedium of our journey was broken only occasionally, when we came across other trainloads of deportees from Poland. Standing alongside each other in the sidings, we had little to offer by way of news. But we did exchange information as to our respective points of capture and departure. After several such encounters we began to comprehend the scale of the operation of which we were victims, and of the numbers of people uprooted. In a spontaneous sort of way there emerged from these encounters a network of solidarity among all those forcibly pushed across the plains of Eastern Europe towards their unknown destinations.

On one occasion, however, an encounter across barred windows was shattered by an incident tragic in its consequences – and at the same time tragi-comic. The *dramatis persona* was our ample guitar-player. She, not realising that the water buckets of the other train were in the line of fire of our 'sanitary chute', was moved to make use of this. There were no facilities for washing or disinfecting, so the train standing along-side ours was denied its precious supply of water. It was a terrible setback for them. The guitar-player's desperate apologies had little effect. The inmates of the other train were enraged. There were no exchanges of gossip with them...

After Ufa we began a long climb towards the Urals. Having never before seen real mountains, I returned to my observation post at the window – despite a cold easterly wind. I was impressed to learn from a fellow deportee that we were actually traversing one of the world's richest sources of gold and platinum, not to mention such mundane commodities as iron ore and oil. Chelyabinsk, our next port of call, was a grim industrial city, engaged in processing these fabulous natural resources for the benefit of the Proletariat. After Chelyabinsk we began the descent towards the West Siberian Lowlands, entering on 26th April our first major Asian city. I applied myself to the deciphering of its name – Kurgan – which I then announced to my mother. The effect was electric. She said: 'This is where my father was deported...'*

On 27th April we reached a small station called Petukhovo, some 200 kilometres beyond Kurgan and 3,000 kilometres due east of Słonim. Here we were ordered to disembark and settle on the ground beside the

* The story of his deportation is told in chapter 6, pp. 81–2

railway line. We had finally arrived. Our truck-load was lucky. There were no deaths in transit. Elsewhere, I gathered, there were many. In such cases Soviet funeral rites were simple. Two guards would take over, push back the family, and toss the body out of the truck, preferably while the train was in motion. For a child one guard was deemed sufficient. The survivors that reached Petukhovo held on, huddled together for warmth under a starlit Siberian sky. Morning ground frost covered all those sleeping bodies, concealing misery under the glamorous sparkle. I remember being shaken by the loud blasts of engine whistles within feet of our encampment.

After two nights in the open, a lorry drew up and we were bundled onto it with two or three other families, including the Naumowiczes. It was late afternoon of April 29th. We set off across the empty steppe, the dirt track skirting the occasional stunted forest, and reached our name-less destination very late at night. An empty barrack-like dwelling, described as the 'veterinary centre', was opened up, and we settled there for the night. Here, by the will of the rulers of the Soviet Empire, we were to toil and die. Early death was an integral part of the formula.

～

The next morning I was the first to wake up. I crept out while everyone was still asleep to have a look at the new surroundings. The morning was sharp and a little misty. Before me lay the *maidan*, an open space at the centre of the settlement; enormous, uneven and unkempt. On that spring morning its aspect was that of a recent mud-bath in the process of drying out. Later, at the height of the short Siberian summer, it would turn into a dust bowl, soon after to become a wintry field covered with a thick carpet of dry sparkling snow. At the far ends of the *maidan* I no-ticed some primitive grey dwellings, randomly dispersed; aligning them into streets was not the local preference. There were no orchards or trees except for two stunted birches at one far corner, harbouring the dese-crated village church. The horizon was flat, and the place seemed utterly deserted.Taking in all those early impressions, I suddenly felt very depressed.

Not for long, mercifully. From one of the backyards came the familiar sound of a crowing cockerel. This universal signal of rural life was familiar and reassuring. I saw someone coming towards me across the *maidan*, and I felt the urge to identify the place. So I accosted the man in my broken Russian, and asked him where I was. The question must have sounded eccentric, because he began looking me up and down. But then he understood. And he patiently explained that the place used to be called Nikolaevka, but now was renamed *Kolkhoz Krasnoye Znamya* – The Collective Farm of the Red Banner.

The village might have been named after one of the two tsars called Nikolai, making it a recent settlement, a hundred years old at the most. Today it features in *The Times Atlas,* so it must have grown in stature. But in the spring of 1940 it was just a large village in the middle of nowhere, clinging to an insignificant lake called Kubysh – its water supply, but not, alas, a source of fish. The latter came in goodly numbers from the river Ishym (a tributary of the great Irtysh), not much more than a kilometre away, beyond the lake. Nikolaevka's link with the outside world was the Trans-Siberian railway, connecting the southern Urals with Novosibirsk and beyond, towards Irkutsk and Vladivostok. Administratively, Nikolaevka (no one ever took the name Krasnoe Znamya seriously) was included in the District of Presnovka of the North Kazakhstan Region. Geographically, it lay on the southern edge of the West Siberian Plain.

The village consisted of three long 'streets' running more or less along the east-west axis, in harmony with the elongated shape of Lake Kubysh on its southern perimeter. Each street was cut into two sections by the *maidan* in the middle. They were known by their traditional names of *Verkhnaya* (Upper), *Srednyaya* (Middle), and *Nizhnaya* (Lower), thus designating their respective elevations above the lake. I recall that Nizhnyaya was renamed by the Soviets *Proletarskaya* (Proletarian, I suppose), but this ideological allusion was generally ignored. The other two streets must also have been similarly dignified. The three streets were mirror images of the *maidan* – no more than wide stretches of rough ground, uneven and, in bad weather, impassable.

The dwellings were clustered irregularly along the edges of the streets. Some of them could be described as cottages (*izba* in Russian) but most were primitive hovels thrown together with no attempt at making them look tidy, let alone pleasing to the eye. The better *izbas* were made of wood, but the majority fell back on the staple building material in those parts: an unfired brick of clay and straw. The roofs were covered with *plasty* – pieces of turf harvested in the surrounding steppe during the summer, and applied so that the earth was exposed to the elements. Roofing of this kind was an inventive local speciality; and an effective answer to the rigours of Siberian winters. The search for suitable raw material required some skill, and so did the shaping of the chosen pieces.

Two or three dwellings were proper houses remembering better times. One of them – the residence of a pre-revolution grain trader perhaps – was converted into the main office of the Commune. It had large windows, high ceilings, and some old birches at the entrance. The other became the main building of the local *desyatiletka*, the Soviet-style secondary school taking children from the age of seven to eighteen.

Nikolaevka's newest architectural embellishment was a wooden pedestal with a red star on the top, marking half a dozen or so unnamed graves of revolutionary heroes who had died for the cause of the Prole-tariat. This memorial was placed at the head of the *maidan* close to the desecrated church, presumably to supersede the latter as a new spiritual and social focus for the 'gatherings of the masses'. As such it clearly failed: I never saw any official functions in its vicinity. Unofficially, however, the memorial became a gathering point for the local exchange market, to which neighbouring Kazakh *auls* (villages) brought their garden produce – and anything else saleable. This commercial enterprise was officially frowned upon, but in fact tolerated in the face of over-whelming popular demand.

The seat of Soviet power, concentrated near the memorial across Verkhnaya street, comprised two forbidding wooden dwellings: the office of *Sel'sovet* (pronounced 'Sielsoviet' – the governing body of the *kolkhoz*) with the private quarters of its chairman under the same roof, and the *Radiotochka*, a separate building housing the single central radio transmitter/receiver and its shadowy operator.

Nikolaevka's chairman was a woman. She was lame, domineering, and skilled at deploying her Wagnerian baritone. It was common knowledge that the radio operator was the local NKVD agent in mufti, whose principal job was to keep a malevolent eye on the village and on the chairman of its *Sel'sovet*. This sinister duo was served by a dedicated bureaucrat, the *sekretar'* (secretary) of the *Sel'sovet*; he, too, was lame. The ruling triumvirate was surrounded by an exclusive circle of courtiers: the *kolkhoz brigadirs*. These were robust frontiersmen of the Siberian plain, placed in charge of the agricultural teams (brigades) allocated to different geographic or functional sectors of the enterprise. Officialdom was served by a fleet of horse-drawn light vehicles exclusive to each member. In these handsome conveyances our oligarchs crisscrossed the village and their fiefdoms at break-neck speed. The rural proletariat observed their betters with a mixture of fear and oriental respect.

The *kolkhoz* establishment ruled with two levers of power. One was the allocation of grain surplus – after heavy dues to the state – among the households of the *kolkhozniks*, members of the collective. The other was the control of information. Newspapers came late and irregularly, and the only contact with the outside world was in the gift of the radio controller. Loudspeakers were encouraged in private dwellings, through which selective propaganda was fed to the households at the discretion of the controller. This sophisticated system was imposed on a village which at the time had no electricity.

Lavka, the village shop, could have been another economic weapon, but it was not – due to chronic shortages of consumer goods. The only two commodities readily available were colouring crayons and books on Leninism-Stalinism. What Nikolaevka really craved was vodka, and that precious nectar occasionally appeared on the shelves without warning. Work would then cease, and an enormous queue would instantly form, panting with anticipation and occasionally erupting into conflict. More often than not the queue would degenerate into a seething crowd. I remember one such occasion when an old man, crazed by desire, climbed onto the heads of those milling in front of him. Touchingly, he removed his boots – a sign perhaps that residual politeness still lingered on among the older generation.... To our great surprise the occasional availability of *odekolon* (eau-de-cologne) was greeted by the male population of Nikolaevka with almost equal enthusiasm. We soon discovered that it was consumed in lieu of vodka. Men transiently acquired sweet breath – presumably at the expense of life expectancy.

Close to the central offices was the tiny post office hidden behind the *Radiotochka*. For us this soon became the most important life-line. Nearby was the *bol'nitsa,* a tidy cottage hospital run by a good paramedic. It dispensed warm and dedicated terminal care and little else, because there were no medicines, let alone any up-to-date equipment. For me the *bol'nitsa* will always remain associated with my earliest introduction to the Russian language. My new local friends insisted that I should memorise their latest pop song which began thus: *'Na gore stoit bol'nitsa / pod bol'nitsoi burdachok...'* , of which the English translation would be: 'There on a hill stands a hospital / and behind it – a little bordello.' The song went on to list the services available in this establishment, together with their prices. Nearby stood the veterinary centre. There was also a dairy, equipped to separate cream from milk (our *kolkhoz* had a small herd of cows, inaccessible even to the members of the collective; no one quite knew the destination of the cream.)

On the northern perimeter of the village the 'motor park' held large quantities of rusty farm equipment, and the occasional tractor – usually under repair. Beyond, at the high edge of the open steppe, stood four windmills, watching over the village at their feet. Three windmills were old and magnificent in their decrepitude. The fourth was a recent investment by the *kolkhoz*. It was equipped with an advanced multi-blade propeller, and Nikolaevka was justly proud of it. Close to the oldest windmill lay the village cemetery, which in due course took in those deportees that were not strong enough to bear the cold and the hunger.

Nikolaevka had its own Soviet-style class system. Members of the *kolkhoz* were the privileged class. Indeed, the *kolkhozniks* and their families had access to the one overriding privilege: the means for survival. They qualified for the collective's grain and potato surplus, and for an allocation of *kizyaki* – dried cowdung-and-straw brickettes used as fuel. They were allowed modest private gardens, in which they grew cabbages, carrots, onions, and more potatoes. Some kept chickens, and occasionally a goose or two. The ownership of a cow – a sign of wealth beyond the dreams of ordinary mortals – was rare.

In comparison with the living standards of our smallholders in eastern Poland, the life of a *kolkhoznik* of Nikolaevka was no more than harsh subsistence, a subsistence subjected to the vagaries of the Siberian climate and to the ruthless and erratic exploitation by the economic dictatorship imposed from Moscow. But to the underclass of our village the status of a *kolkhoznik* seemed one of extravagant luxury.

The underclass consisted of two groups, the deportees, and the *odinolichniks*, who were the original 'refuseniks'. Not prepared to trade political subservience for permission to subsist, they would not – could not – join the collective farm. The enraged establishment declared them social pariahs, to be left to fend for themselves and to be discriminated against at every turn. In Nikolaevka there were only one or two of them and no wonder. They survived mainly because of the surreptitious help extended to them by their relations and friends in the collective.

Such help was not available to the lowest caste of Nikolaevka's social pyramid: the deportees. We were the untouchables; the undesirable flotsam resistant to re-education. The NKVD kept us under constant surveillance, but at arm's length. We were not allowed to leave the *kolkhoz*. There was no need to force us to work. The powers knew very well that the deportees would be desparate to do anything for bread. But these 'rewards' were insufficient for survival. This was a well-tried Soviet formula, through which the 'enemies of the people' were deliberately drained of their ever-decreasing strength.

On the first morning of our exile my mother ventured out to look for accommodation. Someone told her that *Odinolichnik* Samoilov would probably take her family in. The sly message that the underclasses belonged together went above her head because she did not know as yet what an *odinolichnik* was. But she duly went in search of the Samoilov cottage, and found it on Lower Street, which refused to be renamed *Proletarskaya*, on the very edge of Lake Kubysh. On the doorstep of that cottage my mother met her prospective landlord, they looked each other up and down, and each recognised in the other more than a match.

I remember that meeting very clearly. Rodion Samoilov was a tall bearded man in his sixties. I do not know his patronymic – my mother addressed him as *Khozyain* (Landlord), which for all of us became his appellation. He called her *Barynya*, the Russian for Lady of the Manor. It was a signal of recognition. Later he upgraded it to *Panya*, a light-hearted derivative of the Polish *Pani* – which approximates to 'Madame'. *Khozyain* had a soldierly bearing: we later discovered that he had been an NCO in one of the Imperial rifle regiments. A photo of a young Corporal (or perhaps Sergeant) Samoilov stood in the 'corner of honour' of the kitchen, that place in every Orthodox household where the family Icons hang. In a sketch portrait of him, my mother caught perfectly his bright humorous eyes.

Samoilov's *izba* was made of timber; very modest, and very run down. It had two rooms. The smaller, directly behind the entrance door, contained an enormous Russian-style *pechka* (a stove for cooking, with places to sleep on the top), leaving just enough room for a single bed and a small table at the window. This was the room into which Khozyain proposed to crowd his own family in order to vacate the larger room for us. His family consisted of his much younger second wife, whom my mother named *Khozyayushka* (Little Landlady), their two small boys Misha and Kol'ya, and the stunning Liza, aged 13 or perhaps 14, the youngest daughter of our landlord by his first wife. The other room had three windows, a modest stove (not for cooking, just for heating), and a splendid set of family Icons in the far corner. The main entrance to the cottage was protected by a large ramshackle lean-to, opening onto the vegetable garden stretching down to the lake. The back fence provided a screen for 'natural functions', which took place on the bare earth. The lake beyond the fence was a handy source of water, which was hauled up to the house by the females of the *izba* (carrying water was below a Russian male's dignity) in buckets suspended at each end of a yoke.

Khozyain explained that he desperately needed the rent, and he named a modest sum which was beyond my mother's means. She said that she would arrange for three families of deportees to move in to share the cost. The deal was done and my mother proceeded to recruit the Naumowiczes and Mrs Halina Skotnicka with her daughter Inka as joint tenants.

That very day the nine of us moved in, to begin our new, very crowded, existence in the front room of the cottage of Rodion Samoilov the *Odinolichnik*. The Naumowicz family we knew well. We had travelled together over those three thousand kilometres between Słonim and the Kolkhoz Red Banner east of Kurgan. Mrs Naumowicz – Pani Nadzia – was charming, kind, and always first with the communal daily chores. Her daughter Zosia, about sixteen, was round and jolly. The son Władek, a railwayman like his father, had one great advantage: he was a man; and therefore an anchor for this random collection of women and children. Władek considered himself – with reason – to be upwardly mobile. He talked with élan about his recent service in the Polish Army, had a repertoire of romantic songs to his own accompaniment on a guitar, and had an eye for my sister Tereska, who was flattered by these attentions. Old Mr Naumowicz found his way from a distant prison to Nikolaevka after the German attack on the Soviet Union in 1941, thus bringing the headcount of our commune to ten. The Naumowiczes were Orthodox and, I think, considered themselves more Belarus'ian than Polish.

Hala Skotnicka was something else. An attractive socialite in her thirties, she was keen to be included in my mother's entourage and to win Tereska's friendship. Having ditched her first husband, a bland younger son of a landed family, she married into the senior echelons of the Polish Army. She was amusing, and wrote clever doggerel. One example was a poignant description of our daily routine. Today I remember only the first four lines:

> *Pierwsza wstaje Pani Nadzia*
> *Bierze miotłę i zamiata,*
> *A na szelest starej miotły*
> *Wnet się budzi cała chata.*

> First to rise is Pani Nadzia,
> Broom in hand, she starts a-sweeping.
> Gently rustling comes the message:
> Time to rise! The end of sleeping!

Hala's daughter by her first husband, Inka, aged eight or thereabouts, was a spoiled brat. Her mother insisted that Inka was a beauty, and more than once suggested that in the fullness of time she would become my wife. To begin with, my mother was amused by these antics; later she had no choice but to tolerate them. It was the tactful and helpful Pani Nadzia who became my mother's real friend.

The Giedroyć family occupied one corner of the room, screened only partially by the stove. There we managed to squeeze in two ancient beds. The larger wooden one belonged to the Samoilovs; the other – small and uncomfortable – was the result of my mother's newly discovered skills for barter. The Naumowiczes settled on the other side of the stove, having acquired another bed, and also a narrow bench. The latter was available for general use during the day, and reserved for Władek at night. To sleep on it was a challenge. The fourth corner, with a small table under the Icons, was occupied by Hala, her disgruntled daughter, another bed, and the many Skotnicki bundles. During the long winter nights a small barrel was discreetly placed near the table, to act as a communal chamber-pot. Its removal in the mornings, through the Samoilov half of the cottage, required diplomacy and logistics. It was a very crowded existence, but one marked by tolerant peace. That peace was not easy to win. As time went by it became a precious asset cherished by both sides: our little commune and the Samoilovs.

I do not know for certain how large was the Nikolaevka contingent of Polish deportees. We all kept our heads down and only gradually established contacts. Mrs Bazylewska turned up at the other end of the village with her guitar. Mrs Tubielewicz, an army wife, and her two daughters struck pretentious attitudes and kept themselves apart. The wholesome and noisy wife of a policeman, accompanied by three burly sons, proved more congenial company. There was a sporty woman called Mrs Machaj, who later impressed us with her swimming prowess in the river Ishym. To her eternal chagrin her son, a contemporary of mine, was no athlete.

A well-known Jewish grain trader from the town of Oszmiana introduced himself to my mother on discovering her family connections. He vividly remembered his business dealings with my grandmother's family. Another Jewish friend was a contemporary of mine called Hirshko Palej. Chameleon-like, he soon switched to the Slavic Grishka. In mundane matters he was vague and disorganised. In due course, at the local school, he and I began competing for the highest marks in mathematics. This race became a salutary experience for me, because I soon discovered that Grishka was capable of outperforming me effortlessly and with nonchalance. He was a brilliant logician in the making. The fact that I was able to beat him in other subjects helped to cement our friendship. I often wonder if he ever had the chance to fulfil his great promise. I suspect he did; he had the makings of a survivor.

There were other Polish Belarus'ians among us, apart from the Naumowiczes. I remember two in particular. One was an elderly carpenter who soon established a strong and ever-growing market for his services. It was sheer joy to watch him swiftly dismantle a dilapidated wooden *izba* and then reassemble the bits into something shapely, almost elegant. His favourite tool was a light axe, which was as sharp as a razor. Once he demonstrated to me its quality by shaving the hair off his left forearm. The other Belarus'ian worked as his assistant. He was young and slippery, and we soon discovered that he was receiving official favours. Among these was a licence for a shotgun – an unheard-of indulgence by the NKVD towards a deportee. We wondered what kind of *quid pro quo* he was able to offer his friends in high places.

We Giedroyćes were too inquisitive to remain cooped up in the Polish ghetto. We soon developed friendly contacts with locals, beginning with our landlord. My mother was appalled to discover that immediately after our move to his cottage Rodion Samoilov was ordered to give up half of his garden – the garden which was his only source of food. This might have been a routine ploy in the campaign of intimidation against this uncompromising dissident, but more likely it was a punishment for daring to accommodate three families of deportees. Typically, he refused to evict us – and a new bond was forged between the parties under siege. Soon my mother and her Khozyain became firm friends – not an unexpected development between two people impressed by each other.

The first thing that my mother noticed about him was, that – unlike most of the men of Nikolaevka – he was not a drunkard. He merely enjoyed the occasional drink; which for financial reasons remained very occasional. He was also blessed with a magnificently robust sense of humour. Someone dared to suggest – it was probably the flirtatious Hala Skotnicka – that at his patriarchal age he should refrain from further procreation (our Little Landlady was just recovering from her most recent confinement). His reply was: 'As it happens, I have to repair the house. While I'm at it, I had better use some of the clay-plaster to seal Khozyayushka's nether regions.' I watched my mother's attempts at registering disapproval. But I also noticed her efforts to suppress her giggles. The business of procreating late in life was part of his total image: here I am, an old man, and still full of vigour. He was a domineering disciplinarian, in the best Russian tradition. I watched him dispense rough justice to cats, dogs and his own children. Except to Kol'ya, that is, the youngest of them all, aged a few weeks. Father and son would retire onto the *pechka*, where the old man would recite little rhymes composed specially for the little boy. I remember one in particular: *Kol'ya, Kol'ya, Nikolayushka / sedi doma – ne gulyayushka!* for which my translation would be 'Little Kol'ya, mend your way! Stay at home and do not stray!'

Old Khozyain wore his traditional views on his sleeve. Once he announced that the earth was flat. Faced with my mother's gentle objections, he put forward two counter-arguments: the authority of his Church, and empirical evidence ('Panya, just look around!'). My mother had to concede defeat. Khozyain was a devoted member of the Russian Orthodox Church. The statuesque ex-NCO was endowed with a high tenor, a fact which I found incongruous. But his best friend (whose name I do not remember) was blessed with one of those magnificent basses that only Russia can produce. The two of them were the focus of a small prayer group – three or four of them – that used to meet at Samoilov's to sing the Orthodox liturgy. I was allowed to listen in. It was a great privilege; and the beginning of two lifelong loves: Russian church music, and the lowest registers of the human voice.

These people were brave. They offered their services publicly at village funerals. I also suspect that they administered baptisms. My mother, encouraged by all this, soon began her own prayer meetings in our communal quarters. Outsiders began joining in, but that was too much for the authorities, who were alerted by village informers. My mother was summoned to the office of the chairwoman of Krasnoye Znamya and threatened with punishment. Apparently a local *odinolichnik* would be tolerated – just – but not a Catholic deportee. In fact Khozyain had some support in high places. His eldest daughter Grusha (which means 'pear tree' in English) was married to one of the *kolkhoz* elders. Their son, the handsome twenty-something Andrey, qualified for an official vehicle. Grusha's father could just get away with his devotions, but not his 'Panya'.

Grusha befriended me and allowed me to listen to the sanitised information booming over the loudspeaker in her *izba*. In the course of these visits I discovered that she subsidised her father and his second family with regular gifts of bread and potatoes. Occasionally I too was the beneficiary of these handouts.

Grusha to this day remains for me a symbol of the best in Russian womanhood, although in the official stakes she had to give way to another outstanding female of Nikolaevka, whose fame travelled even as far as Moscow. A neighbour in Nizhnaya, she was then nursing her latest infant – the twenty-second. Her eldest son was a full colonel in the Red Army. The Socialist Motherland, stunned by this awesome performance, gave her a medal. Perhaps as a Hero of Socialist Labour...

~

Our survival, and paying the rent, were my mother's two preoccupations. Or rather, two great burdens, which at this early stage of our exile she had to bear alone, because we three children had not yet fully grasped the gravity of our circumstances. Survival just above the starvation line was all that she could offer, but not freedom from hunger. The diet consisted of some rye bread, augmented irregularly with a helping of *kasha* (porridge) or potatoes. Of milk, butter, eggs and the like we could only dream. Which I, for one, did fervently. The daily ration of bread was no more than one thick slice. The temptation to eat it all at once was enormous, but I soon learned the discipline of dividing it into three equal parts, representing three 'meals'. The difficult part was the interminable waiting for the next one. But then I hit on the idea of hiding my bread behind one of the Icons; not from the others, but from myself – in a make-believe sort of way. This helped a little. Further self-help came with the discovery of garlic, which was easy to find. I took to rubbing it onto the bread and then closing my eyes, imagining that I was eating bread-and-sausage.

My mother provided for us by gradually using the small cache of roubles she had assembled in Słonim, and by bartering some of our less essential possessions for flour and potatoes. In this way she secured just enough time to establish a practice as a skilled duvet-maker. Discreet orders began to flow (although she and her clients had to be careful, because this was the officially despised 'private enterprise') and with them modest earnings in kind. At the same time my mother repeatedly tried to make contact with her two sisters, presuming that they were still in their house in Wilno. She was right. Letters began filtering through and then parcels with foodstuffs such as smoked bacon and boiled sweets. Not many of them reached their destination, but the few that did became a life-line; bringing joy in the knowledge that we had not been abandoned. From then on our life became measured out in intervals between letters. A cry of *'Pismonoska idet'* (Here comes the postwoman) would go up along the Nizhnaya to alert the deportees at the Samoilovs. People knew how desperately we clung to these contacts with the outside world.

Anuśka and Tereska also tried to find work. One or two odd jobs at the *kolkhoz* came their way, but there was no continuity in it, and no reward to speak of. And the jobs allocated to them were beyond their physical capabilities. Their early attempt to enter the brave new world of collective farming was not a success. I too looked around for something to do. I noticed other boys of my age (I was just eleven) going fishing. My early attempts at making contact with them were inconclusive: the language barrier made me timid.

At this time, the first summer of our exile, at least the climate was on our side. The steppe at the bottom of our garden exploded into a display of wild flowers. It was breathtaking. The carpet-like phenomenon lasted only a couple of weeks, after which the steppe turned dry and spiky. A heat wave followed, the Ishym river went down and became invitingly serene. We three ventured out once or twice to join some of the villagers on its sandy beaches. There contacts became easier, and when Anuśka – not a strong swimmer – found herself in difficulties, local young men gallantly went to her rescue. From then on relations with local youths relaxed. Some of them became friends.

In spite of hunger and hardships, to us three the summer of 1940 still seemed generous. But not to my mother, who alone had to face the cold hostility of the outside world. German successes in Western Europe were broadcast by Hitler's Soviet allies with relish. The *Radiotochka* blared out contempt for rotten Western democracies on their knees. To this accompaniment the local authorities began closing in on 'Barynya'. It was suggested that the former organiser of May prayer meetings should demonstrate her goodwill by encouraging her daughters to join in the activities of the local 'social club'. It was a provocation, because the social club met in the desecrated village church. My mother prayed, consulted her Khozyain, and came out with a formula: her daughters would go to a dance in the former church, but they would precede their arrival with a quiet prayer, asking God to forgive them and their mother for this piece of pragmatism; also asking Him to protect the Orthodox Church from its enemies. To the best of my recollection, Anuśka and Tereska got away with only one visit. In the meantime my mother was faced with the demand that she should accept a Soviet passport. It was not a real passport, because it did not confer on the holder any civilised freedoms such as travel. But the acceptance of this caricature of citizenship was a ritualistic act of submission. The matter was serious because refusal carried with it the threat of a 'corrective camp', today known to the rest of the world as the Gulag, and separation from the children. My mother retired to her prayers – Rodion Samoilov could not help here – and unveiled another of her formulae. She would accept the 'passport' on condition that her nationality would be described in it as Polish. The local scribe went along with this demand. I am not sure if my sisters were issued with similar documents.

These trials were as nothing in comparison with the constant anxiety about the fate of my father. This burden my mother chose to bear alone. All we knew was that as she stitched she prayed. She prayed especially through St Anthony of Padua, and to him she offered a total fast every Tuesday. In our circumstances this was self-denial indeed. Outwardly she remained stoical and serene. There was little laughter left in her; the only person who could still make her smile was our Khozyain with his outrageous ditties.

CHAPTER 5

Hope

The Siberian autumn struck quite suddenly. The temperature dropped, mornings became misty and the days shorter. The sky filled with cries of geese flying low over Lake Kubysh. This type of autumn was hardly a season: it was no more than a warning that winter was about to reclaim the Eurasian land-mass. There was no time for clouds and rain, and for that reason it was different from the Russian autumn evoked in Pushkin's *Evgeny Onegin*: '*Uzh nebo osen'yu dyshalo…*':

> More often now the sun was clouded;
> The sky breathed autumn, sombre, shrouded;
> Shorter and shorter grew the days;
> Sad murmurs filled the woodland ways…

Nikolaevka's autumn was as beautiful as Pushkin's. But the difference between them went further than clouds and rain. The southern edge of the Western Siberian Plain lacked trees, purveyors of colour and providers of a carpet of leaves. In my exile, whilst bowled over by the sharp autumnal interlude, I still longed for Pushkin's – and Łobzów's – leafy, leisurely season of transformation.

At about this time, and quite suddenly, I discovered that I could speak Russian. I am told it was a case of learning by osmosis. It was totally painless. Wisely, my mother chose this moment to suggest that I should go to the local secondary school. I was included in class 3, no questions asked. We were accommodated in an annexe – in effect a huge log cabin with two large classrooms and a generous corridor. Furniture was basic: tables, stools and a blackboard. There was some heating – for me a luxury even though it was minimal – but there was no lighting. Classes were enormous, about forty at the junior levels, and still the school was overcrowded; a two-shift routine was unavoidable. We were regularly switched from one shift to the other, because the late shift had little daylight. Each pupil on the late shift had to bring his personal *puzyrek* – a small bottle fitted with a wick and filled with paraffin. Of an evening the classroom became a sea of flickering lights. It was smelly, hazardous, and very pretty.

My mother's decision to send me to the Soviet school was a radical step. Most deportee children were kept at home through a mixture of defiance and fear of indoctrination. My mother was prepared to take the risk. She explained to me that she expected selective learning, without submission to brainwashing. I was proud of her confidence in me, and was determined not to let her down.

The opportunity arose soon enough. I was instructed to join the Pioneers, the first step on the ladder towards party membership. I refused. The teacher, under pressure no doubt to 'deliver' the children, ordered me to stay behind after lessons. She sat at her table, I at mine. She told me that I would not be released until I signed up. So we sat there, eyeing one another. Time went by and my teacher became tired and hungry. Eventually I was released – and on return home commended by my mother. I had won my first confrontation with the System.

But this was only a prelude. During my second year of Soviet education I was elected by my peers (no doubt with some encouragement from the authorities) to the office of *klasnyi organizator* (head of class). I did not seek the job and I declined to accept. This was unheard of, and my classmates became concerned for my future. Sure enough, I was hauled before *zav-uch,* short for *zaveduyushchii uchennikami* – the all-powerful political boss of the school. He told me to sit down, moved over close to me – his legs wide apart – and began shouting: *'Tebya nassy izbirayut!'* (You are being elected by the masses!) I stood my ground, only just, and was eventually released. My mother was very pleased, but also worried about possible repercussions. There were none, and I was left alone to get on with my studies, which by then I was starting to enjoy.

In September 1940, I was still unable to read or write in Russian. I was extremely unsure of myself. My first dictation was a disaster, and my chances were pronounced bleak. But I was fascinated by this new language, and I began applying myself. In the spring of 1941 my grade in the Russian language rose to 'good' (second in the scale of five). Other subjects were no problem. At the end of the school year I was declared one of the two *udarniks* of my class: the two that is, whose grades were at least 'good'. There were no *otlichniks* – those with only 'very goods' – among us.

The other *udarnik* was a Kazakh boy called Akhmetov, a village aristo in shiny high boots with beautifully soft leggings. Our relationship was one of mutual respect, which eventually, and slowly, blossomed into friendship. In the meantime I was befriended – swiftly this time – by Kol'ya Glotov. He had only one eye, but in spite of this disability – indeed perhaps because of it – he was a boy of some standing. We two co-opted Grishka Palej, the maths wizard. The three of us set the tone, so to speak: the two deportees delivering results, presided over by the street-wise and respected Kol'ya. The fourth member of the class deserving a mention was our Hercules, Karpachev. He was good-natured but not too quick-witted, and for that reason disqualified from our inner circle. On one occasion he challenged me to a friendly wrestling match, presumably to win some respect. Everyone assumed that I had no chance. But then I remembered one particular 'throw', shown me by my riding instructor at Łobzów. It was more of a Ju-Jitsu throw than a legitimate wrestling hold, and it amounted to locking one's right arm around the opponent's neck and then twisting the victim anticlockwise onto the ground over one's right knee. I deployed this against Karpachev – and soon had him on his back. My success became a sensation. Karpachev demanded several replays, and each time I was able to pin him down in exactly the same way. It still puzzles me why he failed to apply the same ploy against me – I was much smaller and not at all strong. But he was a good-natured giant, and we remained on the best of terms.

Winter arrived early. There was nothing tentative about snow east of the Urals. It came down suddenly and copiously, and soon muffled the *izbas* to the rooftops. It was like an instant 'make-over', to use a modern term. Ugly blemishes and wrinkles were buried. Temporarily. Relentless frost followed soon after, settling at below 20 degrees Centigrade, often plunging to minus 40. Old men spoke of minus 60… The snow became hard, and on calm days the sky was blueish – occasionally bright blue. But there was an ugly side to the Siberian winter: the *buryan*, a snow storm without snowfall. At ground level icy wind pumps a dust of tiny particles of hardened snow at anyone who dares to confront it. Visibility is low, frost-bite virtually inevitable. Death is seldom far away. During *buryan* any self-respecting 'Sibiryak' stays inside; and when he has to go out, he makes sure that he wears appropriate clothing: warm underwear, *pimy* (long stiff felt boots), a *fufayka* (padded jacket), a fur hat with ear-flaps, and an assortment of woollen scarves.

To us deportees all these necessities were inaccessible. Indeed, in Nikolaevka *pimy* were like gold-dust, a valued inheritance subject to a brisk repair business, and only very occasionally for resale. So our commune settled down to hibernation, now faced with the double threat of hunger and cold. Anuśka and Tereska huddled in their corner, writing interminable letters, awaiting replies, and taking their turn at the 'Polish flying library'. This involved the few books that had accompanied the exiles all this way (although none had come with us). They were carefully split into many slender instalments, which were then discreetly circulated among the Polish-speaking community, weather permitting. It was the Nikolaevka flying library that introduced me to Sienkiewicz's *Quo Vadis*, the novel that won him the Nobel Prize. Parcels from my mother's family in Wilno were the joyful milestones. We went to bed early: there was no light apart from my *puzyrek*, which in any case was for my homework. Early bed was also a way of keeping warm; and of killing time.

All this time my mother stitched her duvets, and tried to defuse the occasional conflict. There were not many of these. Everyone understood that calm was one of the weapons for survival. Hala produced the occasional poem, and we sent copies to Wilno and elsewhere. I wonder if any of them reached their destinations. My mother was sometimes persuaded to stop sewing, and instead to sketch a little with crayons. She drew her three children, which attracted the attention of our Khozyain. Eventually he too was persuaded to sit for her. His little portrait was the best of them all.

We dreaded the approach of Christmas. Back home it was the happiest event of the liturgical cycle: the exuberant coming together of the material and the spiritual. Tentative, and very modest, preparations were put in hand. Some bits from the parcels were put aside for *Wigilia* – the Vigil celebrated on 24th December at the sighting of the first star of the evening. There was no problem with that: the cold Siberian sky was crystal-clear. Khozyayushka invited our women to make (under her supervision) some real Russian *bliny*, delicious pancakes. Władek's bench was commandeered and transformed into a banqueting table under a white sheet. There was plenty of hay under the 'table cloth', a reminder of the stable at Bethlehem. The Samoilovs, after ritual refusals out of politeness, were persuaded to join in. Prayers were said, and *opłatek* (a wafer symbolising Communion, safely received from Wilno) was shared. Wishes were exchanged (along the lines of 'next year in Jerusalem'), carols were sung pianissimo and tears were shed. Our first Siberian *Wigilia* remains a happy, bitter-sweet memory to this day.

Two years later, at the age of fourteen, I wrote a description of our daily life in Siberia: 'During the winter, in a small room covered with mould where the ten of us lived together and where hands were stiff with cold, I studied by the *puzyrek* from the occasional textbook which I was able to borrow from some fellow-deportees. Most of the time we were hungry. The fight for survival was interspersed with illnesses. Deported from Poland without warm clothes, we suffered during Siberian winters regular frost-bites on the face, the hands and the feet.'

I faced frost-bite every day on my trek to school, which I persisted in attending because I had discovered the pleasures of learning. My clothes were inadequate; other children had *pimy*, I had to make do with my father's old riding boots. But clearly I was prepared to pay the price. There was little in me of pure dedication to knowledge; I had simply discovered the pleasure of winning against the odds and performing better than others – not a pretty sentiment, but a powerful motivation. The Russian language was the main challenge, and its conquest a source of exhilaration. This in turn led me to the school library, stocked mainly with Marxist-Leninist texts, but containing some classics of Russian literature, and even a few foreign books. In my spare time I began my systematic forays into Russian *belles-lettres*: Pushkin, Lermontov, Gogol, Tolstoy... The fascination is still as intense as it was then. In Nikolaevka I also discovered Shakespeare, Dickens, and Robbie Burns – in Russian translation.

Maths was my other passion, although there I had to defer to the superb Grishka Palej. We were both rated as 'very good', but his grade, unlike mine, was effortless. We used the excellent pre-revolutionary text-books by Kiselev.

My 'third subject' was the exotic Kazakh language, still employing Latin script. I found it fascinating and can still name the fingers of the hand: *bas parmak, bere uluk, onton kerek, shin-shin shmok, kishkintai bubok.* The rhyming sounds slightly suspicious, but I have no reason to question the bona fide of our fearsome Kazakh teacher. I also remember *aman* – the Kazakh equivalent of 'shake hands' among the village boys *(bala)* and girls *(dzhimurtka).* Lovely sounds. Other subjects I treated as a tedious necessity. I did well in all of them, although I missed practical science. But then we had no labs, or indeed any other aids to lighten the burdens of learning.

Winter gave way reluctantly to spring. *Buryans* were succeeded by wet and bitingly cold winds. Our rock-hard streets now turned into mud-baths. The way to school became an assault course. For me it was a hateful season, and it seemed to last for ever.

On 4th March 1941 my mother wrote to her mother-in-law in Wilno, who had sent two pairs of stockings and some boiled sweets. This is the only surviving letter of our exile. A great deal of it concerns my father: 'So far I have no news of Tadzio, but I wait patiently… Poor Tadzio – thrown aside by evil people but – I fervently believe – under Divine protection… Nothing wrong can happen to him. He will survive these terrible trials, as shall we all. I pray every day with all my heart that we may have enough strength. May God hear our most fervent prayers for the reunion of all families… Poor dear Tadzio – he must worry about our fate.' The letter also gives some idea of our daily life as we emerged from our first Siberian winter: 'We try to manage our daily affairs very prudently, so that things to eat may last as long as possible. Thank God we are all well again. Tereska no longer complains of palpitations – in my view a sign of nervousness. Anuśka's temperature is back to normal. Michałek is well and so far my own health has not failed me once; may it continue so… Better food has a lot to do with good health and good sleep… We have early signs of spring, so the girls are beginning to make preparations for their summer employment: cutting down trees (in the forest) and sawing them into lengths. I sew as much as I can; Michałek's results at school are excellent – just like his father's used to be – in spite of difficulties with a foreign language.'

My mother goes on to express concern for the health of her mother-in-law and her entire family: 'May God protect you all.' Her gratitude for the offerings is fervent. 'We know that you, our dear ones, deny yourselves to help us. We think with deep gratitude of those who come to our rescue.' And now comes the most poignant passage: 'Such nice things (the sweets) we normally divide into four equal parts and then each of us manages her/his own share; but this time we allowed ourselves only one sweet each; the rest will be put aside – perhaps Tadzio will make contact, and we would then have something to send him...'

~

Within days of the outbreak of German-Soviet hostilities in June 1941 the Wehrmacht captured Wilno. Our line of communication with my mother's family – in other words, with the outside world – was cut; and the life-giving food parcels ceased. From now on our life would no longer be a bloody-minded battle for survival, but a desperate struggle to delay the inevitable approach of death. Many years later my mother admitted to me that during that summer of 1941 she went out begging. She insisted that this happened only once, or maybe twice... She desperately persisted with her stitching and sewing, and Anuśka (then just 21) and Tereska (19) went out to join the 'woodcutting brigade'. This was really man's work, beyond the strength of any girl of that age, however robust and well fed. Neither of my sisters was robust or well fed. But they bravely struggled on with their quotas, weakened by hunger and pursued by clouds of midges, until work ran out later in the summer. Soon after, Anuśka was engaged as a housekeeper by an old widower who owned a cow, and was therefore rated a *kolkhoz* aristocrat. That job became a burden because the old man would regularly get drunk. There may have been some harassment. Anyway, one evening Anuśka came running home and said that she would not go back to the old drunkard. A modest opportunity for some 'cross-subsidising' (some milk, even a little cream) had to be forfeited.

I too, at the time aged 12, joined one of the *kolkhoz* 'grain brigades'. We were housed out among the fields of wheat in a temporary shack –

little more than a roof over our heads. In theory food was provided, but it was no more than thin cabbage soup, to which regular *kolkhozniks* added bread and other provisions of their own. I had none of those. I soon discovered that I was unable to keep up with my older and better-fed companions. Not quite knowing what to do with me, the kindly *brigadir* (foreman) gave me the job of oxen-driver. I found myself carting loads of wheatsheaves and loudly directing the animals with either a *tsop*, or a *fsaba* – left or right (I do not remember which) in the Kazakh language – which the oxen understood and reluctantly obeyed. But my pair remained much slower than the rest. And then one of the other drivers took me aside and explained that to achieve results one had to poke goads up the backsides of the unfortunate animals. Soon my pair were trotting – and I am still ashamed to recall this particular shortcut to efficiency. In due course one of my oxen took revenge on its tormentor – a fact which I now accept as deserved justice. One lunch-break the ox stood on my bare foot. The torture was long – oxen are ponderous and the pain was excruciating. Mercifully no bones were broken because I was pinned down on soft ground.

My first pay in kind (a small sack of wheat grain) was derisory. We realised that the *kolkhoz* was paying the likes of me much less than its members. So I did not bother to go back. Instead I spent a lot of precious time waiting at one of our three ancient windmills for my turn to have my grain converted into flour. And as I waited, I explored openings for odd jobs in the 'private sector'. My friend Kol'ya Glotov invited me to join their fishing syndicate – a great honour, rather like being invited to become a member of an exclusive London club. I went out with them, but it was no good. These boys were after sport, and I was looking for food. In the meantime a really promising opportunity came my way, which was also an unintentional contribution to the anti-German war effort. A lot of men were called up, and their wives could not cope with their gardens, or with the occasional execution of a hen no longer able to lay eggs. I stepped in and soon became a useful – if unskilled – gardener, and a swift despatcher of poultry. In a previous existence I might have been employed by the Tudors: I used the axe. The earnings, though irregular, became sufficient to keep me at it. In time I acquired a small reputation as a promising odd-job man; a reputation sealed the following summer with an invitation to dismantle the roof of the 'milk centre' – a major coup for a 13 year old. For this job I recruited a helper, and at the end of two hectic days each of us came home with a bucket of skimmed milk.

At the height of the summer of 1941 the outside world of war and politics began to intervene, providing distractions from the daily grind. We welcomed the setbacks of the Red Army (as did some locals, including our Khozyain), forgetting that it was the other deadly enemy who was administering the blows. I remember hearing on a loudspeaker that Smolensk had been abandoned to the Wehrmacht after fierce fighting, and saying to myself: 'serves the bastards right'. It took me two years to spread these sentiments evenly between the Soviets and the Germans: 'let the two bastards bleed each other to death'. Driven by this primitive ferocity, I was nevertheless still able to distinguish between the Russian people and the Soviet system. This pleases me today.

At this time Nikolaevka received its second influx of deportees: a contingent of Volga Germans, deemed by Moscow to be a risk on the Volga – i.e. not far enough from the advancing Wehrmacht. Actually, these people, unlike us, were a part of the fabric of Russia, having been imported by Catherine the Great in the late eighteenth century. We and they watched each other with interest; at arm's length, but without hostility. The German deportees were followed by a contingent of refugees from Leningrad – an altogether different additive to our social mix. These newcomers from the 'second capital' seemed to us extremely sophisticated. There was a residual chic about them, and affectations reminiscent of another era. They were given to bathing in the nude on the far side of Lake Kubysh. Kol'ya Glotov's gang (which included me, naturally) devised observation posts, and from these we indulged in some joyous peeping. In the autumn one or two teachers were found among the Volga Germans and the Leningrad sophisticates, and our local school – all credit to the headmaster – invited them to join its staff. The newcomers were of high quality, among them a fearsome Volga German with a face like a waffle. He was told to teach German – the second foreign language alongside Kazakh. I fancy that my smattering of German, acquired east of the Urals and long since forgotten, would have borne the stamp of the eighteenth century Volga dialect.

There were also some new additions to the Polish-speaking community of Nikolaevka, no more than three or four families. They were not deportees under NKVD supervision, but Jewish refugees who managed to move east ahead of the German advance. These newcomers were comparatively well off and well dressed. Our local authorities treated them correctly. In fact, a young lady doctor among them was immediately asked to take charge of the cottage hospital, whence – even though denied medicines and facilities – she was able to offer much-needed professional care. She was assisted by another elderly Jewish newcomer, long retired but apparently with a brilliant medical career behind him.

And then came the Rudskis, mother and her teenage son. Their provenance was shrouded in mystery. They too may have been Jewish, and they certainly had important connections in Moscow. The Rudskis were civilised, and the son Edzio tumbled for Tereska which we took as proof of the young man's good taste. My mother did not ask any questions, her relations with Mrs Rudska were correct, and Tereska's admirer and I struck up a friendship. No doubt my position of 'the kid brother' encouraged Edzio to be nice to me.

The summer was coming to its climax and we knew that autumn was just round the corner. My mother was becoming apprehensive, and unusually withdrawn. She knew that this winter would be even more difficult than the previous one: there would be no help from her relatives. She feared for our survival.

Then, quite suddenly, news arrived of the Sikorski-Maisky agreement, signed on 30th July 1941. The Soviet Union desperately needed help against the Germans, and by this agreement, signed by the Polish Prime Minister in exile and the Russian Ambassador in London, Stalin provided for the release of Polish prisoners and deportees so that a Polish Army could be formed on Soviet territory. Our community was at first stunned; and then, as the news sank in, euphoric. My mother was convinced that the miracle she had been praying for had happened. Soon after, Uncle Henio, since mid-1940 in a Soviet Prisoner of War Camp ('Kozel'sk II') wrote to my mother from Moscow that he was on the staff of the Polish Military Mission. The two of them launched a frantic search for my father.

One day a bearded man in rags arrived on the Samoilov doorstep. To our amazement, he turned out to be old Mr Naumowicz, released from prison (or a Gulag). He had a long journey behind him and was very weak. Our little commune, now joyously expanded to ten, began fussing over him. He soon perked up. Other Polish ex-prisoners, younger than he – tens of thousands of them – began streaming from all the corners of the Soviet Union towards a small town called Buzuluk, where General Anders – until August 4th himself a prisoner in the notorious Lubyanka – had set up his headquarters in early September.

To us the name Anders was familiar. He was 'our general', the commander of the splendid Nowogródek cavalry brigade which we had watched on exercise around Łobzów during the 1938 manoeuvres. We soon heard of his – and his brigade's – excellent record during the September 1939 campaign. Now all these starved ex-prisoners in rags who wanted to fight for Poland flocked to him in thousands. They knew that they were placing their lives in good hands. News travelled slowly in those parts, but eventually – around Christmas in fact – a copy of *Orzeł Biały* (White Eagle), the newspaper of Anders's army, arrived in Nikolaevka. It was the very first number, and it described the visit of General Sikorski, the Polish Commander-in-Chief as well as wartime Prime Minister, to his newest and most eccentric army in exile. My sisters shed tears over it; and so, I expect, did my mother.

In the depth of our second Siberian winter a consignment of used warm clothes (a gift from America I think) arrived in Nikolaevka via the Polish Embassy to the Soviet Union. The Polish community spontaneously elected my mother as their trustee charged with the distribution of these precious offerings. I watched with pride as she assumed command; but I was not surprised: the former *châtelaine* of Łobzów was in her element.

The aid did not extend to food. In the Soviet Union of 1941–42 such supplies did not travel well in bulk, unless of course under NKVD supervision. And it was food that was needed most, because hunger was beginning to give way to starvation. With resistance at its lowest, illnesses became frequent; some of them serious. My mother went down after Christmas with severe abdominal pain. We watched helplessly as the distinguished old Jewish doctor examined her with great care. He said he did not know what was wrong; he also said that even if he did know, he could do nothing without medicines. So we prayed as we looked after her; she who was struck down for the first time in her life. Eventually the pain subsided, and she was able to go back to her sewing. Soon after, our Pani Nadzia became very ill. She was taken to the cottage hospital where she died peacefully in Zosia's arms. Rodion Samoilov and his friends sang at her graveside.

Driven by last year's successes I went back to school, where I found new challenges which came with the higher standards imported from Leningrad and the Volga. Our first lesson of Kazakh was opened with a resounding declaration from the teacher that Latin script had been joyfully abandoned by the Kazakh people in favour of Cyrillic, so that the two nations, the Kazakhs and the Russians, could be bound together by even stronger ties of brotherly love; and so on... The speech was passionate and very long, so I decided to amuse myself by firing dried sun-flower seeds from my new catapult. The very first missile hit the teacher smack in the forehead; and all hell was let loose. I kept my head down, and managed to avoid detection. But I could not avoid the extra-mural initiatives of another teacher (a nice young female) who took it upon herself to make us behave *kulturno* – politely – and on one occasion proceeded to demonstrate the use of a handkerchief: she spread hers on the palm of her left hand – and then blew her nose through the fingers of her right hand onto it.

Although I had acquired the reputation of a refusenik my academic results were getting better and better, and I was not molested. Wishing to serve my class in my own way, I offered to start a wall newspaper. Permission granted, I recruited Grishka Palej and the two of us wrote down innocent classroom gossip (quite a lot of it invented), which was duly posted – and received with rapture. In our small way Grishka and I pioneered the introduction of the joys of the popular press to Soviet youth. I suspect the authorities were unaware of the subversive nature of our venture. We covered our tracks by diligently applying ourselves to basic military drill – a new subject introduced to the curriculum to increase the commitment of the young to *Velikaya Otechestvennaya*, the 'Great Patriotic War'.

For me all these goings-on at school were a blessed distraction from the grim realities of our existence. My sisters had no such escape. For them the daily grind must have been unbearable. My mother clung to the hope that the new Polish-Soviet understanding might yet bring our release, and this she offered to us – and to herself – as an antidote for depression. She continued to search for distractions nearer home. One day she triumphantly produced a three-string balalaika, and challenged me – the musical member of the family – to play it. I soon accumulated a basic repertoire of chords to accompany such current favourites as *Katyusha* and *Tri Tankista* (a song in praise of Soviet tank crews). There was another in praise of their equipment (*Bronya Krepka i Tanki Nashy Bystry* – 'Our Armour is Strong and Our Tanks Are Swift'), but I avoided the Polish army repertoire.

My mother also encouraged me to try my hand at sketching. For my subject I chose battle scenes, and soon discovered that there existed in Nikolaevka an untapped market for my kind of art. My first commission came from Kol'ya Glotov's parents who asked for a bloody but victorious encounter with the Germans. This, my first serious exploration of the genre, was extremely violent, and much praised. The reward was a large slice of fresh bread. Other commissions followed (so did the 'emoluments') and I became something of a local war-artist. More than that: an artist who lived to see his work displayed in Nikolaevka's front rooms, under the Icons.

In the early spring the husband of Mrs Tubielewicz arrived in the village. An ex-prisoner, he was now a Polish officer in a splendid British uniform – which created a sensation. He came armed with official papers declaring his wife and daughters to be 'dependents of the Polish Army', and immediately took them away to Uzbekistan. It was to Uzbekistan that General Anders was allowed to move his men in search of more humane conditions. Soon afterwards Captain Bazylewski arrived in Nikolaevka to fetch his wife and her guitar. We watched them depart, envied their luck, and hoped that maybe one day our turn might come… Władek Naumowicz and one or two other young men took the opportunity to volunteer, and presently set off. We were left to face the Siberian spring, which in 1942 was to be not only tedious but downright treacherous.

One sunny afternoon Tereska and I went for a walk along the far bank of Lake Kubysh. We did not realise that the ice was already melting. I began showing Tereska how to skate on one's heels. Suddenly the ice gave way. I just managed to stay afloat as she rushed towards me and stretched out her hand to pull me to safety. There was no time to be frightened. The trek back in wet and ice-cold clothes was far more distressing. A few days later the river Ishym broke its banks, flooded the steppe, engulfed Lake Kubysh, and began creeping towards the Samoilov *izba*. The scene was breathtaking: a vast expanse of huge floes charging northwards in close formation and noisily crunching as they collided. Some people in Nizhnaya began moving out. Samoilov sent his family away but decided to stay on himself. As did my mother. It went without saying that we three remained with her. The battle of nerves began: our Khozyain and his Barynya willing the river to submit and retreat. It was the Ishym that eventually gave way.

~

Early summer of 1942 came in, and still we had no news of my father. I saw in my mother's face deep concern. Then a telegram arrived from Kuibyshev. The date is difficult to decipher, but it must have been 30th May. It was signed by the Polish Ambassador to the Soviet Union, and it read: 'Transferring by telegraph one thousand two hundred roubles. Confirm receipt. Am sending a letter. We are searching for your husband. Ambassador S. Kot.' The money was a god-send, of course, but infinitely more important was the reassurance. Now we knew that President Raczkiewicz, and with him the Polish Government in Exile in London, not only remembered Tadeusz Giedroyć and his family, but also knew where my mother and her children were exiled. The promised letter never reached us, but instead we received a food parcel which was an instant sensation. It came from China. It was sent by Tadeusz Romer, until recently Polish Ambassador to Japan, who had launched an aid programme for the Polish deportees in the Soviet Union. These signals gave us new hope and strength.

The school year ended on a high note: I was declared an *otlichnik*. All my grades were 'very good' – in Russian, *otlichno*. Akhmetov remained an *udarnik*. Neither my mother nor I expected this high honour, because I had acquired a reputation as a dissident-in-the-making. But our secondary school in the middle of nowhere was brave enough to give justice to results. The *zav-uch* did not have his way. Today I remember with gratitude, and pay tribute to, my teachers and their headmaster, whose name I no longer recall.

Now aged thirteen-and-a-half, I thought of myself as a young man, ready for a serious round of odd jobs and the occasional artistic commission. My self-esteem received a further boost when I discovered that the lovely Liza Samoilova was now aware of my existence. She had a slight squint which I found particularly attractive. But I did not know how to acknowledge my good luck. And soon new events turned my attention elsewhere.

Late in June official documents arrived by post from the Polish Army (already in Uzbekistan) summoning my mother and her three children to a place called Guzar. We had some difficulty in finding it on the map: it is located halfway between Samarkand and Termez on the Soviet-Afghan border, and less than 50 kilometres from Kesh, the birthplace of Tamerlane. Guzar was the main reception depot of the Polish Army.

My sisters and I declared at once that we were ready for anything, even for a journey beyond Samarkand. Anuśka was particularly vocal in this; and she spoke for the three of us. The decision rested with my mother, of course. It was the second critical decision of her life. She faced the choice either to remain in the middle of this Siberian nowhere, or to risk a journey to the furthest corner of Soviet Central Asia in conditions of wartime chaos. A decision of this magnitude, to be taken also on behalf of her children, confronted a woman without material means to speak of, or male protection. She decided that we should go.

CHAPTER 6

Ania

I have before me some early photographs of my mother salvaged from the debris of World War Two. In the earliest, the round face of a six-year-old smiles from ear to ear, sending a message that it is the whole person, not just the face, that is smiling. In later photographs she emerges as a graceful young woman with a straight back and a characteristically tilted head. In 1919, the year of her marriage, Jan Bułhak, the Cecil Beaton of Eastern Europe, caught Ania's perfect small nose *en profil*. 'Of all three of us,' Aunt Zosia recalled, 'you were the first to attract admirers, and the first to receive a proposal of marriage. Mama had to take you away from your first ball after two young men exchanged visiting cards (a preliminary to a duel), because both asked you for a Mazurka and you took the floor with the one who was not the first to invite you.'

Ania's father, Leon Szostakowski, was born in 1850. He grew up under the care of a French tutor on the estate of Sokółki, some 80 km northeast of Daugavpils in today's Latvia – a property much depleted by his father's lavish life-style, where an atmosphere of patriotic romanticism prevailed. On 8th June 1863 the thirteen-year-old Leon sneaked into the citadel of Daugavpils to witness the execution by firing squad of his cousin, the insurgent Leon Plater, and to carry back to the mother of the condemned man a handful of earth soaked in his blood. He studied law in St Petersburg, began a successful practice as a jurist, and in 1880 asked for the hand of Melania Umiastowska, the daughter of an eminent family, one of the richest in the region. With ancestors holding high public office in Lithuania, the Umiastowskis had inherited a substantial fortune in property, and in due course established several charitable and educational trusts. (These were all dissolved by the Soviet authorities after the war, but one survives in Rome to this day, the *Fondazione Romana Marchesa Umiastowska*, offering study grants to Polish scholars in Italy).

In normal circumstances Melania's parents would have had little to complain about in her suitor. The heir to Sokółki was well-educated and widely travelled (with Berlin and Paris to his credit). He stood at the threshold of a promising legal career. Immediately after his proposal, however, he was placed under arrest by the Tsarist secret police, the *Okhrana*, on suspicion of plotting against the state.

The Russian authorities accused Leon of subversive activities on behalf of the 'socialist revolutionary party'. He certainly was not a revolutionary, nor a socialist, and under interrogation he denied the accusation. On the other hand his 'democratic' views were no secret; neither was his condemnation of the presence of the Russian occupiers on the territory of the Grand Duchy of Lithuania. This was enough for the authorities, in a state of shock only weeks after the assassination of Tsar Alexander II on 1st March 1881. But the prosecutors had no evidence to support their case. As usual in such instances, the verdict took the form of a secret administrative directive, issued on 13th January 1882 in St Petersburg in the name of the new Tsar. Leon was condemned to exile with hard labour in Western Siberia.

While awaiting trial in the notorious Słuszka prison of Wilno, Leon passed the time by writing on the wall of his cell, from memory, long passages from Krasiński's *The Dawn*, the high point of Polish romantic poetry. Thus occupied, he received Melania's acceptance. Elated, he added to his mural: 'But I also had my Beatrice…'

Melania made her father escort her to the perimeter of the prison so that she could wave a white handkerchief at her fiancée. The scene was to be replayed by her daughter – my mother – some sixty years later.

Leon served his sentence in Tyumen', in conditions which he later described as extremely harsh. Melania now faced a difficult test: a five-year engagement at a distance – some distance! – to an enemy of the state. One can imagine the temptations offered by less risky options. Or even pressures towards such alternatives. The couple were finally allowed to meet in 1885, when Leon was released from detention and allowed to take employment on the eastern fringes of the Empire. They married at Ekaterinburg in the Urals – a triumphant ending to a long and unconventional engagement.

Leon was a talented man, determined to break away from the

constraints of his class, which encouraged young landowners to be good shots, good dancers and good farmers, but little else. Of course with his liberal views a career in the service of the Imperial establishment was out of the question. But the Russian legal profession – then highly regarded – offered an alternative with prospects, and also opportunities for public service of an informal kind. And so, after release from Tyumen' in 1885, Leon Szostakowski returned to the law, initially constrained to live in Shadrinsk and Kurgan in Siberia, and then at Perm, just west of the Urals. In 1889 he was allowed to move to St Petersburg, where his career took off. However, when in 1891 after nearly ten years of detention and exile, permission was finally granted for his return to Wilno, he did not hesitate in spite of the opportunities in the Empire's capital. The step was drastic because legal briefs entrusted in Wilno to a former political prisoner attracted the attention – and the hostility – of the ever-suspicious local secret police. But to Szostakowski work within his own community was a call of duty.

He returned home with the reputation of a rising legal star, and was soon acclaimed as one of the leaders of public opinion in the spirit of progressive liberalism. The fact that he had chosen to return to Wilno in spite of prospects in Russia was noted and approved. The 'great romantic' had demonstrated that he was ready for service where it was most needed. He disengaged from the management of the estate of Sokółki by leasing the home farms to a local tenant (retaining the manor and grounds for summer visits), and in Wilno he built a town house, known as the House Under the Swan. The family moved in during the autumn of 1894 – the youngest, Ania, having arrived just in time.

The House Under the Swan – *Pod Łabędziem* – with its terraces and its views of Wilno, was Ania's personal Arcadia. My Aunt Zosia described the decade 1894–1904 as 'the epoch without cares'. The beloved house on Pohulanka Hill had 'a happy atmosphere, where everything was geared towards the education of the children'. Pod Łabędziem became a setting for regular musical evenings (Leon being an enthusiastic cellist), during which Aunt Hela Tyszkiewicz, placed strategically behind Leon's back, would silently imitate his mannerisms to the delight of the children. This Arcadia was complemented by Leon's estate at Sokółki, where the family went for summer holidays. Aunt Zosia remembered it vividly: 'The manor was spacious, of timber and stone; reception rooms beautifully kept; extensive grounds with a park beyond, adorned by a pond; further on, a young forest planted by Papa himself. During our absences the house was under the care of old Peter, the footman; maintained in a state of permanent readiness for the return of the master: parquet floors shining, clocks ticking.'

In Wilno, alongside the usual attributes of wealth (a large apartment on the top floor, numerous servants, two governesses), the children led disciplined, moderate lives. Mela chose to be a partner to her husband in the modern sense – a novelty among their family and friends. She took part in the preparation of his court cases, and learned to type – a skill then judged eccentric – so that drafts could flow freely as speeches were honed. The children – sharp observers – soon realised that the secret of this exceptional partnership was the 'happiness which their parents found in each other' (Aunt Zosia again). The next generation went into the world with a great deal of discreet confidence, freely dispensing good-natured friendliness. The main source of this style must have been the total security of a home associated with a happy marriage.

Mela was there to help when Leon faced the greatest challenge of his professional life: the defence of the victims of the Kroże massacre. In 1893 a Cossack detachment, under orders from the local governor, brutally suppressed a demonstration by the Catholic population of the small Samogitian town of Kroże, who were peacefully attempting to prevent the closure of their church. There were fatalities and rape, and the surviving victims were put on trial *en masse*. The outrage soon became a *cause célèbre*, watched and commented upon by the world press. Two Wilno jurists came forward to offer their services, free of charge, to the accused: Michał Węsławski and Leon Szostakowski, lifelong friends sharing similar views. In the case of my grandfather, a former political prisoner and Siberian exile, it was an act of great courage. The two prepared the case, then invited the best advocates of the Empire to plead under their guidance. Leon's contacts among the progressive jurists of St. Petersburg must have helped them recruit an impressive legal team. The accused were pardoned by the incoming Tsar, Nicholas II, eager for public approval.

I am convinced that the involvement of world opinion saved Leon Szostakowski from further persecution. He was left alone by the authorities. Sadly, however, his health began to deteriorate, no doubt as a result of imprisonment and harsh conditions in Siberia. The best medical care and a long sojourn on the Italian Riviera (where Leon pined for his beloved Wilno) failed to strengthen his resistance to viruses and infections. Soon after coming home, on 3rd February 1904, he died from pneumonia at the age of fifty-four.

At Leon Szostakowski's funeral his brother-in-law General Zenon Cywiński was overheard to say: 'How will Mela manage with five young children?' For the young generation the death of Leon was doubly shocking. Not only did they suffer the loss of a beloved father; their mother now became severe and distant. To the end of her life she wore black. She insisted on visiting her husband's grave alone, afraid of sharing her grief even with her children. It took them some time to understand that this was their mother's way: a search for peace through lonely discipline. Apparently she knew no other.

Harmony was eventually restored through the influence of Mela's mother. In the early 1890s, having sold the Umiastowski town house, Grandmama Umiastowska took an apartment in the House Under the Swan on the floor below the Szostakowskis. Of all her children she was closest to Mela, and the Szostakowski fivesome were to her 'our children'. To them she now brought the missing ingredients of warmth and laughter. During her own long widowhood Ania would be guided by this double model: her mother's dedication to the memory of a happy marriage, but at the same time her grandmother's capacity for happiness even in adversity.

Cywiński need not have worried about Mela's capacity to manage. She proved capable of sound decisions, and of a steady hand. The loss of Leon's income as an advocate coincided with the deadline for the settlement of his sister's share of their joint inheritance. Mela had to decide between the town house in Wilno and the country property at Sokółki. She wisely opted for the town house. The loss of Sokółki was softened by her family's offer of a charming dower house called Michaliszki on the edge of the Umiastowski domain. The House Under the Swan was subdivided into apartments, and these were let to chosen friends and relations. The resulting income, supplemented by the interest on the residual capital from Sokółki, was sufficient for school and university fees, some travel, and a frugal life-style not too different from before.

The two sons, my uncles Henio and Stefuś, were sent to the *École Polytechnique* of Lwów . This was no provincial college sponsored by a municipal council. It was an institution on a par with the best universities of Western Europe. Such institutions carried great prestige; and its graduates, adorned with the title of *Inżynier* (the closest English equivalent being Chartered Engineer), commanded appropriate status.

Of her three daughters Mela expected not just social graces but a baccalaureate – a radical departure from the traditions of her circle. So all three 'Swanettes' were shipped off to Cracow in pursuit of formal education: Zosia studied at the University of Cracow, Maniusia at the School of Nursing, and Ania at the Chyliczki Institute, an establishment that prepared young ladies for the management of a manorial household, and for the gentler aspects of farming. Ania arrived in Cracow in 1913.

The following year the First World War broke out, bringing disruption and difficulty for them all. Henio and Stefuś had no choice but to accept commissions in the Russian Imperial Army. The Szostakowski women subsisted in Michaliszki. During the most dangerous two years of the Russian revolution – 1917-1918 – the House Under the Swan became a sanctuary for friends and relations from the countryside menaced by marauding troops. Relief came in April 1919. The three young ladies and their mother welcomed the arrival in Wilno of the Polish Army under Józef Piłsudski. With him arrived two Polish volunteers: Henio, and Stefuś.

The Swanettes threw themselves into welfare activities for the soldiery. I remember a delightful photograph of Ania dispensing hospitality in a military canteen. And one particular incident related by Aunt Zosia: Piłsudski , surrounded by ladies in summer dresses and men in uniform, taking out a cigarette; several lit matches proffered, including one held by Ania – too late; and the Commander-in-Chief, noticing Ania's failed attempt, immediately putting out his cigarette so that he could accept a light from the young woman. Gentle manners within the sound of guns...

My father, Tadzio, arrived in Wilno in the wake of Piłsudski, but separate from the great man's entourage. At the age of thirty-one he came as Deputy Governor of the Wilno region – in the process of being wrested from the Reds. These were hectic days, during which young people nevertheless sought social distractions. And there, in the centre of Wilno society, Tadzio could not fail to notice Ania. Nor could she fail to notice him – a young man whose exploits were the gossip of Wilno even before his arrival.

Ania was bright, humorous and practical, with a passion for dancing. She had a way of appearing shy, but she was perfectly at ease with the world. She was adored by her siblings, and recklessly spoiled by her two brothers. The atmosphere in their home was one of almost automatic optimism, and of unquestioning – sometimes too simple – loyalties. It was a breeding ground for good works. Tadzio was doubly smitten: by Ania, and by her family; like Pierre Bezukhov in *War and Peace*.

When he came in full dress uniform to propose, Tadzio had to seek Ania out on a distant allotment tending a crop of tomatoes – her private venture. He disliked the dress uniform ('the guards of the Queen of Madagascar'), but he was more than willing to arrive in his official carriage – a coachman on the box, a batman in attendance.

Ania accepted Tadzio's proposal without much hesitation, even though she had known him for only a short time. She was swept up by the whirlwind romance, but she also recognised in him all those traits that she so admired in her own father: contempt for autocracy; liberalism grafted onto an allegiance to the Church – a surprising blend, but not uncommon in that part of Europe; and the prospect of a successful legal career.

Ania did have serious misgivings about one thing: the return journey from the allotment. A young unchaperoned lady in her escort's open carriage before the official engagement! Imagine the gossip! Tadzio however was not to be denied this, the most joyous ride of his life. The tomato-stained apron was tucked away and a roundabout route was plotted to avoid public outrage. No-one spotted the young couple, and a happy acceptance of the offer was formalised in the bosom of the House Under the Swan.

CHAPTER 7

Tadzio

My father was descended from an ancient family. Its founder was Giedrius, brother of Grand Duke Trojden who united and consolidated Lithuania in the 13th century. Giedrus ruled the duchy of Giedrojcie, or *Terra Gedereytha*, a large tract of land in eastern Lithuania covering at least 2000 sq km. Three successive dukes of Giedrojcie fought the knights of the Teutonic Order, who threatened the country from north and south. The fourth duke, Dowmont, quarrelled with his sovereign and was stripped of his status and political power. His title of 'Prince' remained, however, and was passed on to succeeding generations when he died in about 1400.

During the 15th century his descendants, in reduced circumstances and without opportunities for public service, turned to higher education and the Church. Five members of the clan became bishops of Samogitia, the second largest diocese of Lithuania. One Augustinian monk, Blessed Michael Giedroyć (d. 1485), is well on his way towards canonisation after a lifetime dedicated to the sick and the poor. His tomb at the church of St Mark's in Cracow remains a place of veneration.

The Giedroyć clan re-established itself in the course of the 16th century, both politically and materially, and lived as landowners and soldiers through the 17th century. Perhaps the most interesting of them was a pioneering industrialist who built a paper mill that could switch to the production of gunpowder in time of war.

Towards the end of the 18th century the family re-emerged on the European scene in the service of Napoleon. General Romuald-Tadeusz Giedroyć (d. 1824), was a 'particular friend' of the widow Josephine de Beauharnais. According to one of his daughters, he later persuaded her to accept a proposal of marriage from a younger man called Buonaparte.

Romuald's son Joseph was a rising star in the French army; Napoleon's aide-de-camp at Waterloo, he was promoted to the rank of general on the battlefield. Joseph's younger sister, the beautiful Lucy, is believed to have been the mistress of the poet Adam Mickiewicz – according to some the greatest poet of Slavdom (rivalled only by Pushkin). Their sister Cunegund, a lady-in-waiting to Empress Josephine, was the author (under a *nom de plume*) of the first pornographic novel in the Polish language.

Distinguished figures of the early twentieth century were Vera Gedroits (d.1932), a surgeon of world renown and a close friend of Tsar Nicholas II and his family, and Nikolai Gedroits (d. 1933), a wealthy and dynamic patron of the arts who founded four museums in Ukraine. Between the wars of the twentieth century two Giedroyć cousins rose to prominence in the Polish Second Republic: Francis-Dowmont (d. 1944), a pioneer in the history and philosophy of medicine, and Tadeusz, my father.

~

To a ten-year-old boy, my father was a distant and somewhat frightening hero. Friends spoke of his quickness of mind, and of his charm seasoned with a little irony. But there was much more to him than that. He was both a devout Roman Catholic and a political liberal. His sternness and impartiality, which served him well as a judge and administrator, were leavened by a love of music, birds and animals. He could not bear the sight of cruelty to any living creature, and I once saw him react with terrifying anger to a man mistreating a horse. Although shooting had been one of the pleasures of his youth, he renounced it at the age of forty. A commanding and volatile character, he was also, I realise now, a restless and eccentric soul for whom privacy, his family and the sheltering world of Łobzów provided quiet but essential spiritual nourishment, a haven from the storms of public life.

He had a distinguished military record, although he was modest about it. Two of his decorations attracted my admiration when he brought them out – rather reluctantly – on white-tie occasions: the Cross of Independence *(Krzyż Niepodległości)*, equivalent to the British Distinguished Service Order; and the Cross for Valour *(Krzyż Walecznych)*, equal to the British Military Cross, or the German Iron Cross.

Tadzio never spoke to me of his wartime deeds, but my mother and

Marteczka sometimes referred in hushed tones to the capture of an armoured train (together with a handsome pair of riding boots and a bucket of jam). I knew no more than that until I gained access to the Polish Army archives after the collapse of the Soviet Union in 1991. The files on Tadzio told a remarkable story. (It is, however, very complex; the military and political turmoil in the western borderlands of Russia in 1917-18 takes some unravelling. Readers should feel free to skip to the end of the chapter.)

My father was a reluctant subject of the Russian Empire, but this did not prevent him completing his legal studies at the Lycée Demidov, one of the four élite Russian law schools, in 1916. He then received his commission in the Russian army from the Constantine Academy of Gunnery in Petrograd. The commission was dated 16th August 1917, and it was granted not by the Tsar, but by the Russian Provisional Government. This fitted well with Tadzio's youthful radicalism: he longed for social justice, and saw the Russian imperial regime as its enemy. His success at Demidov, and his radical (but not revolutionary) outlook, caught the eye of Vladimir Stankevich, a distinguished Petrograd lawyer close to the Provisional Government. Stankevich decided to bring the young gunnery officer into the inner councils of the Russian high command and high politics: on 16th October 1917 Ensign Prince Tadeusz Giedroyć was appointed head of the Political Office at *Stavka*, the Supreme Headquarters of the Russian army, at that time stationed in Mogilev. He was to report to Vladimir Stankevich, High Commissioner at the HQ, through whom Prime Minister Kerensky hoped to influence the enormous Russian army, which was then in a state of terminal collapse. Tadzio arrived in Mogilev nine days before the Bolshevik *putsch* later to be described as 'the great socialist October revolution'.

My father's appointment at the Russian HQ was surprising, because one month earlier he had volunteered for service in the Polish First Corps, formed on Russian territory with the co-operation of the Russian authorities, but committed to the emergent Polish cause. Thus a *Polish* officer found himself at the centre of *Russian* high politics. This can only be explained by the extreme pressure of events, Tadzio's qualities known to Stankevich, and the common anti-Bolshevik cause uniting the

Provisional Government and the nascent Polish army. The Russian authorities must have realised that Ensign Giedroyć would become a source of intelligence to the Supreme Polish Military Committee, under whose auspices the Polish army was being created in Russia. Nevertheless, the beleaguered Provisional Government was prepared to accept the risks implicit in this arrangement.

Tadzio took up his duties at the Supreme Headquarters on 16th October 1917. He stayed at his post until 19th November, the day the Headquarters fell to Lenin's 'red sailors'. These thirty-four days must have been the busiest of his life. There was the official appointment – a mammoth task for a young ensign, however brilliant. There were also the demands for information and briefings from the Supreme Polish Military Committee (*Naczpol* in Polish), whose chairman Władysław Raczkiewicz was a personal friend.

The position of the Committee vis-à-vis the Provisional Government was extremely delicate. The Polish units were disciplined and efficient, and the Russians hoped to use them either against the Germans or against the Bolsheviks. The Poles on the contrary wished to husband their armed forces for future deployment in a Polish – not Russian – cause.

The precarious existence of the Polish units depended on two things: the continued determination of the Russian high command to resist the Germans, and the attitude of the Russian Acting Commander-in-Chief, General Dukhonin, towards the Poles. Tadzio was in a uniquely advantageous position to offer a view on both these matters. He had access to reports from the commanders on all the Fronts, and to the Military Missions of the Western Allies attached to Dukhonin. He could observe Dukhonin himself at close quarters. Obviously he made good use of the material to hand, because the citation for his Polish Cross of Independence singles out for praise the quality of his reporting. His capacity for analysis, and his overall grasp of the complicated military and political situation of the Eastern front, must have matched the highly influential position to which he was advanced by Stankevich. I also suspect that Tadzio enjoyed this multi-layered challenge, in particular the strong diplomatic element of it; for this, as we have seen, he was well suited, being clever and very good company. Serious motivation, an essential ingredient for success in public service, came from the knowledge that he was working for a new post-imperial order, which would bring with it political and economic opportunities for the former subject peoples of the Tsars.

On 7th November 1917 Lenin made his henchman Krylenko Commander-in-Chief of the Russian army – which consisted of several million men unwilling to fight. R. H. Bruce Lockhart described Krylenko as 'the most repulsive type I came across in all my connections with the Bolsheviks'. This description fits his subsequent career. Krylenko's arrival on the scene in early November 1917 signalled the beginning of the end of the old army establishment, and with it of Stavka, its Supreme Headquarters.

For as long as possible Tadzio's boss Stankevich tried to shield Dukhonin and his staff from danger by blocking the progress of the train bringing Krylenko and his 'red sailors', the Bolshevik storm troops, to Mogilev. He also refused to endorse Krylenko's orders for a general cease-fire on the grounds that the new C-in-C had not yet assumed control on the spot. Tadzio must have been involved in this desperate delaying action, because he said in his own detailed Curriculum that he took part in a mission 'to the headquarters of Krylenko'. It is a some-what ambiguous statement, but I read it as a hint that my father came face to face with that enemy of the old army establishment; an enemy doubly dangerous to Ensign Giedroyć in view of his delicate status as a Polish officer. These were sufficient grounds for him to withdraw, had he wished.

But the brave Dukhonin decided to continue *pro tem*, still believing that something of the army command structure could be salvaged. Stankevich decided to remain with Dukhonin, and Tadzio decided to stay with them. This was no longer an adrenalin-driven adventure. It was now a confrontation with a deadly enemy who had time and resources on his side. But during these last few days attempts were still made in Mogilev to galvanise the army, and to put together a credible political alternative to the Bolsheviks. These matters were extremely important to the Supreme Polish Military Committee, and Tadzio remained their primary source of information to the last. The citation for his Cross of Independence speaks of 'dangerous tasks' carried out in 'extremely risky circumstances'. In the last days of Stavka the young ensign, burdened with responsibilities well above his station, revealed his capacity for dangerous living.

The last 48 hours of Stavka have been described hour-by-hour in several books, with Stankevich's own memoirs as one of the main sources. In them I find a vignette which describes Tadzio's role in these whirlwind events. In the early hours of 19th November, only hours before the surrender of the remnants of Stavka troops to Krylenko's reds, a hasty meeting was arranged by Ensign Giedroyć in his hotel room to decide how best to smuggle General Dukhonin out of Mogilev to safety. Dukhonin himself was present. After some discussion Dukhonin declined to take advantage of the car made available to him by the aides. Having dismissed the last half-a-dozen or so officers that stayed with him, he hid his general's epaulettes under his raincoat (rebel soldiery were already roaming the streets) and walked back to his office. Tadzio and Stankevich slipped out from under the noses of the Bolsheviks and went their separate ways. Two days later Dukhonin was recognised by mutinous soldiers at the railway station and lynched on the spot.

Tadzio re-emerged in Kiev on 4th January 1918. Raczkiewicz and his collaborators arrived in Kiev at the same time, which suggests that Naczpol remained in contact with its star agent. Indeed, within two days Tadzio was appointed deputy head of Naczpol's intelligence service. Circumstances however prevented him from assuming his new responsibilities at once.

Within a week the battle for the city of Kiev began between the Bolsheviks and the troops loyal to the Ukrainian Central Council. Tadzio's instant inclination was to abandon his desk for the front line. He secured his release 'for the duration' and proceeded to recruit a band of Polish volunteers – less than twenty men – over whom he assumed command. A gunner by training, he armed the little group with a piece of field artillery which was soon to prove extremely useful. Within days Tadzio was ordered to assume responsibility for the defence of 'Kiev 1' railway station, a key objective which the Bolsheviks were attempting to capture with the help of an armoured train. The citation for Tadzio's Cross for Valour has this to say about the events that followed: 'At the head of his small detachment, he held the station for five days against the attacks of a superior enemy force; with accurate fire from his single field gun he disabled the armoured train brought into battle by the Bolsheviks. He then proceeded to capture the train, and man it with his own volunteers. Under his personal command the train became [for the next three days] the central element of the station's defences; when ordered to do so, he withdrew his unit from the station in an orderly fashion.'

Such then were the deeds behind Tadzio's light-hearted story about his spoils of war: the riding boots and the bucket of jam. The Cross for Valour, gazetted in 1921, reflects the true extent of his leadership and bravery.

The Cross of Independence was awarded in 1932 as the final recognition of his wartime services. This took notice of his role in the defence of Kiev. Naczpol simply declared: 'During the siege of Kiev he displayed physical courage and cool nerve'. Many years later Mme Raczkiewicz, who was at her husband's side during the siege, remembered how Tadzio moved to and fro under fire, 'sometimes unnecessarily; but then, he was very brave.'

I realise now that my father's role in the early struggle for Ukraine's capital has some historical significance. It was in fact one of the first instances of active help, extended spontaneously by the Poles towards the Ukrainians, in support of their struggle for freedom. Today, when bridges are being built between the two peoples after the bloody conflicts of the 1940s and the subsequent decades of hostility, the memory of the small band of Polish volunteers under Ensign Tadeusz Giedroyć fighting in defence of Kiev, 'the mother of all the cities of Rus',' should be remembered as a signal for the future.

On 25th January Tadzio handed over his command, rejoined Naczpol, and stayed on with them in Kiev to begin underground work under the Bolshevik occupation, which came to be known in history as 'the period of red terror'. Tadzio, the seasoned intelligence officer, was now recognised as a soldier of quality and a leader with a facility for improvisation. He returned to his duties as head of intelligence, clandestinely serving the Polish cause.

With the Treaty of Brest in March 1918 hostilities between Russia and

Germany ceased. German troops moved in to Ukraine, and showed little sympathy for Polish initiatives.

Early in April Tadzio was given a senior staff appointment at the head-quarters of General A. Osiński, Commander-in-Chief of the Polish Forces in the Ukraine. These consisted of two army corps, Second and Third, into which trained men declaring allegiance to the Polish (or rather Polish-Lithuanian) cause, were being transferred from the Russian army. The units were undergoing intensive re-organisation in the face of increasing German and Austrian hostility. In the meantime the First Polish Corps under General J. Dowbór-Muśnicki, the largest and most effective of the three Polish army corps, had established itself around Bobruisk in Belarus', from whence it looked for a *modus vivendi* with the Germans. The geographical separation of the Polish units was an obstacle, and there was a need for liaison between Kiev and Bobruisk-Minsk. Ensign Giedroyć played an active role in this risky undercover enterprise. Even before the arrival of the German occupying forces on 1st March 1918, it was he who first established contacts between Kiev and Bobruisk-Minsk, forcing his way across the Bolshevik lines in order to deliver important documents. This feat is also noted in the citation for the Cross of Independence.

The Polish authorities based in Kiev had grounds for suspicion that the Germans were making plans for the disbandment of the three Polish corps in the East. The future of the First Corps was of particular concern, because its commander (General Dowbór-Muśnicki) was drawn into unilateral negotiations and was thought to have taken a rather soft line. The Kiev Poles decided that drastic measures were needed. A plan was hatched to replace the pliant Dowbór-Muśnicki with a man who would be prepared to stand up to the Germans. The man chosen for the task was the brilliant young Polish colonel, Przemysław Barthel de Weyden-thal, hiding in Kiev under the pseudonym 'Barta'. The cover was neces-sary because the Germans thought him dangerous, and were already on his trail.

Disaster struck in early May. The Second Corps was dispersed by the Germans after a pitched battle (11th May 1918) in which General Osiński was taken prisoner. Meanwhile the Austrians were dismantling the Third Corps (still in early stages of formation). The decision was taken to smuggle Barta to Bobruisk, stage a coup, remove Muśnicki, and attempt to disengage the First Corps from the 'German embrace'. The immediate task was to smuggle Barta over a distance of more than 300 kilometres, infested with Germans already looking for him. No mean task, this; and an opportunity for Tadzio to stage the last – and most outrageous – of his three Eastern Exploits. Around 14th May Ensign Giedroyć managed to cross German-held Ukraine and Belarus', taking with him Colonel Barta disguised as his batman. The escapade was successful, and was duly singled out in the citation for the Cross of Independence.

The *coup* to save the First Corps was not successful, however. Muśnicki was reinstated and his units demobilised by the German authorities on 26th May. Yet from the point of view of the Polish cause it was not a total disaster: the men were offered repatriation to Poland, and the majority, over 23,000, found their way into the regular Polish Army being formed under Piłsudski .

Tadzio refused repatriation; in Kiev there was still work to be done, both official and clandestine. The time had come to wind up the affairs of Naczpol, and on 30th May 1918 Tadzio joined the Commission entrusted with this task. On 1st July he was appointed Commission secretary. Concurrently, he became involved in the provision of aid for the Polish refugees in Belarus'. All these activities, demanding in themselves, gave Tadzio freedom of movement across the vast territories of Belarus' and the Ukraine, which enabled him to discharge his clandestine tasks: the removal to safety of the men from the disbanded Polish units – mainly the ill-fated Second and Third Corps but also some from the First. These men had to be located, assembled into inconspicuous groups, and spirited away to either the Allies in Murmansk, or to Kuban' on the Black Sea. The transfers of manpower had to be carried out across enormous distances still under control of either the hostile Germans or the even more hostile Bolsheviks. These enterprises, too, were in due course highlighted in Tadzio's citation for the Cross of Independence. Naczpol fulsomely recorded 'Prince Giedroyć's extraordinary energy, perseverance and great organisational talents' He finally left Kiev, his work complete, in late November 1918, to re-emerge in Warsaw soon after at the side of his friend Władysław Raczkiewicz.

In the early summer of 1919 he arrived in Wilno (Vilnius) to take up the appointment of Deputy Regional Governor. His reputation preceded him and – I suspect – helped him to win the heart of Ania Szostakowska. Their marriage on 10th September 1919, in the Cathedral Church of the former capital of the Grand Duchy of Lithuania, was the first post-war event of the Wilno social calendar.

CHAPTER 8

Beyond the Oxus

For my mother the decision in the summer of 1942 to travel to Central Asia must have been painful. She always considered it her first duty to be as near to her husband as possible; now she was about to abandon that duty. But circumstances had changed. She knew that my father was neither in the Polish Army nor in the Embassy. If he were still alive, he could be anywhere between Archangel and Kamchatka. She alone could not mount a search of this magnitude. And she was encouraged by assurances from the Polish authorities that they were acting on her behalf. In these circumstances she decided that her next priority was to get her children out of the Soviet Union; in other words, to attempt a journey from Nikolaevka via Novosibirsk towards Tashkent and beyond, all the way to the Afghan border. Responding to the summons from Guzar was a step in that direction. Obviously, it was risky, but she had papers from the Polish Army and she assumed that these were endorsed by the Soviets. In fact this was far from the case, and it is just as well that she did not know how far Soviet-Polish relations had deteriorated since those papers were issued.

In the summer of 1942 Stalin and his henchmen were far less malleable than twelve months earlier. In December 1941, with the assistance of Russia's traditional ally 'General Frost', the Soviets had made a stand at the gates of Moscow, and managed to stop the German advance. Allied assistance was beginning to flow. There was no longer any desperate need for Polish help. At the same time this unusual ally on Soviet soil – thousands of semi-starved men in rags just out of Soviet prisons and Gulags – was recognised as a potential embarrassment. Stalin was already hatching new plans for Poland. In the meantime the NKVD was instructed to become less accommodating.

Anders was allowed to move his men to Tashkent in search of better conditions for convalescence. But in early March 1942 he was suddenly informed that his rations would be reduced from 70,000 (the number of men under his command) to 26,000. This was a tragedy of major proportions because the soldiery were already sharing their food with the Polish civilians gathering around the camps. Anders appealed directly to Stalin, secured an interview, and on 18th March renegotiated the rations up to 44,000. At the same time Stalin agreed to evacuate the balance of Anders's men, about 30,000 of them, to Iran for recuperation and training.

There followed the so-called First Evacuation. It was a Soviet *tour de force*. Within a week 34 trains were laid on by the NKVD, and between 24th March and 5th April half the Polish Army on Soviet soil was transported to Krasnovodsk, then to Pahlavi, an Iranian port on the Caspian Sea, in 17 or 18 shiploads. The extraordinary aspect of this exodus was that Anders managed to include in it some 11,000 civilians. Stalin certainly knew about this, but chose to ignore it. Not so the Polish Government in London. Orders were issued that no civilians were to be evacuated. Apparently the London Poles did not wish to upset the British Government, which had expressed doubts about its capacity to cope with a sudden influx of humanity in great distress. Anders ignored the orders of his political masters, and more than 11,000 old men, women and children were saved. To those thus rescued, Anders became a latter-day Moses. The rest of the world came to call this event 'the Polish Dunkirk'. The British – presented with a *fait accompli* – coped with their side of the task in their usual way: humanely and without fuss.

Back in Nikolaevka we knew little of the First Evacuation. For a long time I found this puzzling until, quite recently, I discovered that the Polish Embassy to the Soviet Union, fearful of an uncontrolled southward rush of the civilian population, deliberately suppressed the information. Neither did we know that relations with the Soviets had by then deteriorated to such an extent that Anders began doubting the rationale of fighting the Germans on the Eastern Front. He feared that his men would not give of their best alongside their recent jailers. Watching the Germans' swift advance towards the lower Volga and the Caucasus, he became doubtful of the Red Army's capacity to prevent a German breakthrough into the oilfields of Iran and Iraq. He therefore suggested to

General Sikorski that his entire army should join the British in the Middle East to help protect the oil.

On 8th June a telegram from the Polish Prime Minister in exile in London arrived at Jangi-Jul' near Tashkent, General Anders's HQ, ordering the Polish Army to remain in the Soviet Union. This was a political decision, taken 4,000 miles away by men unaware of local realities and unable to read the Soviet mind. Anders knew better, and decided to ignore the order. He suspected that the British authorities had already arrived at the same conclusion. So, on his own initiative, he requested an interview with Sir Archibald Clark-Kerr, British ambassador to the Soviet Union, to take the matter further. This act of insubordination took place on 7th July – and had an instant and dramatic effect. That same night, the night of 7th–8th July 1942, Stalin gave his agreement to the transfer of Anders's entire army to Iran. Orders for the Second Evacuation were issued to the Polish units on the 15th.

Stalin's motives for these decisions are unlikely ever to be fathomed. The instant response to the Anders – Clark-Kerr conversation suggests that in this case British and Soviet objectives were identical and urgent. The Polish historian Zbigniew Siemaszko recently suggested that Stalin's intelligence service anticipated the discovery by the Germans of the Katyń graves. Stalin would have been seriously concerned about the effect of this news on the Polish Army within the Soviet Union. So he chose the 'lesser evil' – the removal of Anders's 80,000 or so men from Soviet territory.

For us the last few days of June were extremely busy. My mother called on the chairwoman of the *kolkhoz* and, having secured her counter-signature on our precious papers, proceeded to convert her 'iron reserve' – the few gold coins put aside for a crisis such as this – into wheat flour to be transformed into dry biscuits, and into a Soviet currency more stable and even more valuable than gold: pure alcohol. There was no money left for transport to the rail station at Petukhovo. So, in anticipation of a 100-plus kilometre trek on foot, we reduced our bundles to a minimum. My balalaika had to go. By then my mother was not too strong on her legs, and the prospect of a long walk was extremely daunting. Help came unexpectedly from the Jewish merchant of Oszmiana. He offered to hire a *podvoda* – a one-horse cart – on the understanding that we would 'repay him sometime, somewhere... ' It was an act of great generosity. I do not remember the name of our benefactor, but 65 years later I still offer a prayer for him every Sunday.

The *podvoda* appeared at midday on 2nd July, complete with two silent and sullen Kazakhs. The bundles were placed on the cart, my mother was deposited on top of the bundles, and we set off across the village, past the *Radiotochka* and on towards the three rickety windmills, saying our goodbyes on the hoof as we passed the dwellings of various friends. The windmills waved their last farewell as we confronted the steppe and set off into the unknown. As the sky darkened, we began our second great journey.

We stopped for the night on the edge of a Siberian forest, sharing the shack of some hospitable woodcutters. If I remember rightly they were deportees from Lithuania. Early next morning we set off again under a heavy sky. Soon the rain came down, and our march became a muddy slog into the wind. Late in the afternoon we were overtaken by some fellow-travellers in a cart pulled by two strong horses. They took pity on us foot soldiers, and offered a lift. We accepted happily – and soon disappeared beyond the brow of a hill where our next staging point was to be on the edge of a small lake. My mother followed behind with the two silent Kazakhs.

After her children were lost from sight, my mother's two minders stopped the cart, un-harnessed the horse, and told her that the three of them would spend the night where they stood. My mother sensed danger and – after a short and particularly fervent prayer – said to the duo: 'Look up there. That person on the top of the hill is my son who is coming to be with his mother.' And so it was. Feeling uneasy about leaving her behind on her own, I began retracing my steps. As I marched down towards them, the two Kazakhs quickly re-harnessed the horse and resumed the journey. Thereafter my mother insisted that on that wet afternoon I saved her life.

Towards the end of the next day, 4th July, we reached the railway station of Petukhovo, where two and a half years earlier we had been tossed out of the cattle truck. The two Kazakhs were paid off, and we spent the night in an outbuilding of a house belonging to a railwayman.

The next morning we joined a large and impatient crowd of would-be passengers besieging the ticket office. A few dispirited Poles assured my mother that our chances of getting tickets were virtually nil. But she persisted, joining the crowd at the ticket booth whenever the news went round that the next eastward train was due. We took turns to accompany her during these depressing vigils.

The routine was becoming monotonous, but then a burly NKVD man appeared on the scene. Wishing to restore order, he shouted: '*Kto zdes' voennyi?*' (Any military personnel here?) In the hush that followed I heard my mother's tremulous voice: '*Ya voennaya*' (I am military personnel). The representative of internal order looked her up and down and said, 'Come with me.' The crowd parted and my mother was ushered to the window where her papers were scrutinised – and four tickets issued to Guzar at the end of the world. The price was minimal. With the tickets came *kompostirovka* – the NKVD endorsement – but only for the first leg of the journey to nearby Omsk. The full significance of this limitation was to become apparent at our next stop. In the meantime we happily clambered up to a real passenger carriage designated *zhostkii* – a Soviet euphemism for third class. My mother said: 'Tadzio's sign of the cross from the Słonim prison has launched us on our way.'

I was ecstatic. The sun was shining, the wheels were tappety-tapping along. From my vantage point on the steps of our carriage – strictly forbidden, of course – I was taking in the Siberian summer countryside rolling by at a leisurely speed. We stopped almost casually at Petro-Pavlovsk (now for some reason renamed Petropavl) and eventually arrived at Omsk very late on 6th July. Here we became specks in a large crowd heaving and pushing for access to trains. This was our first experience of the Soviet wartime 'railway way-of-life'; to which Petukhovo was a gentle introduction. What was now required was a double endorsement from the NKVD: the next *kompostirovka* and a *sanobrabotka* (sanitary inspection) i.e. a delousing-cum-shower.

After several attempts it became obvious that the NKVD were routinely refusing *kompostirovkas* to Polish civilians attempting to travel to Tashkent and beyond. My mother decided that the time had come for her pure alcohol. By diluting a measure of this nectar, she converted it into a *chakushka* (quarter litre) of respectably strong vodka. With this prize she proceeded to corrupt the station personnel – in the event a surprisingly easy task. *San-obrabotka* and *kompostirovka* were brushed aside and in the depth of the night we were smuggled by our relaxed new friends onto the train destined for Novosibirsk, some 700 kilometres due east. My mother did not know that *en route* we now faced the risk of being picked up by the NKVD as illegal passengers. The train pulled out of Omsk in the early hours of 8th July; the very night during which Stalin issued orders for the Second, final, Evacuation.

The race was on. We had been extremely lucky so far: there were no ticket checks along this sector of the journey. But in comparison with Omsk, the station of Novosibirsk was a nightmare. And for us, a critical point of the whole undertaking. Novosibirsk was an important rail junction, besieged by a mass of humanity demanding transport. Because of its strategic significance, it was strictly controlled by the NKVD. My mother soon discovered that her *chakushkas*, though welcome, were not enough. For a day or two she fought for official permits, while we three, and our bundles, were continuously moved by the police around the pavements near the station. We seemed to have reached the end of the road.

Then a Polish sergeant in a British uniform came up to us and asked if he could be of any help. I do not remember his name but I feel bound to put on record his talents as a sculptor. Learning of our predicament, and showing little surprise, he produced a potato, on which he proceeded to carve a replica of the *kompostirovka* stamp. The result was impeccable. He then applied this stamp to our tickets, added signatures with a flourish, and said to my mother: 'The secret door to Tashkent is open.'

My mother understood how dangerous this was. But in Novosibirsk she had come to the conclusion that our journey was no longer a battle of wits with hostile authorities, but a hazardous game with life itself as the stake. Our cicerone escorted us with full pomp onto the train bound for Tashkent – 2000 kilometres away. Over the next few days he travelled with us. Inspections were frequent and the tickets were scrutinised with great care. We missed several heart-beats at every check, but the potato stamp created by our guardian angel in battledress passed the test every time.

⁓

For citizens of the former Polish-Lithuanian Commonwealth, the eastward journey towards the salt-mines of Irkutsk had bitter associations. It was therefore with relief that in Novosibirsk we broke out of the 'east-west straitjacket', and turned sharply south onto the 'Turk-Sib' Railway. It was then a tedious single-line route, interspersed with occasional 'waiting sidings' and windswept towns. Of these I vaguely remember the depressing Semipalatinsk. Progress was slow and stops at the sidings long – we always seemed to be early for the rendezvous with oncoming traffic. During such interruptions I developed the habit of getting off to stretch my legs. I was the only one to do so, or so it seemed. It was enjoyable but could be risky. On one occasion – our driver having moved off with no warning – I had to run along the moving train in order to remount it several carriages downstream of ours. I did not tell my mother about this incident. Sometimes I perched on the steps of our carriage, sharing this illegal pastime with the conductor. We sat there, silently observing the dry limitless steppe slowly roll by. The vigils became soporific as the temperature rose steadily.

The other distraction was the pursuit of food at the stations. Some of these offered a soup kitchen, but the demand was such that a thirteen-year-old had little chance in the mêlée. So I developed a cunning plan. I would wait for the final whistle when the crowd would rush back to the train, get my bowl filled, and then run very fast to clamber back onto the moving wagons – more often than not pulled up by friendly passengers. My mother was pleased with my street-wise exploits. I do not think she quite understood the risk. But then she too was a risk-taker. Perhaps she knew, and quietly approved.

One afternoon a limitless expanse of water appeared to starboard. Someone explained that it was Lake Balkhash. More of a sea than a lake, really; and for me a new experience of water on such a scale. On that day the lake was restless, and its waves lapped quite close to the wheels of our carriage. I was mesmerised. Later, past Alma-Ata, the snow-clad approaches to the mighty Tyan-Shan range came into view. Our journey now acquired a dramatic backcloth. The train turned westwards and travelled along the foothills of these majestic mountains all the way to Tashkent.

Fifty miles short of our destination, at Chimkent, we were confronted for the first time with an abundance of watermelons, and also jugfuls of rough local wine; all very cheap. Alas there was no bread… The sight was seductive and we – inexperienced newcomers – overdid the melons. The price was diarrhoea, to which many succumbed, including myself. My mother, not quite knowing how to deal with the situation, told me to try some red wine. I put away a large mug, fell sound asleep, and woke up several hours later totally cured. From that moment on I trusted implicitly in my mother's powers of improvisation, not to mention the healing qualities of red wine.

We rolled into Tashkent station exhausted by the long journey and disoriented by the heat. The huge square in front of the station was full of squatters waiting for their chance of onward travel. There we established our private space. Around us we noticed many Poles in uniform. Indeed, Tashkent station seemed almost Polonised, which was not surprising because General Anders's HQ was in nearby Jangi-Jul', no more than 30 kilometres away. It was cheering to see the NKVD take a back seat.

Tashkent seemed full of clanging trams. Ever since visiting the city of Lwów I had associated great cities with trams. Clearly, Tashkent was another, and I was determined to explore it. My mother, now in deep conclave with our sergeant-cum-guardian over the next fake *kompostirovka* – and confident that my street-wisdom was adequate for *ad hoc* tourism – let me loose. So I leapt on the next tram and began my exploring.

The new Soviet-style squares I found overbearing, and the old Tashkent, with its low houses and high walls of sun-dried mud, uninviting. But the bazaars were magnificently colourful. I could not keep my eyes off the men's *tibeteikas* (skull-caps), the sultanas and dried apricots arranged in pyramids, and the tea-house sub-culture around the edges. But the day had a sinister epilogue. At one of the tram stops I had to reach with both arms for the hand-rails, pressed by a small crowd of young men suddenly appearing from nowhere. Once aboard, I saw that both my trouser pockets had been slashed with razor blades. I was relieved to discover that my few roubles survived this attempt at socialist redistribution. I returned to our squat outside the station very tired, and full of stories.

In the meantime our sergeant presented my mother, by way of a farewell gift, with fresh fake endorsements for the next leg of the journey. The following morning, after warm good-byes and embraces, we boarded the train for Samarkand.

About 70 kilometres out of Tashkent we crossed the mighty River Syr-Darya. It was an awe-inspiring encounter. At the time I did not quite realise that we were about to enter one of the great playing fields of history: 'Transoxiana' to the men of the Mediterranean. It is a vast stretch of Asian steppe between the ancient rivers Oxus and Jaxartes, today called the Amu-Darya and the Syr-Darya. Most of the region is a desert, the Kyzyl-Kum, stretching northwards to the sea of Aral. Its southern belt is blessed with important oases, Samarkand and Bukhara, and the fertile valley of Fergana. Between 330 and 327 BC Alexander the Great made this fecund corner his staging post *en route* for India. And, as was his habit, he founded here another Alexandria – Alexandria the Furthest – on the left bank of the Jaxartes, not far from where we crossed it on our journey from Tashkent to Samarkand. In 1336, in a place called Kesh about 80 kilometres south of Samarkand, a child was born, later to be known as Timur the Lame, or Tamerlane. He made Transoxiana the hub of his empire.

We caught only a glimpse of Samarkand from the train windows; I remember it as a city nestling among trees. No wonder: it stands in the middle of a great oasis. Here, during a drunken quarrel, Alexander killed Cleitus, his closest friend and best cavalry commander; here Tamerlane established his capital – a city famous for its exquisite architecture. To this day his tomb attracts to Samarkand the historian and the tourist. And here, in Samarkand, our last bag of dried biscuits from Nikolaevka was stolen. By then it did not matter all that much.

We moved on, and eventually got off at a small station in the middle of nowhere called Karshi. Robin Lane-Fox says that at Karshi Alexander rounded up the best local horses for his depleted cavalry. At Karshi, on 15th July 1942, we had no difficulty in catching the local train to Guzar, where we arrived late in the afternoon, 13 days after leaving Nikolaevka. On that day, 15th July, General Anders issued his orders for the Second Evacuation. We heard the news at the station.

~

Guzar is a largish town of no great significance, which at the height of the summer of 1942 claimed the distinction of being a death-trap. General Anders notes in his memoirs: 'In Guzar the state of health of our people (i.e. the men and the civilians) was desperate.' The men of the Polish Reserves Depot and the civilian camp followers were being decimated by typhoid, malaria and dysentery. The busiest department of the local military hospital was the mortuary. Guzar was not a place to linger.

On arrival my mother went to the Polish HQ asking for the Mr Piotrowski who signed the papers summoning us to Guzar. He would have been one of the two Piotrowskis known to my parents before the war – probably the one who was notary public in Słonim. But he was no longer there. Later we discovered that he, too, had succumbed to typhoid. Instead, and by chance, she bumped into Captain Bazylewski, the husband of our guitar-playing acquaintance. He offered us temporary refuge, a lean-to at his married quarters. In the main room of the house, we found Mrs Bazylewska in bed and very unwell. She did not, or could not, communicate with her new sub-tenants. The guitar was silent.

The next morning we all went to Mass at the Headquarters. It was a marvellously cleansing experience. For the first time since April 1940 we went to confession and to Communion. My offer to serve at Mass was accepted, and I discovered that I could still remember all the Latin responses.

My mother was now ready for her fight to be included in the forthcoming evacuation to Iran. It was a daunting task and a physical challenge; the HQ was besieged by civilians pleading for a chance to escape. My mother, exhausted by the journey and weakened by recurring bouts of dysentery, was unable to make any progress. For the first time she began to lose hope.

And then Providence intervened in a miraculously decisive manner. Today I would say it was at my father's prompting. On hearing our surname, an officer came up to my mother and introduced himself as Captain Antoni Giedroyć, a distant cousin and a friend of Uncle Henio. There and then he registered us as his dependants, thus qualifying us for the evacuation, and moved us to his quarters. He also alerted Uncle

Henio at the Polish evacuation base in Krasnovodsk, telling him that we were on our way. Two or three days later the NKVD issued orders for the departure of the Polish Army and its dependants to Iran.

Antoni Giedroyć came from the other half of the family, based in Korwie just north of Wilno. Contacts between us were not close – in fact my mother had never met him before. But in Guzar she had to acknowledge that before her stood 'the most handsome man of the clan'. His wife and two surviving children (one perished in Siberia) were with him already. Andrzej, the surviving son, was a near-contemporary of mine and we got on well together. The ties loosened with time, but Andrzej's son Karol (today a Canadian Mountie) was destined many years later to become a close friend.

Departure was due in two weeks. These two weeks became our final battle. It was no longer a matter of hunger – the army shared with us their daily rice and bully-beef – but of serious illnesses. My mother suffered chronic dysentery, and my two sisters were stricken with malaria. I managed to remain in reasonable health.

The departure was fixed by the NKVD for 13th August. We did not know that ours was the very last train in the rearguard of General Anders's army on its march to freedom. At the station we found the familiar set of Soviet cattle-trucks crudely adapted for humans. Now, of course, we were in the care of the Polish Army, each of us clutching a British iron ration of condensed chocolate in a shiny tin. My three women were too ill to enjoy these delights. Earlier I had to lead each of them in turn to the train, and then help them up the ladder to the truck door. Fully occupied, I did not understand the seriousness of the situation. But at last we were on our way. In the heat of this exceptionally hot August afternoon, the train slowly pulled out of Guzar – a place where survival was a victory.

∼

The Second Evacuation was carried out as efficiently as the First. The first batch of trains departed for Krasnovodsk on 30th July, just four days after the issue of NKVD instructions. The operation took two weeks and a day. Forty-five thousand men and twenty-six thousand civilians were removed from Soviet soil in forty-one train-loads and twenty-five shiploads. An undertaking on this scale must have been planned well in advance.

The conditions in the trains were appalling. There was overcrowding reminiscent of April 1940, but this time the move was accompanied by epidemic diseases and subtropical heat. Yet, harsh as it was, we were now ready to bear anything. Indeed, the attitudes of the passengers on that train were almost sanguine; and the atmosphere near to joy. My mother suddenly seemed better, and Anuśka's and Tereska's malaria subsided. I began to enjoy the countryside.

We travelled back to Karshi, and then on to the oasis of Bukhara – the ancient Soghdiana – famed for its carpets and the beauty of its women. Here it was that Alexander the Great was smitten with Roxane, daughter of Oxyartes, 'the most beautiful woman in all Asia'. Soon afterwards we crossed the River Amu-Darya, the Oxus so familiar to the great Macedonian conqueror, and exchanged Transoxiana for the sands of Kara-Kum. Our next port of call was the oasis of Merv, described by Lane Fox as 'a fertile and strategic pocket of civilisation'. The NKVD now chose Merv as a venue for a farewell feast. It was an extraordinarily naive ploy, through which our jailers attempted to placate their former prisoners and deportees. We were led to long tables laden with most delicious *pilafs* and even some kebabs. In a way it was a chilling experience, but this did not prevent us – even my mother – from enjoying the Turkmeni cuisine.

Of Ashkhabad I remember only its nondescript rail station. A day or two later we caught our first glimpse of the Caspian Sea – busy with cargo ships and transports ferrying wounded soldiers. This was my first sea, an exhilarating sight. Yet to us it had just one meaning: a route out of the Soviet Union.

We arrived at the port of Krasnovodsk early in the morning of 20th August, after a seven-day journey. And there, on the quay, stood Uncle Henio, ready to whisk us away for a day's rest at his quarters in town. To me that day seemed the height of luxury: a bath, a long sleep, and abundant food, although – unused to such things – I was unable to swallow either sugar or butter. That same day, late in the evening, Uncle Henio handed us back to the port authorities, who put us onto an ancient tub of a ship called, if my memory serves me right, *Kaganovich*.

top left The Author, c.1933; *top right* Łobzów, 1935
below Łobzów Manor, right wing, 1929

clockwise, from top left Jan Maurycy Giedroyć, Tadzio's father; Tadzio, Wilno c.1920; Aunt Sophie, Tadzio's sister, 1930s; Tadzio with MG, Łobzów, 1929; Professor Francis Giedroyć, Tadzio's cousin, 1930s

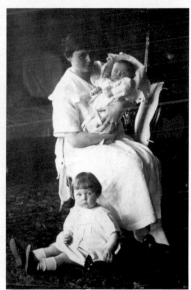

clockwise, from top left
Ania, 1919 (photo. J. Bułhak);
Leon Szostakowski, Ania's
father, c.1904; Ania with her
daughters Anuśka and Tereska
(in arms), "Under the Swan"
1922; Ania, 1930s; uncles
Henio (*left*) and Stefuś, Ania's
brothers

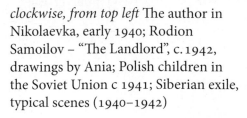

clockwise, from top left The author in Nikolaevka, early 1940; Rodion Samoilov – "The Landlord", c. 1942, drawings by Ania; Polish children in the Soviet Union c 1941; Siberian exile, typical scenes (1940–1942)

top Ania, Michał, Tehran, Autumn 1942; *middle left* Polish children evacuated to Iran, 1942; *middle right* Evacuation across the Caspian Sea, August 1942; *above* Ania with daughters Anuśka (centre) and Tereska at the *Delegatura*, Tehran 1944

The Polish Secondary School (*Gimnazjum*), Tehran, late 1942 (the author in the centre)

Camp Barbara, 194[
top left the author a[
young soldier; *mid[*
"The Aristocrats" o[
Sixth Company;
right Assault cours[

Fifth Company
parading before
General Anders, C[
Barbara, June 1946
(the author, Comm[
Second Platoon,
marked).

The JSK band

(Photos courtesy of *Albu[*
1972, and *Księga Pamiątk[*
2000)

General Anders visits
؛; *middle left* General
ładysław Anders;
ht Passing out parade,
mp Barbara, June 1946,
author, top cadet
ymus) congratulated
Gen. Anders;
ow left Uncle Henio,
iro, 1945; *middle* the
hor at the Pyramids
iza) 1944; *right* at
xor, 1947

Stach Lickindorf –
Tereska's husband

The Author, Beirut 1947   Anuśka (*right*) and Tereska,
Beirut c. 1945

Memorial cross for Tadzio, Ihumen, 26 June 2002.
(Second from left Miko, the author's son.)

Conditions on board were indescribably foul. We were herded onto a deck so crowded that sitting on one's bundle became a luxury. Most people had to stay on their feet. And those stricken with dysentery had no choice but to relieve themselves where they stood... This squalor we had to endure for 36 hours – two long nights and one scorching day. I fear that the voyage on the *Kaganovich*, rather than the banquet at Merv, will always remain our lasting memory of the Land of the Soviets.

Early on 22nd August 1942 we entered the port of Pahlavi, now renamed Bandar Anzali, in Iran. My mother found herself nearest to the gang plank. She was the first to step down onto the welcoming Iranian soil. She insisted on doing it unaided, in style.

CHAPTER 9

Twenty Happy Years

On 10th January 1919 Tadeusz Giedroyć was appointed *starosta* (governor) of the district of Opoczno, half-way between Warsaw and Cracow. He was then just thirty-one, back from his exploits in the war. I suspect that this appointment was arranged so that he could recharge his batteries in a new environment. Otherwise it would be difficult to explain this unusual transplant of a man from the Eastern Marches into the heart of Polish Poland. The new job was far from a sinecure, however. His task was to set up a new Polish administration among the ruins of this recent Russo-German battlefield.

Tadzio's 'rest' was soon cut short. In the late spring of 1919, probably towards the end of May, he was seconded to the newly created post of Deputy Governor of the Wilno region, one of three vast territories in the eastern borderlands of the new Polish Republic.

These Borderlands (known as *Kresy* in Polish) were in a state of flux. After the armistice on the western front, the German armies began a grudging withdrawal, the vacuum being filled by the Poles and Soviets in sharp competition. The Wilno Region, the northern sector of the Borders between the river Dvina and the Pripyat' Marshes, now became a focus for all these manoeuvres. The situation was further complicated by the claim from the young separatist Republic of Lithuania that Wilno (Vilnius) was her capital.

The Soviets arrived first, immediately setting up the so-called Lithuanian-Belarus'ian Soviet Republic, or 'Lit-Bel'. Marshal Piłsudski had other plans. In April 1919 he took Wilno by force, and from that vantage point sought to create a federation of post-imperial states capable of standing up to both the Germans and the Russians. Naturally, Piłsudski envisaged a leading role for Poland in the region.

In May 1919 the Wilno Region was still in dispute. In the north and east, Polish control reached no further than 60-70 km beyond the gates of Wilno. But in September – at the end of Tadzio's tenure as Deputy Governor – the Polish Army was already 130 km further east, on the rivers Dvina, Ulla and Berezina (that same Berezina at which Napoleon lost the remnants of his *Grande Armée)*. It was a spectacular territorial expansion. Tadzio's task was to create a civil administration on the hoof, in the wake of the Polish Army which kept delivering new stretches of territory in a state of postwar devastation. No mean task. As if that was not enough, my father was at the same time in hot pursuit of Ania Szostakowska whom he had met, and tumbled for, on his arrival in Wilno. He was successful on both fronts, personal and public. Just married, he was allowed to take his bride to Opoczno, a more tranquil posting in central Poland. The powers-that-be decided that he had earned a second breather. My elder sister Anuśka was born ten months after the wedding.

The young bride was looking forward to making a new home, but she had to wait. In the spring of 1920 the hostile confrontation between Poland and Soviet Russia erupted into a full-scale war. In August of that year the Reds stood at the gates of Warsaw. Opoczno, the district for which Tadzio was responsible, was close to the front line, and within the immediate reach of Bolshevik propaganda, aimed at the young and naive Polish proletariat. Men like my father, administrators of the areas nearest to the battle, were as crucial to the integrity of the Polish state as men-at-arms. Tadzio held the line and kept the peace. His young wife, now nursing a month-old baby, stayed at his side. From the very beginning it was that kind of marriage.

The Polish counter-offensive, the so-called Battle of Warsaw (included by J. F. C. Fuller among his decisive battles of the Western World), was launched by Piłsudski on 16th August 1920. Within days the Red Army, the self-appointed bringer of 'world revolution' to the West, was in full retreat. The twenty years of peace that followed were Poland's gift to the rest of Europe. Opoczno district could now begin to think of convalescence.

Not its governor, however. The city of Wilno (or Vilnius) and its environs remained the cause of unremitting hostility between Poland and Lithuania. Lithuania claimed Vilnius as her historical capital. Poland also claimed Wilno because – apart from its Jewish community – it was

Polish-speaking, and for that reason gravitated towards Poland. Piłsudski, himself a native of these parts and deeply attached to the land of his forebears, saw the matter in a strategic, not local, perspective. In pursuit of his federal vision, he was prepared to give up Wilno provided Lithuania agreed to renew her historical links with Poland. Lithuania would have none of this: she wanted Vilnius without preconditions. She also accused the Polish Head of State – with justification – of aggressive high-handedness. The Lithuanian David, confronted with the Polish Goliath, fought back with skill, deploying every available diplomatic weapon. Off the battlefield the two sides were evenly matched. One of the Lithuanian counter-moves was a dangerous flirtation with the Soviets. On 11th July 1920, when Poland was fighting for her life at the gates of Warsaw, the Lithuanian government signed a treaty in Moscow under which Wilno, together with a generous slice of the surrounding territory, was ceded (sic) by the Soviet government to Lithuania. But when the defeated Red Army began streaming eastward, Piłsudski reacted. In October 1920 a Polish division, claiming Wilno as its homeland, staged a 'mutiny', took Wilno by force, and proceeded to set up a self-governing enclave under the name of 'Middle Lithuania'. The 'mutiny' was a ruse, behind which stood Piłsudski himself. This act of coercion Lithuania now proceeded to expose and exploit in the world press and in the chanceries of the Allies. The Polish authorities decided that there was a need for careful damage-limitation on the diplomatic front.

So, in December 1920, Władysław Raczkiewicz was sent to Wilno as Delegate of the Polish Government. His brief was to establish an understanding with 'Polish Wilno', and to liaise with the Missions of the League of Nations and the Allied Powers, which now descended on this hot-spot of Europe. By implication, the brief would in due course draw him into multilateral negotiations, which the League was instructed to begin in order to resolve the issue.

The negotiations were launched in Brussels on 20th April 1921 under the chairmanship of the Belgian statesman Paul Hymans. Meanwhile Raczkiewicz asked for his friend and trusted collaborator Tadeusz Giedroyć to be appointed Councillor at the Polish Mission in Wilno. Ania was delighted: she was returning home. The *piano nobile* of the

House Under the Swan in Mała Pohulanka – a sumptuous apartment of thirteen rooms – was hastily set aside for the incoming Councillor and his family. There, exactly nine months later, my second sister Tereska was born. On 21st July 1921, Tadzio was promoted Deputy Head of Mission.

Hymans tabled his Plan on 20th May 1921. It was modelled, under Polish promptings, on the Swiss cantonal system. The Lithuanian Republic would consist of two cantons: the Lithuanian canton based on Kaunas, and the Polish-speaking canton centered on Wilno. The disputed city was thus included in the Lithuanian state, but under a federal partnership between Poland and the new Lithuania.

The Hymans Plan was endorsed by the Council of the League of Nations on 28th June 1921. The Polish Government gave its approval on 15th July – followed by a Lithuanian rejection on the grounds that preconditions (i.e. the imposition of a federal link) were not acceptable. Brussels responded with six weeks of frantic re-drafting. The result was the Hymans Revised Plan, tabled on 3rd September, closely reflecting the Lithuanian position. The two-canton model was scrapped and instead the Wilno region was offered a measure of autonomy within the Lithuanian Republic. On 24th September the Council of the League of Nations recommended the Revised Plan to the General Assembly, and Poland rejected it soon after. Whatever Piłsudski's personal reaction to the idea of Wilno's autonomy, he had no choice but to submit to the pressures from the Polish nationalists, determined on incorporation. Polish-speaking Wilno shortsightedly allied itself with the Polish nationalists, fearful of a minority status within the equally nationalistic Lithuania. Piłsudski's federal dreams lay in tatters.

On 12th January 1922 the disenchanted League of Nations admitted defeat and withdrew from arbitration. Two days later Tadeusz Giedroyć resigned his commission.

On 20th February 1922 the 'Wilno Parliament' voted for the incorporation of Middle Lithuania into Poland, which Warsaw formally welcomed on 24th March. Many years later my cousin Zbyszek Lutyk told me that at about that time my Grandmother Giedroyć accused her son of 'handing over Wilno to the Poles'. The accusation, even though kept within the family circle, must have been doubly distressing for

Tadzio, because his personal position was close to that of his mother and her milieu.

It must not be assumed that the winter of 1921-2 was all gloom and despondency. My parents knew how to protect their happy private life from the incursions of politics. The Szostakowski family and their friends, gathered in the House Under the Swan, plunged into the social whirl, made even more frenetic by the presence in Wilno of the various foreign missions. My parents found themselves at the centre of it all, and after the arrival of my sister Tereska (born on 3rd January 1922) they decided to give a christening party to outshine all parties.

It was in fact an all-night ball, opened by Raczkiewicz and my mother with a polonaise. It ended with the traditional 'white mazurka' as dawn broke over the city below. The event did not entirely escape notoriety. At one point my mother decided that the gentlemen were becoming a shade too exuberant. So she rounded up the many jugs of punch and poured them down the sink. In the meantime my uncle Stefuś had to be rescued from a delicate conversation with a police patrol asking for re-assurances that the event was under control. The rescuer was the redoubtable Aunt Hela, who dropped one or two names. But she had to explain why she was barefooted and Stefuś was clutching her dancing shoes ('too much waltzing, very sore feet').

Tadzio's resignation was not just from his current commission, but from the Polish Civil Service – a far more drastic step. My parents were able to stay on in the House Under the Swan because the legal fraternity of Wilno immediately invited Tadzio to establish his own law practice in the city. The new venture proved successful, both professionally and materially. Some of my mother's best jewellery dated from my father's spell at the Wilno Bar. So did her splendid Persian lamb coat.

This period of opulence was not to last, however. After just one year Tadzio became restless. He complained that his briefs came to him because of his notoriety and contacts rather than his merits as a lawyer. I see it now as a case of excessive sensitivity, because he proved himself to be an accomplished advocate. But he withdrew once again and, cap in hand, went back to his former employers: the Polish Civil Service.

They took him back, but with reservations. He was now offered the modest governorship of the Augustów district, with a small town of some 8-10,000 inhabitants, close to the Lithuanian border; or rather, to the hostile line of demarcation. The posting was a trial, and a tricky one at that. Tadzio on probation had to reassure his old employer.

He was now thirty-five, wiser and less radical. The year at the Wilno Bar had been an opportunity for reassessment. The 'Red Prince' (Tadzio's nickname at university) had edged towards a view of the world almost identical to that proclaimed by Ania's late father at the turn of the century; a view of centrist liberalism in harmony with progressive Catholicism. The measured stance, purged of agnostic and anti-clerical overtones, was fairly typical among the 'democratic' elite of Wilno. So the Augustów enclave received a reflective and not too impetuous administrator. My cousin Jerzy Giedroyć told me that when, in the late thirties, he visited the area on behalf of a Ministry in Warsaw, my father's stewardship was still remembered warmly and gratefully.

For the next two years Tadzio and his family found themselves in a corner of Europe that was close to idyllic. The *Guide Bleu* of 1939 says, *toute la région environnante, dite 'Puszcza Augustowska', particulièrement celle située au Nord de la ville, abonde en lacs glaciaires renommés pour leur beauté.* ('The entire surrounding region, known as the Virgin Forest of Augustów, and particularly the area north of the town, is rich in glacial lakes renowned for their beauty.') My mother's memories of their stay in Augustów – no more than two years – are all of picnics on the lake, social events devised by the officers' mess of the local lancer regiment, and a never-ending succession of house-guests attracted by the setting (and, let me add, by the hospitality).

Tadzio's rehabilitation was swift. In 1924 he was advanced to a far more substantial job: governor of Białystok. The town, a big railway junction and textile-manufacturing centre, had a population of nearly 100,000, including a large and important Jewish community. My father had to deal with problems at the interface of raw capitalism and a comparatively inexperienced proletariat; and with issues of race and religion.

After two successful years in Białystok my father was once again on the brink of a career at the centre of the affairs of State, probably through a governorship of a province. It was not to be. In 1926 my parents were confronted with the prospect of inheriting the estates of Łobzów and Kotczyn; both on the brink of ruin. This burden they could not avoid. Tadeusz Giedroyć tendered – this time irrevocably – his resignation from the Civil Service.

I shall skip over the six years that followed, when my mother and father restored their estates to health. During this time my father served as magistrate for the local town of Dereczyn. In 1932 he was invited to become Deputy Chairman of the Regional Court in Białystok – the town where, from 1924 to 1926, he had been Governor. The job was a challenge but its setting was familiar, and my parents' memories of Białystok were good. It was also a flattering recognition of this gentleman-farmer's record as a dispenser of justice in the backwoods. The invitation was well timed, because Tadzio, having successfully rescued Łobzów from oblivion, was no longer feeling stretched; he was ready for a new challenge.

My mother was taken aback by this threat to our life in the country: she knew that she would have to be at Tadzio's side during the long winter Court Sessions, and of course the children would have to go along too. But she also knew that confining her husband to bucolic routines would be counterproductive.

There were two further attractions; first, the prospect of a career and a good income, which would enable the family's horizons to be broadened beyond the charmed but restricting rounds of country-house existence; and second, the opportunity to give Anuśka and Tereska a good, structured schooling at the Białystok *gimnazjum* for girls.

When we moved to Białystok my life became restricted and monotonous. I clung to Marteczka as the visible link with my real home. Only once was I allowed a glimpse of my father on the job, a distant figure gowned and gold-chained, presiding over an incomprehensible court-case. During our long walks Marteczka and I would occasionally bump into my mother. These were joyous encounters, and I particularly remember one: the smart lady in a long fur coat opening her arms to catch a small boy rushing towards her. Otherwise it was a strictly controlled and, in comparison with the joys of Łobzów, boring existence, brightened only when Marteczka attracted the attention of a nice policeman whose beat included our end of St John's Street. I encouraged his advances, but Marteczka remained distant, and not at all amused.

In comparison with Łobzów, my memories of Białystok remain fragmentary and out-of-focus. Except for one event, that is: the arrival of the news of Marshal Piłsudski's death. On that cold and overcast morning – it was 12th May 1935 – my father, visibly moved, came into my room to tell his six-year-old son about it. I realised that something very important had happened. The memory of this interview remains with me as the one clear item in the otherwise loose and disjointed catalogue of reminiscences of my father's first term of office.

Soon after this, he was offered the chairmanship of the Regional Court at Zamość. After three winter Sessions at Białystok his success as a senior judge and administrator must have been noticed. The offer was a major step forward, and naturally he accepted. My mother and I both attempted to conceal our sadness at the thought that Zamość was even further away from Łobzów.

After only one Court Session (1935-6) my father was asked to be chairman of the Regional Court at Łuck (pronounced 'Lootsk'). Before he went, he was able to do a kindness to a fellow lawyer which none of us knew anything about until much later. In London in 1950, quite out of the blue, my mother received a substantial sum of money 'for a charity of her choice' from a person unknown to her. It transpired that the donor, a senior Warsaw lawyer named Garwin, was a member of the Zamość Jewish community. He told my mother that her husband, hearing of a local Zamość conspiracy to deny Garwin the right to practise his profession, immediately ordered an inquiry, punished the culprits, cleared the name of the victim, and in this way saved him from further persecution and financial ruin. Mr Garwin's letter is one of my cherished possessions: 'In the interwar period, when 'western winds' [i.e. German anti-Semitism] had already begun to sweep across Poland, such a spontaneous intervention by Tadeusz Giedroyć, on behalf of a Jewish lawyer unknown to him, speaks volumes for his sense of justice and his integrity. I shall always remember him with deepest respect.'

Łuck, my father's next posting, was the capital of the province of

Wołyń – an important part of interwar Poland which had the potential to become the granary of the Republic. But it lacked political balance. Seventy per cent of its population was Ukrainian, whilst the politically dominant Polish minority amounted to just sixteen per cent. The Ukrainians voiced dissatisfaction with their status. Mutual suspicions were fed by memories of recent acts of terrorism by Ukrainian nationalists, and by the severity of the police response. Tadeusz Giedroyć was brought in from Zamość with a mission to ensure transparency and evenhandedness in the judicial service.

The trappings of his job matched the task. The lodgings were within a former monastery of the Trinitarians built in the 18th century. The rooms were spacious certainly, although monastic rather than palatial in style. The staff included two official valets and a full-time gardener. My father also had at his disposal a carriage-and-pair, in the charge of a moustachioed coachman called Antoni, whose driving skills and punctuality were legendary. Antoni was particularly kind to me. During the winter he allowed me to follow on skis his sledge-and-pair, the arrangement involving two ropes trailing from the back of the sledge, with me hanging on to their ends. Thus we promenaded at a trot up and down the main street of Łuck to the amazement of onlookers.

My two sisters came to Łuck to complete their secondary education. Marteczka and I came in their wake, and I too was soon placed at the local private school. I remember little of my early academic endeavours, but quite a lot about my early contacts with this new world. The school was fee-paying, and therefore its classes very small. The dominant boy of the class was too forceful for my comfort, and I tended to avoid him. This was not difficult, because a challenger for leadership called Zbyszek Horewicz offered me his friendship. We became inseparable, and subsequently Zbyszek regularly visited Łobzów. The cleverest of the class was Jaś Titow, gentle and helpful. The surname suggests a Ukrainian, or even Russian, background. He and I were on good terms, but our relationship was inhibited by the interventions of Jaś's older brother Witek. He was three years senior to us, also extremely clever, and king of the school. Witek and his entourage decided to single me out for teasing. I can see now that I was a sitting duck, because I was set apart by my parents'– and Marteczka's – excessive fussing. Imagine: my daily arrivals at school by carriage; Marteczka's hovering presence right up to the classroom door; my mother's insistence that I should continue wearing *rajtuzy* – babyish tights – long since discarded by my bare-kneed contemporaries; and, worst of all, my reckless boast that our family had once owned half of Łuck. Witek and his posse began calling me 'the man from Mars' – and the name stuck for a while. I had never been teased in public before, and my initial reaction was one of surprise rather than hurt. But I soon discovered the discomfort of being laughed at. By a strange twist of fate, Witek Titow and I came together again in 1944 at the Polish Military School in the Middle East. But by then our relative positions had changed in my favour.

In the spring of 1938 Anuśka gained her *matura* and began preparations for her debut in Warsaw in pursuit of higher learning and social diversions. For me it was an opportunity to get closer to Tereska. But this was not to be; not just yet anyway. She was still recovering from two accidents which struck in quick succession. During the summer at Łobzów she suffered a bad fall while riding at full gallop in front of an admiring audience. Later, in Łuck, she was knocked down by a car. Convalescence and tedious young brothers do not mix. My mother sensed that I was at a particularly tricky loose end, and offered to read to me aloud. She chose Sienkiewicz's *Trylogia*, a great 19th century historical novel. In this we immersed ourselves to the exclusion of the world around us. On one memorable occasion, for the first and only time alas, my father took over from her. He was a brilliant reader. At last I was admitted to my parents' company, and my gratitude was intense.

Proof of their caring interest in me came on 25th May 1938, the day of my First Communion, when my mother gave me a prayer book, in which she wrote on behalf of them both: 'May this little book always remind you that he who remembers God, and prays fervently, never strays.' The prayer book is here with me in Oxford seventy years later, having survived many a transcontinental adventure.

~

Politics now began to play an increasingly important part in my father's life. Poland in the late 1930s was young and still vulnerable: the German threat, and ways of countering it, were the one overriding concern. (The

Soviets seemed a lesser danger, no doubt because the Polish victory of 1920 was fresh in the memory.) My father believed that the integrity of the Republic, essential for its security, would depend to a large degree on the loyalty of the Borderland 'minorities': the Ukrainians and the Belarus'ians. So he began to look for a political platform where the integrity of the Republic was a shared objective; an objective, in time of peril, overriding any divisions. Early in 1938, he joined the Camp for National Unity (*Obóz Zjednoczenia Narodowego*, or OZN), a movement which had at one time attracted nationalist extremists, but was now led by more moderate men.

He was quickly invited to stand for election to the Senate. My mother remembered how he agonised over whether or not to accept the invitation. Eventually he agreed to stand, and was duly elected. The Polish Senate was 96-strong, half of it appointed by the President and the balance chosen by Colleges of Electors. At the time this system was said to have brought forward 'the most distinguished hundred in the land'. My father was about to exchange the status of a big fish in a smallish pond for membership of a select body at the centre of events. We all listened to the swearing-in ceremony on the wireless (shouts: 'Here he comes!'), and glasses were raised by the entire household in celebration.

My father was then elected to the chairmanship of the Polish Parliamentary Association of Wołyń, which included both Senators and Deputies. There also emerged a parallel Ukrainian Association. Tadzio was determined that the Polish Association should take the lead in the process of 'bridge-building' between them. He saw this as a step towards a new relationship between the two communities of Wołyń.

Our family now became geographically split. It was decided that Tereska should sit for her *matura* in Łuck, so my mother (and with her Marteczka and I) stayed put. Tadzio began commuting by train to Warsaw, where Anuśka was already an undergraduate; a role which she seemed to take lightly. My parents decided there was a need for fatherly interventions. One proved salutary. At the time the Warsaw student community was being infiltrated by extremist groups with anti-Jewish agendas. One of these groups sported a handsome badge called the Sword of the Brave. Anuśka was offered this badge and she started wearing it, much taken with its decorative qualities but unaware of its significance. My father swiftly put a stop to this, and very firmly. Another intervention was less serious. Anuśka had her eyebrows enhanced at a fashionable hairdresser. When my father saw the result (in my view very pretty, and in my mother's and Tereska's quite innocent), he hit the roof. There were sharp words, tears, and a need for peacemaking from my mother – no easy matter by letter or telephone from Łuck.

On March 9th 1939, my father made his maiden speech to the Upper House. He used it to present his political agenda for Wołyń, in the context of the wider issues concerning the Eastern Borderlands. The Wołyń Ukrainians accounted for some seventy per cent of the region's population of about two million. Most of them were rural smallholders. Wołyń's Polish-speaking community – a politically dominant minority of landowners, servants of the state (in and out of uniform), and professionals – made up sixteen per cent of the population. The Jewish community accounted for ten per cent (which was also the average percentage for the Republic as a whole); in addition to a strong presence in the professions, they controlled over seventy per cent of urban commerce and crafts.

My father's speech opened with a reminder that the well-being of the Republic required 'organic integration' of the Borderlands into the rest of Poland. Such integration was a precondition to the economic growth of the Borders. Then came a well argued programme for investments in the infrastructure of Wołyń – an essential preliminary to economic development. The proposed investment programme was to be backed by a policy of positive discrimination in favour of hoped-for Polish arrivals from other parts of the Republic, and (by implication) of the Ukrainian community – both aspiring to advancement in business and the professions. The strengthening of the 'Polish element' in Wołyń – and indeed across the Eastern Borderlands – was to be welcomed as an essential step towards Poland's integrity and therefore safety. The Polish element was to be the 'binding agent' of the multiple body-politic.

The policy of positive discrimination was put forward as a means of correcting the imbalance of urban business, dominated, as we have seen, by the Jewish community. In today's climate of post Holocaust sensitivities and political correctness, my father's proposal to favour the new

Polish 'immigrants' (and indigenous Ukrainians) might expose him to a retrospective charge of anti-Semitism. Such a charge would be absurd, of course, in the light of his record, which speaks for itself. The proposal should rather be viewed as a means towards assisting the underprivileged; a means preached and practised by many groups and agencies throughout the world – including Jewish communities. However – and I venture to speak here as a former adviser on economic development – positive discrimination can be dangerous medicine: it is potentially inefficient because it can inhibit the best talent within the communities excluded from benefits; it may also encourage state intervention, thus compromising the latter's obligation to remain even-handed. And my father appears to have allowed for state involvement in his proposals for positive discrimination. Today, for these reasons, I am prepared to cross swords with the Senator for Wołyń.

He ended his speech with an impassioned appeal to the Ukrainians and the Poles of Wołyń to engage in 'brotherly and harmonious co-existence' – on condition that the Ukrainian community within the Polish State offered its full loyalty to the Republic in her hour of need. This appeal, proclaimed in the Senate on the eve of World War II by one who in 1918 took up arms in the cause of Ukrainian independence, I now put on record without any qualifications.

In the spring of 1939 Senator Giedroyć gave a public address in Łuck. His subject was Poland's perilous situation. The largest hall, *Teatr Miejski* (City Theatre), was filled to capacity: my mother sat in the front row, Tereska in the gods (by choice), and I alongside my mother (no choice). I was overwhelmed by his performance, his first public address on this scale. He was totally at ease, master of the subject, sparingly amusing. Tereska later reported that as the audience rose to applaud, a voice boomed above her: 'That grey-haired Senator! What a gift of the gab!' *(Ten siwy senator dobrze gada!)* The following morning the local press had this to say: 'Senator Giedroyć's subject, 'The International Situation Forces Us to Rearm', attracted huge crowds, which gave him an enthusiastic reception'. Elsewhere in the same paper gushing praise was showered on his 'deep analyses and splendid presentation; mastery of the subject; and personal charm and ease of contact with the audience' *(Kurier Wołyński*, 20th March 1939). The paper expressed the hope for as many such future occasions as the speaker's time would permit.

Tereska gained her *matura* in June 1939, and we all repaired to Łobzów for a long summer. My father returned from Warsaw, dead tired. He brought the news that he had been granted an official residence in the grounds of Parliament. The apartment was on the first floor of the so-called White Pavilion, in a stretch of parkland called Frascati. My father seemed very pleased: this was a signal that preferment was imminent. My mother was happy for him. Resignedly she began making preparations for yet another move at the end of the summer. Our last summer at Łobzów...

∼

In the spring of 1943 a partisan body calling itself the Ukrainian Insurgent Army (*Ukraińska Powstańska Armiya*, or UPA) began the slaughter of the Polish civilian population of Wołyń. It was a well-planned and efficiently executed campaign of ethnic cleansing over a period of nearly one year. Between 40,000 and 60,000 people – men, women and children – were murdered in circumstances of indescribable brutality. The Polish Underground Army (*Armia Krajowa*, or AK) retaliated in kind, killing several thousand Ukrainians. This was the start of the Ukrainian-Polish civil war, which raged on for nearly five years.

I have asked myself many times: was this explosion of barbarism inevitable? And if so, were the efforts of Tadeusz Giedroyć on behalf of Wołyń a lost cause?

Between the two world wars, when the territories of Belarus' and Ukraine were divided between Poland and the USSR, the policy of discreetly encouraging peaceful national independence movements was more successful in Wołyń than elsewhere. The formula for a *modus vivendi* between the Ukrainians and the Poles of Wołyń may have been unsustainable in the long run, but it was feared by Stalin as a tempting Polish alternative to Soviet rule. In the Wołyń experiments there must have been seeds for a non-violent progression.

Now we know that the Wołyń tragedy of 1943 was not an inter-war time bomb doomed to go off. In 1941 the Germans began in Wołyń (and everywhere else east of the River Bug) the wholesale slaughter of the Jewish population. According to the historian Timothy Snyder, 'About twelve thousand Ukrainian policemen assisted about fourteen hundred German policemen in the murder of about two hundred thousand Volhynian Jews'. Most of these young Ukrainians, thoroughly trained in the procedures of inhuman brutality, became in 1943 the backbone of UPA. It can plausibly be argued that the tragedy of Wołyń was the outcome of the corruption imported into the region by the Germans, on the back of earlier brutalisation that arrived with the Soviet invaders in 1939. It seems to me therefore that, in the context of the 1930s, the attempts by Tadeusz Giedroyć as judge and senator to encourage co-existence between the Ukrainians and the Poles of Wołyń were fully justified.

CHAPTER 10

The City of the Pomegranate

On 19th August 1942 General Anders left the Soviet Union, never to return. In the course of that year he led to freedom 120,000 citizens of the Polish Second Republic: 80,000 fighting men and 40,000 dependent civilians. In the period 1939-1941 the Soviets had imprisoned or deported about one million Polish subjects. By 1942 half of them were presumed dead. Anders was therefore leaving behind him around 400,000 of his compatriots. At the time he was often faced with the painful question: was it right to take out of Soviet clutches only a quarter of all those recent prisoners and deportees? Time and again he made it clear that he never doubted the correctness of his decision, taken in defiance of his political masters. He was convinced that within months his men would have been returned to prisons or Gulags. He quoted as evidence the growing Soviet hostility towards his army, and the tragic events of 1943 – the discovery of the Katyń graves, and its political consequences. In the circumstances he acted to save those within his reach. And he had the comfort of knowing that all those staying behind were no longer prisoners or deportees, nominally at least. Less than a year later – in June 1943 – General Sikorski, the Polish prime Minister, conceded that the Anders Exodus was in fact 'the most realistic and positive result' of the 1941 Polish-Soviet agreement.

On 28th August, a few days after our arrival in Pahlavi, General Anders visited the transit camp. I did not go to cheer him because I was ill, but I am sure that my mother and sisters did. He remembered his visit thus: 'I was deeply disturbed by the sight of men looking like skeletons, and by those destitute children... Everywhere there were tangible signs of disease.' The inmates of the camp saw his concern for them; and all those soldiers, old men, women and children, a microcosm of the Second Polish Republic, responded with unqualified love for this latter-day Moses who had opened a path for them across the sea.

I like to imagine that my mother tossed the despised Soviet 'passports' overboard as soon as we entered international waters. It would have been a fitting gesture. In any case, as we stepped – dirty and infested with lice – onto the shiny army lorries waiting for us at the quay-side, we no longer felt tainted with Soviet paperwork or subjugation. The journey was short. We found ourselves at the gate of the 'dirty camp', where new arrivals were to be stripped, disinfected, fed and dressed in new clothes provided by the American public. The accommodation consisted of open-sided shelters, with matting on bamboo poles for roofing. The floor was the sand of a Caspian beach. This al fresco arrangement matched the blue skies of a perfect subtropical August. The total effect was one of a jolly adventure.

Jolly, that is, to those who were well enough to appreciate it. I was not one of them. As we trekked on foot from the gate to our appointed quarters, I suddenly felt weak at the knees. Unnoticed by the marching column, I dropped my bundle and slumped at the nearest shaded corner. I do not remember how long I sat there. I was dazed and comatose: it was a strange state of detached peace; a not unpleasant experience. Anuśka found me there, took up my burden, and patiently helped me along to our new shelter. I stayed with the three of them long enough to see my mother succumb to her most serious attack of dysentery. When she was no longer able to walk, a neighbour from under the shared matting approached her. She was a young Jewish doctor who at once understood the seriousness of the situation, and gave my mother some of her own precious medicines. This act of anonymous charity saved my mother's life. Soon afterwards I was admitted to the improvised field hospital.

The hospital ward was identical to our quarters. The patients lay on the sand close to one another, rather like freshly caught fish laid out in tidy rows. Death was a frequent visitor. I vaguely remember stronger patients laying claim to a dead man's next meal – before the kitchen staff could catch up with the declining head-count.

I was not interested in food. The symptom that I remember most vividly was the pain at the ends of my bones; especially the heels. I had to negotiate the longish walks to the latrines on tiptoe. The doctors, not knowing what was wrong with me, prescribed a tablespoon of brandy three times a day. This was dispensed by cheerful nurses in very short tropical shorts. I am sure the sight was pleasing to those on the verge of convalescence. Many years later my condition on the Pahlavi beach was tentatively diagnosed as rheumatic fever.

My mother was a frequent visitor; she tried to conceal her anxiety. On one occasion she brought Uncle Henio, in transit with the army to Iraq. The two of them made me laugh – and I think this visit was the turning point. Slowly I began to improve. The authorities decided to move me – behind my mother's back, I might add – to a 'convalescent centre', a forbidding and almost empty house on the edge of the town. There my mother caught up with me, and forcibly declared that I should convalesce in her care. She took me with her to our new quarters in the 'clean camp', this time under canvas. I was fussed over and fed with rich food, such as rice and lamb stew. I began venturing out onto the beach, where one day I was approached by an officer leaning heavily on a stick. He told me that his name was Stanisław Wnęk and that he was a friend of my father's. The meeting was a happy reminder of our old life.

By mid-September we were all well again, and ready for the overland journey to Tehran. Transportation was contracted out to local bus entrepreneurs. They ferried the Polish civilians to the capital in convoys across the forbidding Elburz mountains. Our family was allocated to a particularly rickety bus with a driver who had a taste for the spectacular. With him, on a sunny morning, we began our climb towards the mountain peaks, along a narrow un-surfaced road. General Anders had travelled this same route just a few days before us. He described it as the most breathtaking road he had ever encountered. This is no exaggeration. As we passed the picturesque villages immersed in lush vegetation nurtured by the moist breeze from the Caspian Sea, the locals lined the road to wave; some of them tossed exotic fruits into the open windows of our buses. In this way these far from opulent smallholders and shepherds expressed their friendship towards the Siberian exiles upon whom Fate had smiled. Rolling in the opposite direction were endless convoys of American lorries with Soviet drivers at the wheel. This was aid from the West *en route* to the Soviet Union, the new ally; and for us a reminder of our very recent past. But that morning the valleys and slopes of Elburz were bathed in sunshine and nothing could disturb our rediscovered capacity for simple joy.

The crash happened as we began our descent from the peaks towards the plateau on the far side. Our bus ran into a lorry awkwardly parked just beyond one of the hairpin bends. I remember the screams, the sound of breaking glass, and the sudden disappearance of the entire left wall of the bus, ripped off by the protruding corner of a solid Detroit vehicle. I caught a glimpse of our back wheels perilously close to the precipice.

It was a miracle that no one was killed, or even seriously hurt. The only victim was the driver: he succumbed to shock – but only briefly. The passengers of the damaged bus were transferred to a spare vehicle at the end of the column. In the meantime our driver announced that his bus was still capable of unaided progress. On hearing this, my mother suggested that we four remain with him. Our driver accepted the offer eagerly. It was a welcome face-saving device – an important matter in those parts. I was delighted because it turned the journey into an adventure.

Without a hitch we reached the town of Kazvin. Here I was over-whelmed by the sight of late night shopping: brightly lit stalls overflowing with sweetmeats and fruit. Next day, in the same battered vehicle, we came to Tehran.

~

The so-called 'Civilian Camp No 3', to which we were assigned, was the result of our General's endeavours, the latest addition to two earlier camps situated in the city's industrial suburbs. 'No 3' was by far the most congenial. It was set up in the grounds of a magnificent country residence, the property of an Iranian notable whose family had fallen on hard times. A high wall surrounded an extensive park, in which tall cypresses guarded the ruins of the big house. The estate was several kilo-metres to the north of the city, on the newly asphalted road to Darbant, the Shah's summer residence. Amongst the avenues and *aryks* – fast streams of ice-cold water running down from the snow-clad peaks of Elburz – an instant city of army tents mushroomed under sympathetic British supervision. In the centre stood the communal canteen, alongside the administration block, hot showers, and an open-air stage for theatricals and film-shows with a natural amphitheatre of hills around it.

We entered this idyllic setting in a blaze of publicity. The appearance in Iran of former Soviet prisoners and deportees was an event attracting world attention. Film crews – mainly American – were poised at the gates to record our arrival. Only the other day I saw on British TV an old clip showing one such event at the gate of glorious No 3. This particular piece of visual evidence remains today a confirmation of what General Anders said about the state of his civilians: 'My most urgent task was to organise proper medical care and accommodation for the civilian dependents. The condition of the newly-arrived was appalling and often beyond rehabilitation. People were dying of exhaustion and the after-effects of hunger... In a matter of weeks over one thousand crosses rose at the new Polish cemetery of Tehran.'

The young orderly with an armband who took our contingent in hand at the gate was none other than my friend Muś Łętowski, one of our fellow refugees at Słonim and a member of Father Adam Sztark's contingent of altar boys. Later we discovered in Tehran a number of 'fellow-travellers' who had shared the Soviet experience: from Słonim the Łętowskis, the Bitner-Glindziczes and the Rudlickis; from Dereczyn the Zięciaks; from Nikolaevka Mrs Tubielewicz with her two haughty daughters; and, last but not least, Mrs Bazylewska and her guitar! A feeling of camaraderie prevailed.

Muś led us to our new quarters. These amounted to a space on the ground covered with matting, in a long communal tent. There was no furniture in the tent, the nearest 'sitting room' being a bench in the central canteen. Stacks of used clothes of high quality awaited the women – American generosity again. Soon my mother and sisters began to look thoroughly presentable, although the total image took some while to achieve. The other day I found in my mother's papers one of her early Tehran photographs, in which she is topped with an elegant summer hat and tailed with a pair of tired plimsolls.

The plimsolls did not inhibit contacts with Iranian high society. Local young blades sought out the exotic Polish girls. Anuśka caught the eye of a colonel in shiny riding boots, who offered outings in his equally shiny American car. Anuśka was allowed to accept the invitation, but 'her mother came too' – as did Tereska; the collective view being that there was safety in numbers. My mother's chaperoning tended to inhibit these budding opportunities.

I in the meantime made new friends and we began thumbing lifts to the city below. I soon discovered that lifts came more easily to individual travellers, so I began exploring the capital alone. This suited me well until one day a chauffeur-driven car pulled up. I remember its number: 1888. A corpulent man in a striped three-piece suit invited me in with fulsome cordiality, and began making sexual advances. I turned to the driver and demanded that he should stop at once. Which he did. On return I told my mother what had happened, and she reported the incident to the authorities. 'Ah yes', they said with amusement, 'the old 1888 again'. My mother was not amused, and from then on I stuck to group travel.

Otherwise life was blissful. Camp food was plentiful, the weather perfect, and there were good friends galore. As an occasional treat at the camp shop we had a drink called 'Sinalco', a delicious fizzy concoction brewed locally under German licence, to which I became addicted.

There was a serious side to camp existence: the alfresco secondary school organised by the Polish Authorities and manned by devoted teachers who had survived the Soviet exile. Classrooms were pitched under the shadiest trees. In view of my academic successes at Nikolaevka I was assigned to the first year of the Polish secondary system, younger by at least two years than my classmates. This time the Polish language was my main challenge, but somehow I managed to please the demanding Mrs Korczewska. Other subjects presented little difficulty, probably because the course was simplified to give the children a chance to catch up on two 'lost years'.

After a month's hard work I obtained promotion to the second year, which my mother celebrated by giving me a slap-up luncheon at the camp shop, by then extended to include a 'café-restaurant'. The main dish was a Wiener Schnitzel with a slice of lemon on it. This blow-out was followed by a foray *en famille* to Cafe Ferdosi in the heart of Tehran, where the Giedroyćes astounded both the waiters and the patrons by their unrestrained demands for fresh mountains of cakes.

Extramural activities laid on by a school anxious to improve our minds were, on the other hand, less exciting. The well-meant random lecturers we found boring, although we welcomed with enthusiasm the pomp of Bishop Gawlina, chaplain to the Polish Armed Forces, who came to administer confirmations – in most cases long overdue. As was customary, I chose another name, that of my father Tadeusz.

Then there was the memorable performance by the Review Theatre which had sprung up on the fringes of the Polish Army. It featured a number of pre-war artists of high calibre (many of Jewish origin) who came out of the Soviet Union with the Army. The star of the show was a platinum blonde (of Polish-Ukrainian origin) called Renata Bogdańska, the darling of the Polish Forces – and the future Mrs Anders.

Enjoying life as never before, I was unaware that to my sisters, and to my mother, things looked very different. Communal living, and the prospect of a sterile existence as refugees, was not what they – one aged 22 and the other 20 – expected after two and a half years of suspended animation. They became restless and my mother began to look for a means of returning to some kind of normality.

Things came to a head when we discovered that my mother's cousin, Aunt Lila Ciemniewska, had taken a job in the town at a smart hotel reserved exclusively for the Americans. Her daughter, and several other young women well known to us, also found employment there. Materially, the Americans seemed to live on a different planet. Aunt Lila's condition looked unattainably glamorous until we discovered that these genteel young women were employed as maids and barmaids.

In the meantime Zosia Boniecka, another distant relation and a woman of the world, hit the jackpot: she was invited to take up the post of Social Secretary at the Polish Legation. But these ventures split families. Aunt Lila's husband, very unwell, lingered on in Camp 3. My mother tried to keep in touch with him, and even recruited my services as a visitor, although he seemed too ill to notice our calls. Zosia, too, had to farm out her children. She slipped her elder boy Władyś under my mother's wing at Camp 3. The glamour of the capital had its complications.

These complications my mother judged as unacceptable drawbacks; and she had grave doubts about the status of maids and bar attendants.

She decided to leave Camp 3 for Tehran, but on her terms. She and her daughters would seek 'suitable' employment. Naturally, I was included in the exodus – against which I rebelled. My pleas were overruled. Towards the end of October we abandoned the security of the camp, and moved to the city to fend for ourselves.

The Bond Street of Tehran was (and perhaps still is) called Lalezar. Its busy southern end was dominated by silversmiths and carpet merchants. Before the arrival on the scene of Reza Shah, the army officer who usurped the Persian throne, the northern end of Lalezar was a haphazard collection of old houses with walled gardens. In the early 1910s the reforming town planners decreed that Lalezar should be straightened. The process involved some high-handed demolition, of which one victim was a house belonging to two brothers, Ali and Bogher (an unfortunate name to an English ear). I do not remember their surname. In this house, in late October of 1942, our family found refuge.

The house was a fitting successor to the mutilated old bus in which we had arrived a month earlier: the demolition gangs had split it in half. The surviving western part retained its walled garden with a defunct fountain. Access was through a *kuche* – a tiny, peaceful alley typical of Tehran. It was quiet except for street cries – *Portukhare shirin, limun torsh!* (Sweet oranges, sour lemons!) Itinerant sellers of pomegranates would also sing out their call. To this day I associate the capital of Iran with this magnificent fruit.

The slice of the house that was still standing consisted of an abandoned ground floor and two large rooms on the first floor accessible from a gallery with a 'hen run' or wooden external staircase leading up to it. One of the rooms was occupied by Ali and his beautiful unhappy wife, Aurora. The other room was offered to my mother by Bogher, who lived in a modern flat round the corner. She must have met him socially, and said at the time that she found him interesting if difficult. The brothers were officers in the Iranian army: polished, fluent in French and discreetly critical of the British monopoly of Persian oil. They concealed, with some difficulty, a lingering admiration for Germany. But they were gentlemen, and eager to extend a helping hand to exiles from exotic Lakhistan, that is Poland.

Our sliced-off quarter was separated from the new street by a makeshift wooden wall, covered with a decorative hanging which failed to keep out the cold winds from the east. But the rickety floor was covered with a magnificent Persian carpet. And that was it – no beds, no furniture, no kitchen. An outside privy, shared by the two families, was tucked away downstairs under the hen run. There was an urgent need for investment, and my mother's last golden coin was converted into some bedding (mattresses and blankets) and a shiny primus stove. There was enough left for essential clothes. Three smart coat-and-skirts were made for the ladies as a preliminary to job-hunting, and I, aged thirteen, was kitted out for the Polish *Gimnazjum* of Tehran.

My outfit was eccentric, to say the least. I was measured up by a tailor for a pair of plus-fours *(pumpy)* – and a matching frock-coat in pre-war English tweed. This was my mother's personal response to the ugly new world. I did not have the heart to object, and in consequence had to suffer endless teasing from my up-to-date colleagues in long trousers and wind-cheaters.

Life was on a knife edge. To survive we had to find work, and soon. Meanwhile the primus stove came into its own, monotonously delivering meals of hot beetroot with slices of liver – the cheapest ingredients available at street corners. This was augmented by some dates and local halva washed down with native tea from the southern slopes of the Caucasus. Bread was scarce and such luxuries as sugar, butter and milk beyond our means. My mother had grandly forfeited the generous camp rations… Would her latest calculated risk succeed?

It did. Soon my sisters became telephonists in one of the Polish institutions on the strength of their ability to say 'Can I help you?' in an impeccably English accent, even though they could say nothing else. Not for long though. Anuśka turned out to be a linguist, and Tereska – more broadly based – graduated to a secretarial job. My mother in the meantime was engaged by the owner of a cinema, as French tutor to his two daughters, Shaheen and Maheen. It was not a full-time job, but with it came the occasional invitation to her employer's table. I was included on the understanding that lunch would be followed by a game of volleyball with my mother's charges. I did not mind in the least: the girls were charming, if giggly.

At this stage my mother had enough time on her hands to spend a part of each day with our neighbour Aurora, who clung to her for company. When not chatting to her, Aurora would sing sad songs reminiscent of Paris boulevards. Soon after our departure from Lalezar the news reached us of her suicide.

~

Kitted out in my Edwardian tweeds, I faced the Polish *Gimnazjum*. It was a small school, no more than 30 children in two junior forms. The city attracted families that wished to re-start their lives and get on, among them some outstanding teachers. At least a third of the children were Polish Jews, who brought with them the ambition to learn and advance. The normal academic year was reinstated, although there were few books or other aids: all we had was paper and HB pencils.

Pressure for results was strong. I had already discovered the pleasures of learning and success, and now began competing as never before. I soon made new friends, three of whom I remember particularly well. Ignac Abramowicz was a robust Polish Jew two years older than I; the sort with whom one would not mind sharing a slit trench. His parents were kind and hospitable, and I remember generous tea parties at their flat. The handsome Żenek Klar was also Jewish. He was even older than Ignac, and something of a role model, because he was worldly and dressed in a three-piece suit. My mother often, and somewhat wistfully, referred to Żenek's mother as 'that glamorous Mrs Klar'. She was a platinum blonde, better off than any of us, and an *habituée* of high places. Our paths were to cross later at the Polish Military School because Żenek's family were totally Polonised and he volunteered for the Army; unlike Ignac, who on arrival in Palestine embraced the cause of Israel.

My third friend, Ryś Straszak, had extramural attributes which impressed me. He was a natural sportsman, with a deep voice, and was integrated into the ways of Iran because his father had been in the Middle East since well before the war. Ryś was fluent in Farsi and had no difficulty in keeping juvenile street gangs – something of a menace to us foreign children – at bay. He taught me useful Iranian phrases such as *man tora dust daram* (I love you), the Iranian national anthem

(*Shohan Shohe Mo Zende Bod*, Long Live the King of Kings), and a jolly little song which began thus: *Ostot-lie Bannoh / Begu yo alloh*, (Foreman Bannoh, please go away). In due course Ryś also entered the Polish Military school.

The belle of the school was Maryla Krzywańska, elder daughter of a distinguished doctor destined to become the Commanding Officer of Forward Field Hospital No 6 at the battle of Monte Cassino. Many soldiers of the Second Polish Corps owe him, and his staff, their lives. Maryla was a serene blonde. The queue of eager young blades offering to escort her, carry her books, etc., was long. I joined it timidly at the tail end.

Friendship with Roman (Romek) Puzyna, a contemporary of mine for a change, and a distant cousin, was special. Sadly, the Puzynas soon departed for Isfahan, but Romek caught up with me at the Military School in late 1944 or early 1945. Our friendship survives to this day.

∼

In the Tehran of 1942 young Poles in uniform were in short supply: the Army had moved on to Iraq. But the dashing Captain Andrzej Czaykowski of the 1st Lancers, a friend of the family, did manage to steal some leave and visit. He and Tereska were seen together. After the war Czaykowski went back to Poland to join the anti-Soviet underground. He was captured and shot.

Another admirer of Tereska's was in an altogether different mould. His name was Eftekhary and he was an Iranian violinist of note. His playing moved Tereska, but not sufficiently. Neither did the romantic Djafar (straight from *The Desert Song*) who came to call on horseback, bearing chocolates. The chocolates were welcome, but Tereska was choosy and kept her distance. Anuśka meanwhile embraced variety. I attempted to keep a register of her escorts, but soon gave up under pressure of numbers.

Naturally, all this took place under my mother's watchful eye. To calm things down she encouraged this social butterfly of a sister to take up 'pen-pal' correspondence with an unknown Polish officer, another lancer called Stach Lickindorf. Anuśka soon tired of a relationship on paper. Kind Tereska stepped in and took over the correspondence. I suspect that initially she attempted to impersonate Anuśka. At any rate, the relationship blossomed. In the spring of 1945 Stach became Tereska's husband.

Meanwhile local politics also provided excitements. Late in the autumn a coup was staged in Tehran, which we observed with a little anxiety (bullets flew), and much fascination. As soon as the insurgents' tanks moved into the suburbs, the carpet makers unrolled their wares onto the streets. Apparently a mangling from tank tracks gave the desirable finishing touch before these indestructible works of art came up for sale at the smart end of Lalezar. The tanks were of the lightest variety.

We were included in the guest list for the Christmas *Wigilia* at the Polish *Delegatura* – the Ministry of Social Welfare. It was a culinary extravaganza, with tables groaning under dishes of pre-war splendour. My mother found it too much for the circumstances – but to me it was irresistible. I ate and ate, and on the way home, on foot in the middle of the night, I experienced a strange sensation. It was as if the walls of my stomach were about to burst. A lesson never to be forgotten…

The writer Melchior Wańkowicz describes life in wartime as 'grass-shoots struggling on the edge of a crater'. Although he was writing about life between the rivers Dnepr and Oder, the description may be extended to our existence in Tehran; indeed, to the whole of our odyssey. Alongside the fragmented normality that my mother was able to piece together, harsh reality loomed.

Towards the end of 1942 a rumour reached us that my father had been seen in one of the Soviet prisons or camps. Taking advantage of the presence in Tehran of Tadeusz Romer, now Polish Ambassador to the Soviet Union *en route* from Kuibyshev to London, my mother passed this information on to him with a plea for help. Romer replied, on 29 December 1942: 'During my transit in Tehran I received both your letters and through one of my colleagues who is going back to Kuibyshev in a few days I am sending them there with an instruction for both letters to be delivered with care and separately to your husband, and a telegraphic order to our representative in the relevant area to give him urgent assistance in my name. I am extremely happy to hear [from you] that he has been found, because on the telegraphic order of the President of the Republic I recently issued further instructions to search for him. Now I shall be able personally to reassure the President about your husband's fate'. These words must have kept my mother's hopes alive. It was to be another six years before she found out the truth.

Early in 1943 the Lalezar intermezzo came to an end. Bogher and Ali showed my mother the final demolition order. We had to look for new accommodation without delay. Rescue came from the father of Shaheen and Maheen. He offered us – somewhat sheepishly – a cubby-hole above the entrance to his cinema. My mother accepted, as there was no alternative. There was just one smallish room (the 'living room' in the true sense) with a sort of box-room next to it. The lavatory (Persian style, i.e. designed around the squatting posture) was miles down a sinister twisting corridor in bare brick.

We arrived with our bedding, the precious primus and coats-and-skirts, to confront life at its most basic. The 'main' room was small and bare, and its brick floor – no Persian carpet here – was a constant source of dust. The box-room, where our treasured possessions were deposited, had no lock on the door, and was promptly burgled: the primus, and my mother's coat-and-skirt, were stolen.

Mercifully, at that precise moment my mother was offered a modest job at the *Delegatura*, as was Tereska. Anuśka was there already – the star telephonist. With these appointments came food rations and access to the office canteen for good daily lunches. Life was looking up again.

The cinema was situated in Sepah Place, in the heart of old Tehran, not far from the famous covered bazaar. Sepah was crowded and very busy. The street stalls were laden with halva, dates, and pomegranates. There were stalls with hot snacks: I remember testicles of various sizes and diverse provenance grilled on open fires. But the main bonus that went with Sepah Place was privileged access to the cinema below. The owner was either enamoured of, or contractually bound to, Soviet films. These were resistible to my mother and my sisters, but I had no such inhibitions. I immersed myself in Soviet cinematography safe in the knowledge that I was immune to Lenin's or Stalin's siren voices. And so, in the heart of Tehran, I came to know Eisenstein's epics and the Soviet version of *Velikuya Oktyabrskaya* (the Great October Revolution).

I particularly remember the film *My iz Kronshtata* (We from Kronstadt) in which the red sailors come to the rescue of Lenin – the very same sailors who rose against his tyranny four years later – and the welcome newsreels of von Paulus' surrender at Stalingrad. Remembering my reaction to Hitler's onslaught on the Soviets – 'serves the bastards right' – I now savoured the same sentiment in reverse. Hatred of both the Nazis and the Soviets was a reaction exclusive to the Polish exiles; it took the West almost a generation to catch up with us.

Other cinemas in the centre, much smarter and more cosmopolitan, were less accessible to me because I had to pay to get in. But I was given the occasional treat such as Disney's *Fantasia*, and the stirring *Desert Victory*. The most endearing feature of Tehran cinema-going were the Iranian subtitles. These came up frequently on full screen, to be read by the audience in a loud and lusty chorus.

After two or three months we left Sepah (with little regret) to move into a proper flat off Shah Reza. A move to this respectable neighbourhood was made possible by my mother's promotion to a post at the *Delegatura* in education and cultural affairs. This was the beginning of her career in the Polish Civil Service. Its immediate fruit was decent accommodation. Our first floor flat was small: two little rooms, cooking in the corridor, and a communal loo; but we now slept on beds, and enjoyed the view of our landlord's trim garden from a balcony.

The flat soon became a centre of social activity. I witnessed the birth of a salon on a shoe-string. The news went round that my mother was now in a position to receive all those who wished to call on her. They came, in increasing numbers, to her tiny bed-sitter doubling up during the day as her drawing room; young men in uniform – mainly British – in the first instance, for whom civilised girls in Tehran were worth their weight in gold. My sisters welcomed these new contacts. It was fun being escorted by warriors from distant Albion. In their company the streets of Tehran became much safer: Tereska was now able to dispense with her riding crop.

Melchior Wańkowicz, a distant relation, was one of the early visitors. (It was his image of 'grass-shoots struggling on the edge of a crater' which inspired the title of this book; in less than two years he would become the celebrated chronicler of the battle of Monte Cassino.) Aunt

Zosia Romer, the noted painter and sister-in-law of Stanisław, Ania's first serious admirer, came to make a crayon portrait of my mother. Witold Świątkowski, an old family friend from Wilno, brought with him Leon Colonna-Czosnowski. That visit was the beginning of a lasting friendship between Uncle Leon and my mother.

While my sisters danced and I enjoyed the films of Eisenstein, clouds were gathering over the cause of Poland and her Central European neighbours. On 13th April 1943 German radio announced the discovery of the Katyń mass graves. The Soviets blamed the Germans. The Poles asked the International Red Cross to investigate. On 26th April the Soviets broke off diplomatic relations with the Polish government. On 4th July General Sikorski, Polish Prime Minister and Commander-in-Chief, perished in an air crash off Gibraltar. The circumstances of this tragedy are yet to be fully explained, but it is difficult to overlook the fact that at the time the head of British Intelligence for the Iberian Peninsula – and therefore Gibraltar – was none other than Kim Philby, the Soviet agent.

Violence also struck nearer home. One day Antoni Giedroyć – he who had registered us for the Second Evacuation – was walking with a lady along the quiet street between the British Legation and the Soviet Embassy. Quite suddenly a man appeared from nowhere, rushed at Giedroyć, knocked into him, and then withdrew into the shadows. All this took only a few seconds. As they walked on, Antoni reached for his chest and said to the lady: 'He had a knife'. The weapon was aimed at his heart, but struck a pocket filled with personal documents. They were sufficiently thick to prevent the blade piercing his chest; he was not hurt. The attack remains something of a mystery. It is possible that Giedroyć was involved in intelligence work, either Polish or Allied: he knew Russia intimately. Long after the war he was still retained by the Ministry of Defence as a translator.

The lady was Elzbieta Strzembosz, who came to the Polish *Gimnazjum* as form-mistress of Year Three. I joined her class in September. We knew her as Pani Elżunia (Mme Lizzie would be the nearest English equivalent). She transformed our lives. Never before, or since, have I met a teacher with such God-given talent and charisma. Her subject was Polish language and literature, to pupils an unavoidable challenge, and more often than not a burden. But under Pani Elżunia's demanding and enthusiastic guidance, even Polish grammar acquired a measure of romance.

The *Gimnazjum* also acquired the services of Mr Kluk, a qualified PE teacher and a sportsman with a fine record. After Siberia, disciplined sport was a welcome new experience. But Mr Kluk's optimism got the better of him when he challenged the junior national athletics team of Iran to a match. The hype that surrounded the event became unbearable when it was announced that the match would be staged in front of the Shah and his Empress at the city stadium! Confronted with lithe specimens in spiked running shoes (all we could afford were soft slippers from the bazaar), we despaired of victory, but we were determined to put up a fight. They beat us of course, but it was not a disgrace. Soon after, in the same stadium off Shah-Reza, the Polish Army (Middle East) beat Iran at football. We cheered wildly, assisted by a large contingent of GI's of Polish origin. Honour was restored.

November came, and with it the Big Three: Roosevelt, Churchill and Stalin. The city came to a standstill, and a cordon was thrown round the two neighbouring diplomatic compounds: British and Soviet. We did not know that inside that cordon Stalin was being compensated with Poland, not to mention the rest of the eastern half of Europe, for his anti-German exertions.

To us the cordon was a nuisance, so my mother decided to challenge the line of red-capped British military police. One morning she simply sailed passed them with an air of authority. She looked thoroughly respectable, of course, and the security men must have assumed that she was an aide, or a wife, of some standing. As she marched towards her destination along the deserted street of the diplomatic quarter, a cavalcade of open cars glided towards her. Recognising the Big Three, she selectively waved at Churchill. Afterwards she claimed that he waved back.

I had just stumbled on a copy of *Polish Parade*, the glossy magazine of the Polish Army in the Middle East. In it I found an illustrated article on the recently established Polish Military (Cadet) School, the *Junacka Szkoła Kadetów* (JSK), carrier of the tradition of the pre-war Cadet Corps. The School's location was a secret, but the Polish community knew it was somewhere in Palestine. This was a reminder of my father's plans for my future. Nearly fifteen, I felt it was time to break away. The matter was clinched by photographs of cadets in full gear, featuring some of my friends from Camp No 3. I told my mother that I wished to volunteer for the Military School.

My plan involved separation, and for my mother a major break from her principle that families in peril should stay together. She knew at the same time that educational standards at JSK – General Anders's pet project – were high. Faced with her son's first independent decision, she gave her consent with grace and understanding. So did the *Gimnazjum*. In fact, on 19th January 1944 I was given early promotion to Year Four with generous grades, even though the school year was yet to run its course.

On 17th January 1944, just in time for my fifteenth birthday, I was enrolled into the Polish Army as a Junior *(Junak)*, kitted out, and rushed through basic training at Camp No 1 in anticipation of departure for Palestine. My mother came to the railway station to say goodbye. For the first time in my life I saw her in tears.

CHAPTER 11

Martial Arts

Among the civilian ex-deportees that gathered round the camps of the Polish Army in Russia, there were many boys too young for active service. Some came with their families, but many were stray orphans. All were destitute and in bad physical condition. General Anders's response was typically Polish: early induction into military ways. On 12th September 1941 he issued an order establishing 'Junior Formations' *(Oddziały Junaków)* for boys aged between 14 and 17. The analogy with the British category of 'Young Soldiers' was discovered later, and this became a useful legal basis for the future of these formations.

The units of Juniors were included in the First Evacuation and moved to Palestine – for these boys truly a Promised Land. There the Polish Army assumed responsibility for their well-being. The care of civilians, or the education of their young, is not – indeed must not be – the business of any ordinary army. But this was no ordinary army; nor was its commander any ordinary general. Anders ordered the screening of his 80,000 men for teachers and educationalists. Enough were found, many of high quality, to take charge of the Juniors. In the summer of 1942, the process of sieving and classifying the boys began, and several schools were set up to cater for the wide range of talent, age and condition. At this point a suggestion emerged, apparently from several sources at the same time, that one of the schools should be modelled on the pre-war Corps of Cadets.

On 28th August 1942 *Junacka Szkoła Kadetów,* the Polish Military (Cadet) School in the Middle East, formally came into being, initially comprising four companies with a total of 342 Juniors. On 26th November General Anders visited the School and granted it the new insignia: the epaulettes and badge closely modelled on those worn by the inter-war cadets. On 28th November the senior company of the school was issued with arms, and on the 29th, the 342 Juniors were ceremonially promoted to the rank of *Kadet*.

From then on the well-attested Polish talent for improvisation took over. The teaching staff began to compile the curriculum, mainly from memory. The Polish-speaking Jewish community was trawled for text-books – with good results. The loaned copies were reprinted by the ever-helpful British Army. In the autumn of 1942 the School was moved to one of the best military camps in the area. The British Medical Corps stepped in to tackle rampant malaria, followed by British PE instructors as soon as the boys were well enough to face their demanding standards. The Education Corps provided teachers of English. Within a year the School was ready for glossy write-ups in the Allied press.

My long journey to a new life at JSK began at Tehran railway station, where my mother attempted to hand me over to Aunt Rózia Mycielska (*née* Tyszkiewicz) who was travelling with the Polish contingent. She was accompanied by her daughter Zosia, a young woman endowed with a very good figure daringly poured into a pair of tight trousers. I retired politely to the safety of our hotch-potch platoon of Juniors. The unit was looked after by an elderly sergeant who remembered the Russian Impe-rial Army. Better him I thought, than female fussing, which at the time I was desperately trying to shake off. In any case there were the fabulous 150 (or thereabouts) railway tunnels to be admired on the way to Basra through Qum and Kazvin, built before the war by the Germans eager to make themselves indispensable to the oil-bearing Middle East.

Basra I remember very well because it was there that I sampled for the first time the 'full English breakfast' cooked by that superior body of men, the Catering Corps. Fried bacon, and that delicious small pastry that went with it, remain a happy memory. In Basra we were transferred to a narrow-gauge railway and sent on to Baghdad, slowly winding our way through plantations of date palms.

The transit camp on the outskirts of Baghdad was total heaven, because it was presided over by the equivalent of a *Grande Ecole* of the Catering Corps. The pupils of that establishment tried on us their *haute cuisine,* and we embraced their offerings with enthusiasm. Our elderly sergeant wished to return the compliment, and three times a day made us sing in formation as we marched to our feasts. The song was a primitive ballad and we rendered it badly. But it attracted the attention of a British Army padre with homosexual preferences. He began hanging around our tents. The heterosexual, and extremely street-wise, Polish youths treated their visitor with kindly forbearance.

The third and last part of our journey, the 800 kilometres between Baghdad and Haifa, was a desert ride in a convoy of army lorries. These vehicles were manned by Sikhs, and the column was commanded by a dashing British officer in an open staff car. The Sikhs I found fascinating. Each morning they would perform the ritual of winding their turbans. This they carried out in pairs. One man would walk around his partner in ever-decreasing circles, skilfully depositing new layers of regulation khaki cloth over the other man's head. The roles would then be reversed.

Our drivers were individualists. Once the dirt track gave way to open desert, they abandoned their formation and started racing. This apparently was a well established Sikh pastime, indulged by the Army provided the CO was able to keep the lid on. Ours was up to the challenge: with panache he herded his lorries by racing round them like a sheep dog, keeping one eye on his compass – the only navigational aid between transit stops. An admiring audience was continuously at his elbow: the most glamorous ATS girls in the convoy were invited to take turns as his passengers. It was a buyer's market.

These goings-on were enjoyable so long as the weather was good. But Iraq's February can be treacherous. We ran into at least one *hamsin* – a desert sand storm whose lashings are as foul as those of a Siberian *buryan*, though for different reasons. We admired the way our CO was able to find his way to our daily destination – the next transit camp – in such conditions. I gather the technique was to look for the outline on the horizon of the regulation water tank on its high stilts.

On the third day the desert, until now a standard yellow-and-grey, turned dark and then almost black. We were approaching Amman, the capital of Transjordan and our last transit stop. This desert 'overnight' was spent in expectant sleeplessness: the next day we were to cross the River Jordan. The approach to that crossing brought with it a dramatic change of scenery. We were suddenly surrounded by orange groves and green farmland; and then greeted by curious glances, and the occasional wave, from the inhabitants of the tidy Jewish settlements. In Haifa, our destination, we caught our first glimpse of the Mediterranean. It was early evening and we were treated to a spectacular sunset.

At the Haifa transit camp Polish Army lorries were waiting for the Junior Platoon. The drivers were PSK (Polish ATS) girls who, being gossipy, at once told us that our destination was Camp Barbara near Ashkalon, about 20 kilometres north of Gaza, at the other end of Palestine. We drove into the night, gratefully enjoying the smooth and careful handling of the vehicles by our new lady chauffeurs. Only now it occurs to me that the name of that camp was unusual. No one has ever explored its origin. Perhaps the British sapper responsible for the camp's inception gave it the name of his flame; or his daughter; or even his wife...

He was obviously proud of his handiwork, and with good reason. Even in the middle of the night we could see that it was as permanent an establishment as a camp can ever be. There were clusters of well made wooden barracks, backed by regular 'quads' of large white tents. We found the camp fast asleep, but at the same time alert. Cadets on night duty could be seen doing their rounds, and armed guards stood at sensitive points. The place radiated confidence.

We were delivered that night to the Distribution Point, where we would await the Army's decision regarding our future. For the newcomers these were tense days. We were interviewed, examined for physical fitness, and our aptitudes – academic and otherwise – were scrutinised. The platoon distracted itself by exploring the camp and admiring its sights, of which the most striking was the enormous red brick garrison cinema (called for some reason 'Kinema'), and doubling as chapel, ballroom, concert hall and lecture theatre. The other landmark was the huge water tank at the northern perimeter, elevated high above the tents and barracks and incidentally providing a perfect vantage point for the press photographers regularly sent down to record the doings of that intriguing Polish enterprise, General Anders's Cadet School. The garrison shop was a magnet, but only to the rich, or prudent; as was the YMCA club-cum-café dispensing coffee, sandwiches and cakes. Those short of funds could console themselves with free access to magnificent Jaffa oranges at the *pardes* (orchard) just beyond the water cistern. The owner encouraged the cadets to help themselves, because he was unable to export his crop, and free hospitality was preferable to costly disposal.

I shall always associate the Holy Land with oranges, alongside Iran's pomegranates and Iraq's dates.

While waiting for my posting I received an unannounced visit from Uncle Henio, my godfather. It was a joyous and reassuring occasion at a rather delicate moment in my military career. After the Soviet experience Uncle Henio was no longer strong enough for line service. He was currently stationed in Tel Aviv, awaiting a less strenuous posting. Over coffee and cakes at the YMCA he gently slipped into the role of my substitute father. During the next two-and-a-half years I was to see a lot of him. He became one of the most important influences of my life.

I was fairly confident that the Cadet School would have me. In the meantime I sought out some of my old friends from Tehran who had already been admitted, among them Romek Brąglewicz, the pack-leader at Camp No 3, and Władyś Boniecki, whose mother was born to grace the *salons*. They showed me the ropes and warned of pitfalls. My hand-delivered posting to the Sixth Company, First Platoon, arrived c. 20th February 1944, by which time I was well briefed. The bearer of good news was the duty cadet of the Sixth in full fig – epaulettes, white belt and white spats. He looked me up and down (he was much taller than me), and offered to help me with my kit. We Juniors were trained to carry all our gear unaided, but this was obviously a gesture of welcome. I accepted the offer, and the two of us set off happily on foot towards the other, 'senior', end of the camp. There, in the shadow of the garrison Kinema and the water tank on stilts, I was to be initiated into military life.

The cadet school was a five-company battalion. This was an attempt to match the six-year cycle of Polish secondary education (a company for each year) – but with a downward adjustment for natural wastage in the last two (toughest) years. Each company had three platoons, and each platoon was made up of four sections of eight cadets. Total numbers fluctuated: at the beginning of 1944 the headcount rose well over the battalion establishment, reflecting an unforeseen bulge at the end of Year Four. The Army responded by adding a supplementary company – the 6th.

The School curriculum was designed to provide both general education and military training. The former was based on the Polish pre-war model, in which a four-year *Gimnazjum* (roughly, GCSE level) was followed by a two-year *Liceum* (equivalent of A-Levels). The *Gimnazjum* course was broadly based across some 11-13 subjects, aiming at a generalist type of education at the expense of study in depth. A concession was made to the arts / sciences divide, by allowing two kinds of *Liceum*: humanist (arts) and mathematical / scientific. The distinction remained one of emphasis. Interestingly, our Cadet School initially opted for the humanist variant. Presumably the choice matched the traditional self-image of the Polish officer corps. A technological *Liceum* with emphasis on civil and structural engineering was eventually added at JSK in the academic year 1945/6.

Military training was thorough. It amounted to basic infantry training, followed by more advanced work up to the level of platoon command. The more promising cadets could expect promotion to this level while still at school by taking charge of their peers. These were challenging assignments. Four times as many appointments were also available at the less exacting level of section command. All these 'martial arts' (I find the term particularly suitable for my subject bearing in mind the humanist character of our *Liceum*) were matched by demanding PE, with an input from the British Army. Needless to say, the equipment made available for these pursuits – martial and physical – was extensive and of high quality. The academic disciplines were less well equipped. The School lacked even the most elementary science laboratories.

After graduation from *Liceum*, the cadets could look forward to promotion to one of the Cadet Officer Schools of the Polish Second Corps in Italy. There, after some six months of intensive specialist training, the freshly promoted Cadet-Officers would be assigned to their units – usually regiments of their choice.

In normal circumstances the age spectrum for our School would have been from 12 or 13 at entry to 17 or 18 at graduation – almost identical to that of the Royal Naval College, Dartmouth prior to 1955. Interestingly, the British Labour Government of the day raised the age of entry to Dartmouth to 18, on the incomprehensible (to this writer at least) grounds that recruitment at the age of 13 would perpetuate class distinctions. I am digressing with this startling piece of information because our School, too, fell victim to a similar attempt at social engineering. I shall return to this matter presently.

Of course, the circumstances of the boys emerging from Soviet captivity were far from normal. On the academic front, virtually all entrants were behind by at least two years. In my platoon, the normal age of entry would have been 15–16. In fact, the actual average age of my peers was around 18. In February 1944 I was just 15. This created some problems.

~

My first impression of the Sixth Company was the impeccable orderliness of its sleeping quarters. Significant numbers of cadets still suffering from malaria were billeted in barracks, but the majority were allowed to move into tents. These were, I believe, Indian Army issue, spacious and comfortable. The perfect geometric layout- each platoon in four tents in a row – encouraged good housekeeping. In no time small gardens appeared around each tent, voluntarily tended by the green-fingered members of each section. This kind of gardening was a labour of love, because our camp was on the edge of the Negev Desert where plants had to be carefully matched to climatic conditions and frequently irrigated. The favourites were, I think, the eucalyptus and the castor-oil plant.

The company mess occupied the central barrack. Its furniture was basic: enough for dining, but only just adequate to double-up as a venue for the wireless and private study. It was staffed by locally recruited Arabs and supervised by two Polish ATS ladies of a certain age. The cadets discovered that their Arab waiters had a knack for Polish obscenities, and naturally this linguistic sideline was encouraged. Personal animosities among the waiters were stoked in the knowledge that at the height of each quarrel the antagonists would slip into Polish abuse of the most elaborate kind. These were moments to be savoured – with an eye on the reaction of the ATS supervisors.

My new colleagues struck me as extremely well turned-out; they were in fact very concerned with their appearance. This was encouraged by the dress privileges that matched officer standards, made possible by our caring sergeant-quartermaster. My Tehran kit and uniform was somewhat short of these exalted standards, and there emerged an instant consensus that something had to be done about me for the sake of the reputation of the Sixth. The quartermaster saw to it within days. But even in my smart new clothes I was still a *Junak*, a mere Young Soldier on probation. All late entries had to undergo a trial period of three to four months. A probationer had to be on his guard. He was observed by his colleagues, and by his superiors. It was not a comfortable position.

On the very first day I was reminded of my double handicap of inferior status and precociously young age, when I met the other seven cadets of my section. The tone of the welcome, which was merely correct, was set by the most prominent member of this group, one Staś Kaczkowski. He was short, perfectly made, and endowed with a classic profile which he presented to the camera at every opportunity. At the age of nineteen he was also the oldest cadet in the Sixth, if not of the whole School. On that morning the grandest and the least important came face to face.

Age difference made life difficult in the gym and on the playing field. I was fit and well coordinated, but smaller and weaker than my colleagues. I sensed that I was in danger of becoming a company mascot. And that role I was not prepared even to contemplate. The problem resolved itself when I began to deliver good academic results. My position improved even further when my older colleagues discovered that I was also willing to give an occasional tutorial.

The hard core of our teaching staff consisted of experienced pre-war teachers; all of them touchingly dedicated to the task before them: the mental rehabilitation of young men saved from captivity. Alongside these professionals the Army placed at our School's disposal a motley collection of gifted and often eccentric men of stature: university dons, men of letters, one or two senior civil servants – not to mention an outstanding pre-war actor-director. These provided the fizz, and encouraged undergraduate attitudes. The appearance of our teachers was not exactly warrior-like, but this was treated by the cadets with friendly indulgence. By contrast, our English instructors, all seconded by the Education Corps, brought with them standards of military *chic* compatible with our own. And so on the whole did our own military commanders, although they tended to be older men (an unkind wit observed that most of them, as they walked, left behind them a trail of dry rot). The fact was that younger officers were needed on the Italian front. In the meantime we had the benefit of more mature guidance.

Dr Wit Tarnawski, a well known physician, had the most daunting task of all, bearing in mind the physical condition of his charges so soon after release from Siberia. Not only was he responsible for its repair; he also had to monitor the escalation of the targets set by the PE instructors, so that the strength and endurance of the young men would not be over-taxed. The success of the Tarnawski rehabilitation scheme was resounding. Within two years the School began winning matches against senior teams of major Allied units. The doctor always attended home games: watching his cadets win was his reward. He also enjoyed other successes. A true Renaissance man, he was an acclaimed expert on the writings of Joseph Conrad and a man of letters in his own right. Such was the calibre of those gathered together by General Anders to educate his cadets.

Year Four of *Gimnazjum*, which I entered in mid-February, was compressed into five-and-a-half months instead of the usual nine. This was done in order to accelerate the progress of all those delayed by exile. At the same time everything possible was done not to compromise standards: working hours were stretched to the limit, leave was cut to the minimum, and quality was still demanded without excuses. In comparison with Tehran's gentle canter, this was nothing short of the Spanish Riding School. For me it was a challenge on a par with the Siberian *desyatiletka*.

The school was consciously elitist: Anders's breeding ground for junior officers. Other boys were directed to Young Soldiers' Schools offering technical education and army trades. There was also a Preparatory School *(Szkoła Powszechna)* based alongside us at Camp Barbara, from which Year One of *Gimnazjum* was drawn.

The Cadet population was fiercely democratic. Our periodical, *Kadet,* declared: 'For three years our School was home for the sons of cabinet ministers, generals and staff officers; for princes and counts; and for the sons of NCOs and smallholders. There were no differences among us.' It could not be otherwise among young men – one third of them either orphans or unaware of their parents' whereabouts. We all shared the scars of Siberia – we were familiar with hunger and disease, skilled at survival, full of the wisdom of the gutter, and used to its language. We had learnt that solidarity is a powerful weapon, and this knowledge bound us into a community.

The officers and the NCOs in charge of the School saw themselves as a part of this brotherhood. They, too, were victims of the Soviet experience; and for that reason were well qualified to guide the School. The bonds of solidarity were further cemented by the shared *Heimat*: three quarters of the cadets came from Kresy, the eastern Borders of the Polish Second Republic.

The social nuances behind the formal façade were subtle. I soon discovered that to the outside world Fifth Company appeared the most fashionable. The reason, I imagine, was that it held in its bosom the two most senior years (the *Liceum*) – a small and exclusive club within a single platoon. The few families that by-passed Siberia (i.e. those that in September 1939 were able to cross into Romania), and still wielded some influence, tended to push their pampered offspring into the Fifth. In the hands of the legendary Sergeant Major Wilczewski the Fifth was impeccably turned-out, and drilled to perfection. In 1943 it was they who represented the Polish Army before General 'Jumbo' Wilson at the military parade in Cairo.

An informal club, calling itself the Aristocrats, appeared in the midst of our platoon. This group was led by Romek Bràglewicz and Żenek Klar, my old chums from Tehran. The Aristocrats were not enamoured of learning. Driven by hormones, this pack of young blades pursued girls – and there were plenty of them at the Polish Junior ATS School in Nazareth. Our Aristos anticipated the fragrance of today's young males by dousing themselves with eau-de-cologne, dressed sharply, and polished among themselves their social skills, above all others the dancing steps of the tango. One Aristocrat called Szuszkiewicz was particularly conspicuous, because he smoked scented cigarettes – the height of sophistication. He kept them under lock-and-key in a small suitcase under his bed, unaware of the skills of my dear friend nicknamed 'Umfa', who was not an Aristocrat but an expert lock-picker. We never asked Umfa where he acquired this ability, but he was wheeled out whenever Szuszkiewicz was away. In front of an admiring audience Umfa would unlock Szuszkiewicz's suitcase with the help of just two sharpened matches. The Aristocrats would then transform the tent into an impromptu smoking den – at some risk, I might add, because smoking in sleeping quarters was strictly forbidden. I did not qualify for entry into this exalted circle, but I remained on the best of terms with its leadership.

In the classroom I came face to face with Zbyszek Mychal. My friend Bręglewicz described Mychal as 'a mountain of muscles'. This young Samson commanded respect, and I was flattered when he suggested that we should share a desk. It turned out to be a happy arrangement. Under Mychal's wing I found a safe niche, where I could get on with what I liked doing: academic work. On that front, once or twice, I was able to be of some help to him.

I soon discovered how steeped in history was our corner of the Holy Land. The ruins of the biblical city of Ashkalon were within walking distance. The teaching staff tended to stress the Polish associations, however. We lived in the shadow of the great romantic poet Juliusz Słowacki. In the course of his travels in the Middle East he wrote some of his most moving poetry at El-Arish, three stations down the line from our own El-Majdal. We were particularly haunted by 'The Father of the Doomed', in which an Arab patriarch watches as his family falls victim to plague:

> We came and raised our tents upon the sands,
> the camels quietly lying on the ground.
> Our youngest child, a little angel,
> fed sparrows – the tiny birds coming to her hands.
> Can you see that stream winding in the valley?
> Our daughter, straight as a reed
> approaches with a pitcher on her head…

I have no doubt that the echoes of our own experiences in this tale affected us more deeply than we knew.

Another 'Polish' connection was Napoleon – a hero to the Poles generally, and to me especially because of the Giedroyć service in his cause. The well-known painting of Napoleon visiting his wounded men in Jaffa – just up the road, near Tel-Aviv – was brought to our attention by the history tutor.

Religious life was formal and strictly enforced. We were lucky in our Chief Chaplain, Father Lorenc SJ, a clever man who enjoyed his confrontations with those of us who found it fashionable to embrace agnosticism. Being by then a confirmed doubter, I felt no need for closer contacts with the Chaplaincy. In the early 1950s I called on Father Lorenc at the church of Il Gesù in Rome, where he held a senior post, to recoup my losses. But he was out of town, and I never saw him again.

Non-conformism was not confined to matters spiritual. Young men skilled at survival knew very well how to outwit oppressors. The temptation to outwit their own military bosses lurked just below the surface. The School's moods remained volatile, and the young needed delicate handling on loose reins. This is best illustrated by the events of 1st April 1944. Amongst the Poles, *Prima Aprilis* has a long tradition akin to the English varsity rag, but more reckless. On that day, the whole school spontaneously absconded from classes. Five hundred exuberant young men spilled onto the dunes to the accompaniment of lewd songs. The objective was a day on the beaches of Ashkalon. The authorities held their fire until the evening, when their sun-burnt charges, happy and tired, began drifting back in search of rest and a shower. Then came the measured response: the announcement that an all-night exercise was to be mounted immediately, and on the very same Ashkalon sand-dunes. Six companies in full gear were paraded before the CO, who then announced that the order was – *his* Prima Aprilis! The parade was dismissed to three rousing cheers in honour of the staff. A new bond was forged, and the 1st April double-routine became an annual tradition.

Smoking was officially discouraged, and only just tolerated in remote venues favoured by the addicts. One such sanctuary was a secluded patch behind the latrines. There a strange custom, traceable to Soviet labour camps, was observed. It was called *sorok*, Russian for 'forty'. Anyone short of a cigarette could approach a smoker and say the magic word. The smoker was then honour-bound to give not quite a half of his cigarette (about forty per cent) to the petitioner. The penalty for breaking the *sorok* rule was ostracism – a fate worse than death.

The finely balanced equilibrium was disturbed only occasionally. One instance of lawlessness still remains in the School's collective memory.

It concerns the chequered academic career of Cadet Sojka, a persistent rebel of diminutive stature. A civilian teacher of English from Jerusalem informed Sojka that he would not progress to the next year unless his results improved dramatically. The response certainly was dramatic. Sojka, when on guard duty, crept up to the open window of his tormentor, and fired a .303 round towards the darkened ceiling. Next morning the teacher tendered his resignation, and Sojka was arrested. This gave him time to devise his defence; which was, that he had responded to a shadowy intruder whom he apprehended in the sleeping quarters; and that in firing only a blank (not true, according to my sources), he showed commendable restraint. Sojka's detention was longer than usual, but he was not expelled. He was likeable, and a useful forward in the soccer team.

Law and order had to be enforced and our gaol was rather busy. Normally the cell was populated by short-term inmates who absconded to visit their sweethearts in Nazareth. Occasionally a gambler would be apprehended and locked up to think again. The Authorities tolerated a liking for bridge among their budding intelligentsia, but would not allow poker for money. As for serious matters, I heard of only two instances of suspected theft. Tragically, there was one case of rape involving a local Arab girl. The offender was taken away for questioning and we never saw him again. I gather that the father of the victim accepted compensation. This was the only outrageous criminal act of a sexual kind; one too many, of course.

Neither in the Sixth Company, nor subsequently in the Fifth, did I ever encounter active homosexuality. We were fully aware of such practices, having been exposed to advances from the locals since Tehran days. I suspect that these experiences actually strengthened the overwhelmingly heterosexual culture that prevailed at the School. At the same time the attitude to homosexuality remained one of patient tolerance. In the 1940s the street-wise Polish ex-deportees were already anticipating the twenty-first century. In the meantime all my eighteen year-old friends were in hot pursuit of the opposite sex. I was not yet ready to compete with them. But I was happy to participate in social diversions available in and out of camp; and compatible with our miniscule pay.

Excessive drinking was not an option. All we could afford was the occasional beer, or half-bottle of inferior Cypriot wine. Only after graduation *(matura)* did serious binges take place. These were tactfully ignored by the Commanding Officer and his staff. Transport on the other hand was freely available from the army vehicles milling round the Middle East, making Nazareth, Tel Aviv and Jerusalem easily accessible. We went to the big cities in search of cheap entertainment – and to the beaches in search of girls. We favoured those run by the NAAFI: they were frequented by the Allied pulchritude, and their restaurants were reasonably priced. The seaside Army Clubs of Gaza, Ashkalon and Tiberias (close to Nazareth) were our favourite haunts.

The lucky few had friends, or – better still – relations, in Tel Aviv or Jerusalem. I was one of them: Uncle Henio was still in Tel Aviv awaiting posting; and always ready to give his godson fatherly hospitality. I spent several weekends with him, including the long Easter leave of April 1944. Together we imbibed the Jewish atmosphere of pavement cafés, discovering in the process a strong Polish cultural undercurrent. Most of the Jewish population of Palestine had its roots in the old Polish-Lithuanian territories. They still remembered the Polish language, and spoke to us with nostalgia and – it seemed – some pleasure. We were made to feel welcome. At the time a great deal of goodwill was generated in Palestine by General Anders when over 3,000 (out of a total of some 5,000) Polish soldiers of Jewish origin deserted during transit through Palestine. The British Authorities, fearing that these highly trained men would join the Jewish underground, demanded round-ups and court martials. But Anders refused to hunt them down. He, better than most, understood the motivation of people getting ready for independence. The Jewish community responded with friendliness, which they focussed on the cadets left behind by the Polish Army on the northern edge of the Negev. (The British were right, incidentally: one of Anders's deserters was none other than Corporal Begin of the Polish Fifth Borderlands Division, responsible for the bomb at the King David Hotel in Jerusalem on 22nd July 1946, which killed 91 people in the cause of Israeli independence.)

∾

Sir John Colville, Churchill's right-hand man, refers in his book *Man of*

Valour to a conversation of 21st September 1940 between Prime Minister Churchill, Field-Marshal Gort and Air Chief Marshal Dowding. The Prime Minister opined that one Pole was worth three Frenchmen. 'Nearer ten!' Gort and Dowding said. In the dark days of 1940–41 the Polish fighting men were indeed praised to high heaven, and lionised by London hostesses. From 1943 praise became muted (the Soviets were now heroes), but Anders and his 80,000 were still highly valued and encouraged. This led to interest in our School, Anders's unique long-term formula for topping-up his officer corps; and his favourite showpiece. The result was a stream of visits by the high and mighty, both British and Polish. Perhaps there were too many of them, distracting the cadets from their daily routines. But for me personally the parade of 3rd May 1944 was a joyous landmark. Even though still on probation, I was declared good enough to parade under arms alongside my peers. The final accolade came in June with the promotion to the rank of *Kadet*.

Our army life was much more introspective than civilian existence in Tehran. We took little notice of world politics, got on with studies and training, and followed with envy the progress of our seniors on the Italian front. We rejoiced at the news of the capture on 18th May of Monte Cassino by General Anders's Polish Second Corps. *Our* Corps, and *our* General! They went on to capture Ancona and liberate Bologna. We basked in reflected glory. Later, in August, we learned with satisfaction that the Polish First Armoured Division had distinguished itself in Normandy as 'the cork to the Falaise bottle', which trapped the retreating German army and yielded 50,000 prisoners.

In the meantime our own in-house political fringe was raising the alarm. Politics, frowned upon by the majority of the cadets, were nevertheless espoused with fervour by a small minority of clever misfits led by cadets Piesiecki (the aspiring polymath) and Korbusz (a polyglot-in-the-making). These young men should not have come to us. They treated our two-pronged education, military training grafted onto a solid (if generalist) secondary schooling, with barely disguised contempt. They aspired to active politics, criticized party squabbles among the London Poles, and demanded that discredited men of politics be replaced by younger men – themselves? Not much of a manifesto.

But it was they, our own Capitoline geese, who understood better than the rest of us that the clouds gathering over Poland's cause were very dark indeed. Of course no-one knew at the time that at the Tehran Conference the eastern half of the Polish Second Republic was being traded to the Soviets; not even Edward Raczyński, Polish ambassador to the Court of St James. On 3rd January 1944 the Soviet army entered pre-war Polish territory – claiming it as its own. Our political fringe took note when Churchill rose in the House of Commons on 22nd February 1944 to declare that the Curzon Line (along the River Bug) should be the new Polish border in the east. During August and September they agonised over the lack of adequate support from Poland's Western Allies for the Warsaw uprising. And they understood the full implications of the Yalta deal when it came in February 1945.

The rest of us, even though aware of these events, simply got on with our daily lives. The hope persisted that the West would somehow bring itself to face the Soviet danger. General Anders and his lieutenants believed that armed conflict between the Anglo-Saxons and the Soviets was inevitable, indeed imminent. These hopes filtered down to our own commanders. If they did have private doubts, they kept them to themselves. I suspect they knew how vulnerable we still were after our recent experiences; and they tried to protect us from the next shock.

Amidst all these cataclysms, and more or less oblivious to them, I lived my intensive fifteenth year. *Mała Matura,* the Polish equivalent of GCSEs, loomed large but the results, when they came out on 31st July, were more than satisfactory. Long leave in Cairo, where my uncle Henio had now been posted, was to be the reward.

On 1st August, the day the Warsaw rising broke out, those of us going to Egypt gathered at the El-Majdal rail stop. I discovered among them Władyś Boniecki and his friend Witek Jarmołowicz, nicknamed Zośka (Sophie), both from the Fifth. The three of us were destined for Cairo, and this set us apart. Władyś's and Witek's fathers were brother officers in the First Lancers – a regiment with which my parents had particularly close ties. But that was not all: at El-Majdal I discovered that the three of us were going to the same Cairo address: Number 10 Naoual Street. This was no coincidence. Uncle Henio, my host, was staying at the small private pension which Zosia Boniecka (Władyś's mother) had set up in Cairo for the select few. That summer she set aside a large room for the three of us. In this way she was repaying my mother's kindness to Władyś at camp No 3 in Tehran, as well as earlier hospitality: she and her children had been made homeless by the Russian invasion in 1939, and had been given sanctuary in the House Under the Swan in Wilno.

The overnight train journey to Cairo was an adventure. The first half was dusty and soporific, the train trundling across the desert beyond Gaza, past Rafah and El-Arish towards El-Qantara, where a bridge would be lowered dramatically across the Suez Canal to let us pass. El-Qantara, a military base, offered the weary traveller in uniform an early breakfast. It was more of a *réveillon*, because it took place soon after midnight. For us, beyond the clutches of our incompetent Polish cooks, it was a feast: bacon, eggs, toast and marmalade, accompanied by a mug of tea that only the British Army is capable of providing.

The next stop, Zagazig, on the eastern edge of the Nile Delta, was a turning point in more than one sense. It was a major rail junction, at which our train swung southwards to continue its journey towards Cairo, having shed passengers destined for Alexandria. Zagazig was also the place at which the valley of the Nile revealed itself in full splendour. Here sand and dust gave way to the humid corridor of palm trees, canals, and antique irrigation wheels turned by oxen.

Cairo was all noise, clanking trams and petrol fumes. A taxi, grandly engaged by the three young cadets, took us past the Egyptian museum, round the huge Ismaliya Place, and onto the bridge next to Napoleon's Kasr-el-Nil barracks. The driver pointed to the stone lions guarding the bridge, and explained that the lions roar whenever a virgin crosses the Nile; the lions have apparently maintained a stony silence ever since their arrival – a joke attributed to the Allied Armies of North Africa. There was another, less notorious, bridge on the other side of the Gezira Island, beyond which lay the opulent Dokki district. Naoual Street was the dividing line between Dokki and the less chic Agouza district. But Number 10 was right next door to the grounds of the palace occupied by the mother of King Farouk – for Zosia a feature that redeemed the address.

The house was modern and very comfortable; and, to us tent dwellers, the height of mysterious luxury: there was an appliance in it called the bidet. Zosia's large apartment on the first floor overlooked its twin-sister on the ground floor, where another glamorous Polish lady, Pani Marychna Buynowska, also had one or two paying guests under her wing. In August 1944 the extended household of the first floor included the three cadets on leave, Zosia's ten-year-old daughter Terenia chaperoned by a young local governess, the *châtelaine* herself, and the two boarders, my Uncle Henio and his boss at the Polish Red Cross who was also a family friend – a fact which became apparent the first evening over drinks.

The Boss came up to me, looked me in the eye, and said: 'My name is Romer and I should have been your father'. Uncle Henio explained in a stage whisper that I stood before Stanisław (Staś) Romer, the man who in 1913 nearly fought a duel over my mother. Staś proceeded to mix me my first ever whisky-and-soda (I was still fifteen but more than ready). Thus began a long friendship.

The Boniecki establishment was under the control of Zosia's Sudanese manservant Abdul. He was black, clad in white-and-red (the red being the fez and the sash), with three tribal cuts on each cheek. We were warned that Abdul was irritable, and for two very good reasons: at the time he was observing the strict fasting rules of Ramadan; and he was in the middle of difficult negotiations over the purchase of a wife. So we kept out of his way. But he was a professional: his personal problems in no way affected the high standard of his cuisine. Only his puddings were a disappointment; he insisted on serving mango with deadly regularity. To the three young visitors this otherwise delicious fruit soon became anathema. For me it became the heraldic symbol of Egypt, alongside the pomegranate (Iran), the date (Iraq), and the orange (Palestine).

In Cairo I experienced a culture shock that comes with the sudden release from military discipline. The easy-going regime that awaited us in Naoual Street had much to do with the personality of our hostess. Zosia Boniecka, a product of wealth and position, was totally at ease with the world. Siberia had made her a survivor. She was beautiful, stylish, and an irrepressible practical joker. One of her victims was Staś Romer, who styled himself, for the benefit of the outside world, Stanislas de Romer. There was nothing wrong with this: the Romers were a noble Polish family of Baltic-German origins. Mischievous Zosia took to referring to him as Stanislas von Römer (with two dots over the 'o'), rejoicing in the impact of the 'von' on the sensitive Allied establishment of Cairo. Her other victim was Piotr (Pet'ya) Kurnicki of the Polish Foreign Office, a boarder at Marychna's rival establishment on the ground floor. Zosia persuaded the three of us to water her balcony flower-beds with excessive vigour so that Pet'ya, on the terrace below with a drink at his elbow, was generously and regularly sprinkled. I might add that Uncle Henio was never subjected to Zosia's teases.

We on the other hand could not resist entering into the spirit of the party, and soon began making our own contributions. The best one concerned my love life. Władyś and Witek, having persuaded Terenia's governess that I was madly in love with her, made me lock myself up in the bathroom and let off Uncle Henio's air-gun (his deterrent against noisy tom-cats). They then announced to the object of my desires that I had committed suicide. There were some tears and shrieks, and finally a mixed reception when I emerged unharmed.

Zosia was an ornament of the Cairo social round and she tried to include us in it. I remember a stuffy luncheon party in Zamalek and a formal tea party at the Gezira Club. She soon realised that our hearts were not in it, so she handed us over to Uncle Henio who gently pointed us in the direction of antiquities. He told us to face backwards on the tram to the Pyramids, only turning at the last moment. We did as he suggested, and the effect was impressive. But more so was the owner of the camel on which I took the short ride from the Mena House Hotel to the ancient site above. There were three camels, actually, and with them three owners. I naively handed over the payment for all three rides to my minder, who then leapt onto his charger and took off into the desert. The other two mounted theirs, and the chase began. The sight of the three of them disappearing into the distance remains with me to this day.

Our real preferences were less refined. Every day we repaired to the Heliopolis swimming pool, and in the evenings we frequented the open-air cinemas where, at the end of each performance, we would join in the Allied chorus of the profane version of the Egyptian national anthem. I blush as I write this… The afternoons were devoted to watching the world go by from the cafés in Soliman Pasha. Our favourite was Groppi's, the hub of the Middle East. Uncle Henio would occasionally sneak out of the office to join us.

The Cairo idyll did not last, alas. In the middle of August I received orders from the School's CO to return to camp. Władyś and Witek were not included in the summons. I left with a heavy heart on the overnight train, and the next morning reported for duty only to be informed that Major Kulczycki wished me to come with him to 'The Cedars of Lebanon' at Bcharre high up above Tripoli, where the School's summer camp was stationed. It was, I suppose, a kind of favour; a favour that at the time I strongly resented, although the trip in his motor was enjoyable. We stopped in Beirut for lunch at Halabi's Restaurant on the waterfront, full of Polish acquaintances from Tehran. There Helenka Zaleska, fresh from Tehran, rushed up to me with the news that my mother and sisters were due to arrive in Beirut in a matter of weeks. That piece of news was more than compensation for the loss of Cairo's attractions. Up in the mountains of Lebanon I crafted two bread-and-butter letters: one to my beloved Uncle Henio (with the news of my mother), and the other to my glamorous Cairo hostess.

Under the cedars the air was crystal-clear and very dry, and the nights were cool; in other words, here was a perfect opportunity to rest. This opportunity to a fifteen-year-old straight from Cairo seemed bland. Instead of breathing in oxygen and absorbing the panorama, I still looked for distractions. And of these there was only one: a nearby stalactitic cave of world renown. Its aloof splendour was enlivened by the antics of the obliging keeper-cum-guide. Having paid him his fee after a personal tour, I thought it proper to reward him further with a packet of biscuits. The response was overwhelming. He began hacking away at one of the stalactites and before I was able to stop him, a priceless tip was being proffered to me, in truly Levantine fashion, as a counter-present. I had no choice but to accept. I still have it tucked away somewhere, and it remains a memento over which I feel extremely uneasy.

The life-restoring mountain sojourn clearly had its effect, because once again my appetite for work began to reassert itself. When the time came for the return journey to Camp Barbara, I was more than ready. The School travelled in a special train from Tripoli all the way down to our own El-Majdal. Around Sidon and Tyre we made slow progress among banana groves, and I decided to add the banana to my heraldic collection as a symbol of Lebanon. Back at camp I was introduced to the legendary Sergeant-Major Antoni Wilczewski, a 43 year-old Wilno man. A new chapter of my life was about to begin.

Sergeant-Major Wilczewski was short, squat, and afflicted with a slight squint, which he knew how to conceal. He enjoyed a reputation verging on a cult. For a Polish soldier of modest standing he was well educated. His *matura* should have encouraged him to seek a commission, but he never aspired to officer rank. He chose instead the opportunities available to able men at the top of the non-commissioned pyramid. And there he shone. Well read and lucid, both verbally and in writing, he knew better than his peers how to deal with attempts at teasing – a standard pastime of arrogant youth. In a competitive atmosphere his speech betrayed a literary creativeness of a high, if idiosyncratic, order. We were not surprised to discover that his pre-war posting was at the best of the three Cadet Corps: the First, in Lwów.

I well remember the first parade, and the interlude before the formal appearance of the commanding officer. For quarter of an hour Wilczewski had the Fifth all to himself. Ninety-six young men, not easily daunted or impressed. He looked us up and down, and then addressed us with fluent precision: 'The cadets will strap-up their arses!' (*Kadeci – dupy w troki!*) He spoke quietly, and the effect was electric. The Fifth straightened their backs, pulled in their stomachs, and thrust forward their chests. More was to come. 'Gentlemen', he said, and we sensed that this mode of address was reserved for the gravest of pronouncements; 'Gentlemen, from now on I expect your boots to shine like dogs' balls in SPRINGTIME.' (*Panowie, buty mają się świecić jak psu jaja na WIOSNĘ*). When the parade was dismissed, the relationship was sealed with a Wilczewski encore, fired at our 'political fringe' skulking away in disarray: 'Those cadets remind me of a fart trailing down a pair of long-johns!' (*Ciągną się jak smród po gaciach!*) From that day onwards the Sergeant-Major held the Fifth in the palm of his hand. Januszek Jaźwiński, the resident wit, described the effect of that first parade as 'chicory in the pants'.

There is a fine line between the robust and the obscene; Wilczewski knew its importance, and he never crossed it. His robustness was confined to the Fifth – in his eyes the only body mature enough to take full advantage of it. He saw it as a didactic ploy, designed to reassure the young that they were being admitted to adulthood. He also used it as a precision tool on the parade ground, where he turned the Fifth into a perfect drilling machine. During one of the final tunings before an important visit he addressed the Fifth thus: 'Gentlemen – the sound of your step reminds me of a goat shitting on a SMALL DRUM!' *(Jak koza srająca na BĘBENEK!)* We understood instantly, and tightened our timing, but we never discovered why the drum had to be small.

Towards the end of October my mother and sisters arrived in Beirut. This was marvellous news, bringing with it the prospect of Christmas leave in the Lebanese capital. Just 24 hours before departure, however, I was told that my leave had been cancelled. No official reason for this harsh decision was ever offered; the gossip had it that I fell victim to an administrative bungle by an office clerk who assumed that Beirut was located in Egypt; and raised the paperwork accordingly. Anyway, there was I, left behind as a member of a skeleton staff for deployment on a never-ending round of garrison duties.

It was a dismal time, lightened with one compensation. On 24th December our CO included me in the small group selected to accompany him to Bethlehem for Midnight Mass at the Basilica of the Nativity. To the Poles *Wigilia* (the evening before Christmas Day) is more important than the feast-day itself, and we were grateful to Major Kulczycki for this opportunity. I must confess that the solemnity of the occasion did not inhibit our enjoyment of the sideshows provided by the various Christian denominations jockeying for position around the sanctuary. The return journey to camp in the early hours of Christmas Day was memorable for the intense cold.

The summer of 1945 brought peace to Poland's allies, but not to Poland. We watched our homeland, now overrun by the Red Army, being forced into the straitjacket of Soviet rule. The Polish soldier felt betrayed. But youth has little time for matters of state. I yearned for some long leave, and was particularly well placed to take it, having both Cairo and Beirut within my grasp.

First I went to Cairo to join Uncle Henio, who had moved downstairs to Pension Buynowska. This time I was on my own, which enabled me to spend more time with my uncle. I loved being in his company. I spent my days at the Heliopolis swimming pool, and late afternoons at Groppi's, often with Uncle Henio. In the evenings we chatted on the terrace over drinks. I enjoyed being treated as a grown-up.

Then came Beirut. That summer the resident Polish *jeunesse dorée* (most of them undergraduates at Beirut's two universities) repaired to the mountain resort of Bloudane, and my mother tried to persuade me to join them. I refused, preferring to remain with her in town where at the time she was the administrator of the Polish House. It was an opportunity to have her all to myself. But there was also another, entirely egocentric, reason for my reluctance to escape the heat of this Mediterranean port. I did not feel confident enough to be thrust into a worldly group of strangers. My mother – ever understanding – arranged alternative distractions. Through her influence my sister Anuśka and I could use the private tennis court of Mr Bayard Dodge (of the car company), President of the American University. She also secured for me entry to the French Officers' Club, the *Bain Militaire,* endowed with a private bay around which one could swim and sunbathe in safe anonymity.

At the end of August my sister Tereska was going to take Uncle Henio (in need of a rest) to Bloudane. I would have joined them like a shot, but this second opportunity came too late. Within days I was due back in camp to begin *Liceum II* – the final year of my military education.

Liceum II now became the First Platoon, the most senior of the School, and I was named Platoon Commander. This was a challenging appointment. Of the command opportunities open to the cadets, section command was the most congenial introduction to leadership. It was the least strenuous, being confined to a small unit within one tent, and at the same time totally independent because at this level there were no senior commanders. At the other end of the scale there was the position of junior company sergeant-major. This was the most demanding post in terms of workload, and far from independent because it amounted to a day-to-day dialogue with the senior company NCO. In short, it was first class training, but at NCO – not officer – level. Potentially the most demanding post was that of junior platoon commander. Here a cadet was expected to impose his will on his peers with only distant help (on an as-required basis) from the nominal senior commander who was at the same time the form-master. Learning opportunities were extensive provided access to the senior was unimpeded. In my case, I was placed in tandem with Dr Kazimierz Lic, an academic happy to give me total freedom; perhaps too much of it, bearing in mind that I was two years younger than my colleagues-cum-subordinates.

It was indeed the deep end. To give opportunities to others, and to protect academic performance, command of Platoon 1 was rotated on a termly basis. When Januszek Jaźwiński took over, I went back with renewed gusto to my revision for *matura*. Then, after the final exams in May 1946, I was returned to platoon command. The involvement in the unit's concluding engagements was enjoyable. I must confess that I did not expect this final preferment; but I cannot deny that I found it gratifying.

The curriculum of *Liceum II* included a new and exotic subject: Introduction to Philosophy. It came to us with the most sophisticated of outside tutors: Dr Stanisław Kapiszewski of the Jagiellonian University. Always polite, on one occasion he lost his cool: 'Gentlemen' (this mode of address recalling the Sergeant-Major, and therefore instantly focussing attention), 'Gentlemen, you are a band of cretins.' *(Panowie są bandą kretynów.)*

The subject, and Kapiszewski's teaching of it, fired my imagination. I began reading round it with the help of my father's old friend from Łuck, Stanisław Wnęk, now one of the administrators at HQ. Under his guidance I even tackled Bertrand Russell. How well I remember my first experience of mental exhaustion.

At HQ level (I mean the HQ of all Polish military schools, ours being one of them) we observed changes. This, I suspect, came with the swing of the Polish Government towards the left of centre. Out went our founder-father Lt. Colonel Bobrowski, and in came Lt. Colonel Ryziński. Soon the School's CO, Major Kulczycki, was removed to make way for

Ryziński's social experiment: the eradication of the special 'Kadet' status in the name of equality. There followed a series of steps aimed at diluting legitimate differences between our School and the others; differences deliberately encouraged by Ryziński's predecessor, and endorsed by General Anders himself. The matter came to a head when on one formal occasion Ryziński greeted us (Polish Army fashion): *Czołem Junacy!* (Greetings to Young Soldiers!) The five hundred young men who had worked hard for promotion from Young Soldier (*'Junak'*) to *'Kadet'*, responded not with *Czołem panie Pułkowniku!* (Greetings to the Colonel!) – but with total silence. It was the end of a working relationship. The school could not be disciplined: how can one discipline the five hundred on the parade ground? For the rest of the school's existence (i.e. till July 1947) behind-the-scenes diplomacy was pursued to repair the damage, but to little effect. After that fateful confrontation we saw little of Colonel Ryziński.

My mother knew that Witek Jarmołowicz and I had become close friends, so she invited him to spend Christmas 1945 with us in Beirut at the White House. This was a new hall of residence for Polish ATS girls seconded by the Army for study at the American university of Beirut (typical of General Anders to look beyond matters military). My mother had set up the White House during the autumn and now she was warden to a large group of young ladies. This was a daunting prospect for a sixteen-year-old cadet as yet not too sure of himself. I was glad of Witek's company. And it was he who stole the limelight when one evening the communal Christmas tree in the hall caught fire. Witek was first on the scene with a bucket of water, thus acquiring glory and quite a following among my mother's charges.

We took our final exams in late May. A string of demanding vivas followed, to be concluded on 6th June. I was given top grades in all eleven subjects; an *otlichnik* once again; memories of Nikolaevka... The most gratifying 'Very Good' was for PE, to me a supremely important area. I had arrived at long last. Having been declared *Prymus* of the senior year, I was released for long leave in Btekhnay, a Druze village in the mountains above Beirut where my mother was spending the summer.

This tissue-restoring interlude was interrupted by a summons to return to camp immediately. I was to parade before General Anders, who came to Barbara to mark with the school the twilight of its sojourn in the Holy Land. On that occasion I received from him my passing-out (i.e. *matura*) certificate with the following endorsement: 'I certify that Lt. General W. Anders, commander of the Polish Second Corps, visiting Camp Barbara at the conclusion of the school year 1945–6, signed this certificate and personally presented it to Cadet Michał Giedroyć in recognition of his exemplary conduct and results. Signed: W. Winiarski, Major, CO of Cadet School.'

This was the General's second visit to the School in quick succession. He was with us a few weeks earlier, just before the final exams, to bid us adieu before moving his Second Corps from Italy to England. Although we expected to join our seniors within the next year, the parting was poignant, because it marked the beginning of the end of an extraordinary educational experiment. The Fifth was the 'Company of Honour' and, drilled by Sergeant-Major Wilczewski, we performed as never before. For that occasion I was reinstated *pro tem* as Platoon Commander. It was a great honour.

The event attracted hostile comments in the Polish communist press subservient to the Soviets. The Red hacks called us 'Janissaries of General Anders'. The trading of insults amounted to an admission of defeat. People's Poland had obviously lost all hope of luring us back into the clutches of her masters – the NKVD. The suggestion that we enjoyed the status of our Commander's legendary shock troops – exaggerated though it was – gave the 'Janissaries' immense satisfaction. It also, involuntarily of course, fuelled our desperate hopes for some kind of deployment under his command in not too distant a future. Hopes that were to remain dreams.

CHAPTER 12

Ad Mare Nostrum

My mother had found speedy promotion within the Polish *Delegatura* from a menial job to an established post. This happened soon after my departure for Palestine, and it marked the beginning of her career in the Polish wartime Civil Service. She was already Head of Department concerned with education and culture when she was posted to Beirut. Her boss wrote: 'Throughout her tenure Mme Anna Giedroyć displayed exceptional initiative and energy. Her application, thoroughness and dedication was recognised and much appreciated not only by her superiors, but also by all the Allied institutions with which she came in contact.'

During that summer of 1944 my sister Tereska met Bill S. He was older than her other escorts – a major in the British Army. Tall and good looking, he was polished, kind and totally smitten with her. My mother's instinct told her that here was a man who was serious and reliable. She accepted him into her inner family circle, and probably saw him as a candidate for her daughter's hand. Tereska grew very fond of Bill, they saw a lot of each other, and I am fairly certain that he asked her to marry him.

The answer was no. Tereska felt that she was in no position to make a commitment of this gravity while being absorbed – indeed fascinated – by her distant Polish hero on the Italian Front. Stach Lickindorf was a lancer, an aviator, a *pro tem* diplomat, and a promising writer (he had just made his debut in a London weekly under the *nom de plume* of Stanisław Lenc). On 19th May he was badly wounded at the battle of Monte Cassino and from his hospital bed – promoted and decorated for his exploits – he wrote to Tereska clever and amusing letters. She was entranced. Her mother, sensing that Tereska was about to be swept off her feet, was concerned: she knew that Stach was a formidable ladies' man. In the meantime Bill wrote sad and moving letters to my mother.

While Tereska agonised, Anuśka played the field. She was now employed by the British Council, headed at that time by Christopher Sykes; a very suitable launching pad for her social career. And while Anuśka socialised, my mother looked for her next port of call. She prayed for a niche around the Eastern Mediterranean, because her son was in Palestine and her brother in Cairo. She was also anxious to get away from the Soviet troops in the streets of Tehran. Her prayers were answered soon enough. The Polish *Delegatura* put forward her name for the task of launching the Polish House in Beirut.

∽

The mountains of Lebanon protect the Mediterranean from the desert of Syria. Their snow-covered peaks generously sustain the narrow coastal plain and the Bekaa valley with life-giving water. The Phoenicians, the earliest inhabitants of this small paradise, invented the alphabet, founded Carthage, and are reputed to have sailed all the way to the British Isles. They also built Solomon's palace of their most precious export commodity, cedar wood. There are no fewer than seventy references to it in the Bible.

On the site of Beirut Emperor Augustus settled his most meritorious veterans around 15 AD. The site must have been congenial. Between the 3rd and 6th centuries AD Beirut was famous for its school of Roman Law – a proto-university serving the whole of the Empire. In the 19th century this awesome academic tradition was taken up by Beirut's two modern universities. Université Saint Joseph de Beyrouth (USJ) was established in 1840 under the name of Collegium Asiaticum by Father Maksymilian Ryłło, a Polish Jesuit born near Wołkowysk, not far from Łobzów. The Collegium was first affiliated to the University of Lyons, and in 1881 granted full status. The standing of its faculties of theology and medicine was very high indeed.

Collegium Asiaticum offered its services to all Christian communities of the Levant, and this drew a swift riposte. In 1866 the Protestant Syrian College was founded, to develop in due course, under the name of The American University of Beirut (AUB), into a major outpost of learning. It was affiliated to the University of Columbia, and blessed with a campus of opulence and great beauty. In the 1940s the two universities coexisted in a spirit of happy tolerance.

[169]

The Beirut which welcomed my mother and her two daughters no longer exists. After the war it was corrupted by American capitalism and the Sixth Fleet, then torn apart by political and religious strife. But in the mid-1940s Beirut was a stable cosmopolitan community addicted to commerce, and looking to France for models. Its population of a third of a million was a veritable mixture of races and creeds, with Christians narrowly outnumbering Muslims.

Blue sea, blue skies, green mountains. The city's setting was – and is – unforgettable, on a headland between the bays of St Andrew and St George. The locals claim that St George *did* exist, and that he was in fact their own exclusive saint before the grasping English came and hijacked him. Hotel Saint George, Beirut's most famous landmark, still proclaims this assertion. The *mise-en-scène* is not as dramatic as Hong Kong or Rio, but it exudes harmony. Before the arrival of the skyscraper, the architectural tone was dictated by handsome nineteenth-century houses flanked by almond trees, jacaranda and bougainvillea. Many of these houses had roof gardens. Pines and cypresses dominated the high ground, and resplendent palms lined the Corniche and the Avenue des Français – the Levant's centre of gravity. The precious cedar had gone, but a grove of some 400 specimens lingers on at Bcharre, high above Tripoli, familiar to today's tourists as 'The Cedars of Lebanon'.

The Polish Army and its civilian dependents needed doctors and chaplains. The potential remedy was waiting in the ranks: the pre-war medical students and seminarians. Someone reminded the Polish Authorities of the reputation of Beirut's faculties of theology and medicine at USJ. The University's response was positive: the young men would be welcome to come and complete their studies. Such was the beginning of the Polish wartime presence in the Lebanon. Soon the American University of Beirut joined the scheme, and other disciplines were offered to young Poles of promise in anticipation of post-war needs.

For the Polish exiles in pursuit of learning, Beirut was a place of historical significance. The founder of Saint Joseph was after all a Pole (albeit from the Grand Duchy of Lithuania), still remembered in the Levant as *Abuna Mansur*, or Father Conqueror; and by the French as *l'Homme incroyable*. The poet Słowacki stayed in 1837 at the monastery of Beit-Chesh-Ban nearby, where he wrote his great prose poem *Anhelli*. In the sixteenth century a grandee globetrotter, Mikołaj-Krzysztof Radziwiłł had written an early and detailed description of the Levant.

The Lebanese Government came to like the itinerant Polish students in uniform. Soon hospitality was extended to several thousand Polish exiles. These people were dispersed among the small towns and villages surrounding Beirut. The dispersion suggested a need for a focus. The Polish Legation and the *Delegatura* responded with a plan to establish in the capital a 'Polish House'. Anna Giedroyć, fresh from her Tehran successes, was designated its organiser and first administrator.

Priority visas were issued, and my mother and sisters arrived in Beirut, courtesy of Nairn Brothers' trans-desert coach service, in late November 1944. My mother's dreams of higher education for Anuśka and Tereska were soon dispelled. They were seduced by our British allies into interesting secretarial work at ENSA. All three moved into what was to become the Polish House, and my mother went into action. In December Father Kantak (an historian at USJ) blessed the premises and the new venture, and on 1st January 1945 Anna Giedroyć's appointment was formally confirmed.

The house was imposing. A wide marble staircase adorned by potted palms led to the grand reception rooms upstairs. The location high above the port afforded a view, and the quiet side-street peace and seclusion. It was a prime site, where my mother soon created a social and cultural centre, doubling up at the same time as a transit hotel for the several thousand new Polish arrivals steadily pouring into the Lebanon. 'Here,' wrote Father Kantak, 'in the principal drawing room, we had meetings, cultural events and lectures; here the new arrivals found hospitality and food.' My mother was particularly proud of her small but ambitious catering staff who three times a day cooked for up to a hundred people. The scale was impressive; so was the quality of the food.

All this I observed from the sidelines during my Easter 1945 break from the Cadet School. At that time my mother was totally – and anxiously – absorbed in Tereska's nuptials, arranged (by special dispensation from the Papal Nuncio) for Easter Saturday. The whole affair proceeded at break-neck speed: it was still wartime, and Tereska was determined. The manner of Stach's and Tereska's engagement, which took place only a few weeks earlier, illustrates the romantic intensity of what my mother described at the time as a *coup de foudre*. Stach, still on crutches, arrived from the front determined to take a discreet first look at his faithful correspondent. He managed this at Halabi's in the Avenue des Français, a restaurant favoured by the Polish community. My sister's friend Helenka Zaleska remembers: 'One day, over lunch with Tereska, I noticed an officer unknown to us holding a photograph and making enquiries. I went up to him and discovered that the photograph was of Tereska! Their first meeting took place at our table. Within days they were engaged.'

The arrival of the bridegroom accompanied by his best man – a regimental colleague called Misiewicz – created a stir. The impeccably turned-out young men who had recently fought their way up Monte Cassino came to us marked with that special confidence which belongs to those who have seen battle and lived to savour the victory. After the horrors of the previous six years, this seemingly reckless marriage on Easter Saturday became a celebration of life and renewal. The private chapel of the Nuncio, and later the principal drawing room of the Polish House, provided a worthy setting.

Uncle Henio was to give Tereska away, but his train from Haifa was delayed. He just made the end of the reception. It did not occur to anyone that I should take his place. At the time I was glad to be left alone at the back of the chapel – a vantage point for happy observation. Today I wish I had gone forward to sit with my mother... But I understand how distracted she and my sisters must have been on that day.

Left to my own devices I slipped out of the reception and sought out Monsieur Naim, my mother's majordomo and factotum. Over quite a few glasses of wine we struck up a friendship. This was cemented in due course with joint escapades to local football matches. On one of those occasions the British Army took on the Lebanese national side. I – in British uniform – sat with Naim in a solidly Lebanese stand, agonising over divided loyalties. The star of the local team was a right-winger called Bubul. He was small and extremely fast. Whenever he received a pass, our stand would rise and roar, 'Yallah Bubul!' I suddenly realised that I, too, was bobbing up and shouting with Naim and the locals.

Crowd psychology took over. The match ended in a draw – in my delicate situation a happy outcome.

On the strength of her success with the Polish House, my mother was asked to set up a new hall of residence for Polish ATS girls studying at the American University of Beirut. This came to be known as the White House. One of my mother's charges remembers, 'We liked our White House and we were proud of it. The Warden maintained firm discipline, but at the same time each of us felt able to enjoy a great deal of freedom; we all knew that our shared concerns, and our individual problems, were understood.' This tribute sums up my mother's secret: discipline on loose reins.

The young ladies of the White House were not privy to their Warden's concern about the potentially harmful influence of the Beirut Polish Students' Union *(Bratniak)*, dominated by one or two 'eternal students' – carriers of the less laudable habits of Poland's pre-war university life. There was one particularly resistible individual, an ageing 2nd lieutenant in the Polish Army whose reluctance to return to the frontline was matched by his reluctance to immerse himself in his studies. During this man's chairmanship, *Bratniak* was side-tracked into pretentious social-ising and dubious politics. My mother's worries about the effect of these distractions on her young charges were shared by Father Kantak and the Legation responsible for the conduct and welfare of the students. In the event, the young ladies of the White House survived *Bratniak*'s tempta-tions, and in due course most of them delivered creditable results with cheerful poise.

The White House also benefited from my mother's circle of friends and acquaintances. In Tehran the exiles still lived in the shadow of the Soviet presence. Lebanon, under the control of the Western Allies, seemed a haven of security. Reassured, people rediscovered entertaining and visiting. My mother's position and her comfortable lodgings encouraged social life of almost pre-war quality.

Contacts with the British Language School for Arabists, i.e. future diplomats and spies, were interesting. Sometimes my mother and my sisters joined them on their excursions to historical sites. The young linguists and their minders were congenial company.

When on leave, I found myself included in these activities, which to some extent collided with my private attempts at attracting the attention of one of my mother's charges. She studied music at the American University and gave impromptu Chopin recitals in the lobby of the White House. A sour note came from one of the Polish communities up in the hills above Beirut. Mrs Bazylewska the guitarist apparently complained that my mother no longer wished to know her. She did not appreciate how busy my mother had become. And it did not occur to her that she would have been very welcome at the White House had she made the effort to call. It was a sad epilogue to the long journey from Słonim. Our paths had parted, never to cross again.

With the White House I shall always associate my mother's return to pig farming. The kitchen yielded nutritious left-overs from the generous army rations, which the former *châtelaine* of Łobzów could not bear to see wasted. She decided to start a clandestine piggery at the bottom of the garden. There was an element of risk in this, because half of Beirut's population was Muslim. But faithful Monsieur Naim was prepared to enter the conspiracy. The enterprise flourished, and the White House became famous for its home-made pork sausages.

During the summer of 1946 a letter under the signature of Ernest Bevin, the British Foreign Secretary, was sent individually to every Polish soldier, urging the addressee to return to Poland – the post-war Poland which had just been handed over to Stalin and his NKVD. In Italy and the Middle East the letter was received with derision: nearly all these men had been Soviet prisoners or deportees. However, with the letter came an offer of an alternative: an invitation to settle in England to all those who could not – or would not – submit to a Soviet-sponsored regime. The invitation included the soldiers' families. At the age of seventeen I was old enough to understand the implications that went with the choices. I was flattered when my mother wrote to ask for my views. There was also the matter of my own immediate future in the army, which I wished to discuss with her.

After graduation from the Cadet School, Year '46 found itself in a state of suspended animation. Little was said about promotion to one of the

Cadet-Officer Schools in Italy or subsequent regimental postings. My own hope was to be accepted by the First Lancers, reconstituted in Italy and converted to Sherman tanks. The old ties with the regiment were rekindled with the return from German captivity of Major-General Zygmunt (Zaza) Podhorski, a friend of the family. I judged my chances with the First Lancers to be more than reasonable. But still there was no news of a move to Italy. Instead news filtered through that Anders's Army was about to depart for England and demobilisation. Gossip began circulating that South Africa had offered to take over our training, and presumably the responsibility for our future. Nothing came of it. I gather that the offer was turned down: Anders's Janissaries were an asset too valuable to be traded lightly. Instead, Year '46 was offered a summer course in Jerusalem; and, before its commencement, another compassionate leave.

I went to Btekhnay for the second time to find my mother in charge of administration and catering for the summer colony of Polish students. Away from sources of supply and hardly accessible, Btekhnay became another challenge. It was just as well that she was so busy. Worries over the future were compounded by the departure from Cairo of Uncle Henio, and the imminent departure of Tereska, now a dependent of her husband Captain Lickindorf, for England. Uncle Henio decided to take Ernest Bevin's offer and go back to Poland. His wife and family had been 'repatriated' (ethnic cleansing would be a more appropriate term) from Soviet Wilno (now Vilnius) to Toruń on the Vistula. My mother understood – indeed applauded – his reasons, but was worried about his personal safety. For her, return to People's Poland was not an option. She sensed that her husband was no longer alive. After the Soviet experience she feared communism in its Muscovite version. Her immediate homeland, Wilno and the Nowogródek region, no longer belonged to Poland. There was no one, and nothing, to return to. She told me that she was ready to face exile in England. I was happy to offer her, and Anuśka, the status of my military family.

My mother knew very well that conditions in England would be difficult; we were told that the welcome to newcomers would not be overwhelming. In anticipation of hard times, she took a course in sewing, organised by the War Relief Service and conducted by Mrs

Mróz, Master of Tailoring Arts. Having qualified as a seamstress, my mother then applied herself to the English language, in which she seriously lagged behind her children. Mrs Trenchen (I am not sure of the exact spelling; to us she became 'Trenczenka'), an English expatriate lady with a small daughter called Leila, was engaged as my mother's personal tutor, and brought up to Btekhnay. The tutorials were intensive and the results passable if not exactly brilliant; my mother was a very busy woman with little time for homework. But by the end of the summer she declared herself as ready as she would ever be to start a new life at the bottom of the British social pyramid.

In the meantime I rejoined Year '46, and we presented ourselves in Jerusalem for the Summer Holiday Course in English Language (15th July – 30th August). Behind that innocent façade hid a string of demanding lectures: Phonetics, English Idioms and Grammar, and the English Terminology of Maths, Physics and Chemistry. We were not quite sure whether the course was intended as a preparation for a military career or university studies. Perhaps it was just a sop; or an anaesthetic against the pains of adjustment to what lay ahead… But life – here and now – was good.

The Army negotiated access to the grounds of the residence of one of the Eastern Patriarchs. The garden was on the right of Jerusalem's Damascus Gate, and abutted the Old City wall. There, beside a working fountain, we pitched our four tents. The Patriarch (I am ashamed I never enquired of which Rite) was in communion with Rome, and this helped to clinch the deal. There was, however, small print to the agreement: the Patriarch expected us to attend his Sunday Mass. We were happy to oblige, but then discovered that the liturgy unveiled by the Patriarch was interminable. Not wishing to disappoint the old gentleman, we quietly devised a roster to ensure the semblance of a congregation.

Life under canvas in the shadow of the City wall had its diversions. One was provided by a colleague, who insisted on making his ablutions in the fountain in the nude. The Arab population behind the wall seemed intrigued; large audiences would line the battlements twice a day. The dialogue with the locals was made complete by the cannon of Ramadan just above our encampment. At sunset it would announce the end of fasting, and at sunrise its re-commencement. The evening thunder was bearable – we were seldom there to hear it anyway – but the morning blast was a serious penance. Some of my colleagues claimed to have been tossed out of their beds.

Catering was offered willingly by the nuns in charge of the Old Polish House, just inside the Damascus Gate. We soon discovered the reason for their eagerness. Having laid their hands on our army rations, they soon reduced us to a vegetarian diet dominated by courgettes. 'Where is our meat?' went up the cry. There was a near-riot, defused just in time by a meeting with Canon Pietruszka, the nuns' boss. *Pietruszka* means parsley in Polish, an appellation which we found appropriately vegetarian. After the confrontation our full rations were restored.

A real bonus was the presence of a contingent of young ladies, most of them from Nazareth. The girls were billeted with nuns at the other end of the city, but of course we mixed during classes, and even more so in the evenings. There was a great deal of dancing and flirting; and I, for the first time, was favoured with the attention of one of the belles of the course – *the* belle, according to some. Such was the gossip anyway – I was not even aware of this piece of luck. But a hint at the rite of passage did my ego a lot of good, albeit retrospectively: here I was at long last, a man with some standing on the playing field and in the drawing room. Not that we totally abandoned our 'laddish' habits. The NAAFI was at hand with its cheap beer and Cypriot wine, where we drank from time to time, finances permitting.

During that summer the armed confrontation between the British and the Jews intensified. One of our lunches at the Old Polish House was disturbed by a thud even louder than the gun of Ramadan. I remember nudging my neighbour and saying: 'There goes the King David Hotel'. I was right. The most outrageous act of terror, later attributed to Menachem Begin, a former corporal in the Polish Army, had just taken place.

The position of Polish cadets in uniform, billeted in the heart of Jerusalem, was delicate. Formally we were under British command. But the Jewish community, and in particular its insurgent element, well remembered the indulgent attitude of General Anders towards his Jewish deserters. The terrorists did not wish to quarrel with us, and said so through intermediaries. Naturally, the Polish commanders consulted their British colleagues and superiors, and an informal tri-partite deal was struck: the Poles would stay neutral, and in return they would not be targeted by the Jews, provided they did not carry arms, and remained clearly identifiable. The arrangement worked. I remember one occasion when I entered Jerusalem after absence on leave to find the city under curfew. I was allowed by the British to pass through the road blocks and continue my lonely progress on foot towards the Damascus gate across the deserted city. The only noise was the sound of my army boots – a useful alert for snipers on roof-tops; but I assumed that I would be recognisable. No pot-shots were taken. The walk seemed interminable.

$\approx$

On 31st August we returned to camp to be told that we had been posted to a nine-month course for 'building-site assistants'. The news was received with disbelief. This was the end of our hopes. Deep despondency set in, fuelled by suspicions that we were victims of one of Colonel Ryziński's attempts at social engineering. There is nothing more depressing than a despondent squad of frustrated young soldiers. My own position was further complicated by an unexpected *individual* offer of a place at the American University of Beirut. The Registrar informed me that I had been accepted for 'Sophomore Pre-Engineering' (whatever that was), and that a place would be kept for me until 2nd October 1946. This was clearly my mother's work. I decided in the name of Cadets' Solidarity not to accept the offer. To my mother the decision seemed foolish. But she behaved impeccably: she accepted my gesture with stoicism, and almost succeeded in concealing her disappointment.

Year '46 settled to sullen passive resistance, something akin to the British 'work to rule'. Very little work was done; just the minimum sufficient to avoid sanctions. And I, their *Prymus*, decided to stage a protest. To those subjects which I deemed vaguely interesting – strength of materials, stress analysis and the like – I applied myself demonstratively, scoring good grades. The remaining subjects of the more mundane kind I deliberately failed. It was a silly act of rebellion by a frustrated teenager. The instructors with whom I chose not to co-operate were generous enough to ignore my antics. And the authorities elected to be lenient. I was not removed from the course.

The training of future 'building-site assistants' soon became a smoke-screen for glorious *dolce far niente*. A secretarial course for young ATS girls from Nazareth was set up at Camp Barbara alongside ours, and this provided ample opportunities for the Good Life on the beaches of Ashkalon, Gaza and Tiberias. These were the settings, and circumstances, for romance. Tentative attachments flourished. I, too, became one of the undeserving beneficiaries.

Back in camp we experimented with alcohol. It was not the civilised kind of introduction to drinking under the benevolent eye of older men. Left to our own devices, we found it difficult to stop short of bingeing. I still remember many vicious hangovers. Discipline became lax, and our private routines eccentric. 'Ptak' Szczygieł was the purveyor of distractions. One was his personal wind-up gramophone, which he acquired in mysterious circumstances and concealed under his bed. With the gramophone came a selection of records, half a dozen of his favourite hits. Every morning, half-asleep, he would fumble under the bed to deliver a blast of his choice for the day. The response, within and without the tent, was mixed but on the whole indulgent. The authorities pretended not to notice.

Ptak's greatest coup came at Christmas, which he spent with some elderly English ladies determined to be kind to the brave Poles. He returned with a huge English Christmas cake under his arm. The cake was adorned with a thick layer of rock-hard icing. Brought up on the soft and creamy cakes of *Mittel-Europa,* we did not dare to tackle the icing. In desperation, someone – I think it was Januszek Jaźwiński – struck a match off the icing. It worked. From then on Ptak's cake, ceremoniously installed in the centre of our tent table, became a major attraction for an ever expanding circle of addicts in search of novel smoking routines.

~

In the Autumn Tereska left Beirut and sailed for England to join her husband. We all missed her, my mother especially; it was our third family disruption since September 1939. I missed my outings with Tereska to her favourite café just round the corner from Bab-Idris, where she would treat me to a deliciously thick hot chocolate drink, *chocolat-moux.*

The atmosphere among the Polish community of Beirut was tense. Even those who already claimed the status of military families (my mother and Anuśka included), were apprehensive about the future. There was a rush to put forward late candidates for the Cadet School to secure entry to the United Kingdom.

The course for building-site assistants kept grinding on. The mixture of hectic social life and work avoidance was pleasant but unreal and demoralising. Year '46 reached the stage of no longer wishing for a change. I was luckier than most. Leave in Beirut now became a reminder of real life, dominated by my mother's concerns for our future. I realised that she now depended on my presence. I became a listening post. I even attempted to offer suggestions. In this way we comforted each other. I see now that Christmas '46, and then Easter '47, were holidays well spent.

Back at camp the despairing bosses made one last attempt to amuse us. A visit to Luxor was laid on. After six months of lectures on concrete mixing and so on, it was received as a welcome distraction. In the event, the trip became a breathtaking exploration into history. Not to mention the memory of Luxor's grandest hotel and its inexhaustible supply of toast with marmalade.

In the early summer of 1947 confirmation arrived from London that Year '46 would be eligible for UK university grants. Most of us, myself included, were delighted; the 'year off' was beginning to pall. The Authorities were positively enthusiastic. Here at last was an immediate opportunity to disengage us – the bad influence – from the School. Swift arrangements were made for travel, compassionate leave was generously handed round (in my case the last dash to Beirut), and there we were, *en route* for Qassasin in the Canal Zone, to be 'processed' for embarkation. The date on my Movement Order Gaza-Qassasin is 13th July 1947.

Two days later I was named officer-in-charge of a pall-bearer party for the funeral of a younger colleague. Cadet Jerzy Dybczyński died suddenly at the El-Qantara Military Hospital. The news was a shock; only the other day he had been among us. The short, round, good natured 'Dybczyś' with a broad smile, always in the money and ever ready to advance an interest-free loan. My Troop Movement Order Qassasin-El-

Qantara specified a party of ten, and I had no difficulty with volunteers. We travelled by road along the Canal in total silence. The sad little ceremony was attended by one or two doctors, some tearful nurses, and the distraught father of our Dybczyś, a sergeant in the Polish Army. This melancholy command was my farewell to arms.

About ten days later we travelled to Port-Said for embarkation. The troop-ship *Empire Ken* (to this day the 'Ken' remains a puzzle) was a handsome vessel of a certain age. I distinctly remember her three funnels and the steel-grey camouflage. Later we discovered notices, badly painted-over, saying *Herren* and *Damen*. We concluded that the good ship was a liner, and a war prize.

The tedium of boarding was enlivened by the presence of Captain Dzieduszycki, in whose otherwise distinguished family eccentricity ran deep. He was apprehended struggling with an immensely heavy piece of hand luggage. Challenged, he explained that he was carrying an anvil, from which he would not be parted. 'When you strike it,' he said, 'it responds with a most beautiful sound.' Apparently he had carried it across Siberia and Central Asia. The English, appreciative of eccentricity, allowed him on board with it.

The Polish contingent was sizeable and the captain asked for a full-time interpreter. I was chosen for the job, which came with a comfortable corner in the ship's office next to the bridge. I was instructed to remain on stand-by to duplicate all the English announcements on the tannoy. This was sufficient excuse to avoid emergency drills, tug-of-war competitions and the like. There were plenty of opportunities for reading, chatting up the girls, and watching flying fish from a deck chair. In the bar at night a contingent of Welsh Guardsmen broke into song at the slightest opportunity. Their spontaneous harmony was perfect. The Mediterranean was as flat as a mill pond and I, in the knowledge that my mother and Anuśka were to follow me in a matter of months, felt at ease with the world whatever the future.

At Gibraltar we put on battledress, and were told to brace ourselves for the Bay of Biscay. But even the Bay was kind to us. On 1st August 1947 *Empire Ken* entered the port of Southampton. Later in the day I was told that it was a 'Bank Holiday'. Out of the morning mist there emerged a tall figure in uniform wearing a matching tall hat. I nudged an English neighbour at the rail and enquired who this mysterious personage was.

'It is one of our policemen,' was the proud answer.

That misty Bank Holiday morning in Southampton docks marked the beginning of the rest of my life.

Postscript

Stach, my sister Tereska's husband, welcomed me to England. He rapidly arranged for me to be measured for a tweed suit – a munificent gift because, apart from the expense, it also meant giving up his precious clothing coupons. But that was only the beginning. Realising that my application for a university grant had become bogged down in the Byzantine corridors of the Committee for the Education of Poles in Great Britain, he took up my case with the authorities on the grounds of the quality of my results at the Cadet School. The effect was swift. I was offered not just the grant, but a choice: either the British Army, or a British university. My mother saw to it that I chose the latter. I took a degree in Aeronautics with Applied Mathematics at London University.

Without Stach's help the beginning of my civilian existence would have been much more difficult. There was more to come. He offered sanctuary to my mother and Anuśka in his modest house in the suburbs of London, when they eventually came to England.

In 1951 my elder sister Anuśka married Adam Perepeczko, an agronomist from Wilno who had been an officer in the Polish Army in the West. They soon left England for Southern Rhodesia in search of a better life. Tereska and Stach followed them two years later.

At last, in 1948, we had definitive news of my father. It was as we feared; our hope, so long sustained, was finally extinguished. Over the next forty years, as I grew to maturity and past the age that he had lived to, I pieced together a few precious fragments of his last months on earth.

On 1st April 1940 a young Polish cadet-officer called Juliusz Jasiewicz was thrust into a cell in Minsk prison; a cell like many others. In a letter to me from Reading dated 24th September 1957, he described what he saw: 'Nearly one hundred and twenty prisoners in an area measuring 20 feet by 25 feet; one small window near the ceiling, almost total darkness; extreme heat and lack of air (in spite of attempts to pump some air in); during the day starved, half-naked inmates regularly chant *vozdukhu!*

(we need air) when the pumps stop; at night we lay like sardines on the stone floor, trying to keep away from the walls along which people relieve themselves because the communal pots are overflowing; when taken into the yard, men faint from excess of oxygen.'

Such was the setting against which Jasiewicz was introduced to my father on 2nd April 1940, thirteen days before our train stopped at Minsk on its way to Siberia. I quote from Jasiewicz's letter: 'On my second day I had the honour of meeting Senator Giedroyć. He still looked well in spite of the circumstances, and was full of optimism.... I remember his long winter fur-coat... He questioned me closely about the latest news.' Unfortunately for my father there were some Belarus'ian informers among the prisoners, who apparently knew of his pre-war activities and position. The NKVD was alerted, and Soviet-style questioning began. After the first round, which lasted several days, he returned to the cell much weakened. He said that his persecutors had him locked up in a room filled with water to his knees. The second round of tortures soon followed, and was longer. This time he returned in a terrible state, swollen all over and unrecognisable. Soon after this my informant was taken to another cell.

The only other glimpse of my father at this time came from Włodzimierz Chajutin-Chatwin, a fellow prisoner whom I met in London in 1978. My father spoke to him of his children and confided that he was far too severe with them: 'The one thing in all my life that I regret most.' He said this with tears in his eyes...

Grażyna Lipińska, in her book Jeśli Zapomnę o Nich... [Lest we forget] (Paris 1988, pp 122, 129) reports that early in 1941 Senator Giedroyć was held in one of the death cells. The NKVD did not hurry with the execution. Then, on Sunday 22nd June 1941, Germany struck. The Wehrmacht's eastward advance was swift and the surviving inmates of Minsk gaol were herded out onto the road towards Mogilev. The road is now called The Road of Death. On it, this side of a small town called Igumen (renamed Cherven by the Soviets), my father perished from an NKVD bullet. The event was reported by an eye-witness, Lt. Col. Janusz Prawdzic-Szlaski, and published in Zbrodnia Katyńska [The Crime of Katyń], (3rd ed., London, 1978, p 218). 'On the road we helped along (Tadeusz) Giedroyć, Chairman of the Regional Court of Łuck, because

[184]

he suffered terribly from asthma. Eventually, seeing that he was also endangering us through delays, he asked us to leave him. Realising that he had no strength left in him and that we could no longer help him, we fulfilled his wish and left him at the roadside. We saw his execution.' This killing, carried out most probably on Thursday 26th June 1941, was one of many committed along the stretch between Minsk and Igumen.

A literary prototype – the execution of the peasant philosopher Platon Karatayev on the retreat from Moscow in *War and Peace* – we owe to the pen of Leo Tolstoy. Yet there was one difference: my father accepted death – one might even say chose it – because he wished to save his fellow-prisoners. His last act of personal courage became an act of self-sacrifice.

In the early 1960s I placed a memorial for my father at the family mausoleum in the Powązki Cemetery in Warsaw. In view of the sub-servience of People's Poland to the Soviet Union, the Powązki memorial had to be laconic. A plaque with a more detailed inscription was un-veiled in the Polish Parliament building in 1999, commemorating those senators of the Second Republic who perished during the Second World War. My father's name is among them. In 2002 my son Miko placed a cross in memory of his grandfather near the Belarus'ian town of Igumen where Tadeusz Giedroyć was killed.

∼

The name of General Anders has occurred frequently in this narrative. Without him, there is little doubt that our family and 120,000 other Poles, exiled in Soviet Russia, would have perished. He was an outstand-ing general and a great leader of men in distress. At a time when their 'half of Europe' was abandoned in Yalta to the Soviets, he held his army together and continued the fight. This he did in the belief (mistaken as it turned out) that a war between the West and the Soviet Union was inevitable and imminent.

Anders was also a leader of a community, extending protection to those civilians that he saved from Soviet oppression. In 1945 Churchill wished to give him an honorary knighthood. This was countermanded by the incoming Labour government, afraid to offend Stalin. The general accepted British hospitality and settled in London, where he became the most conspicuous spokesman for the Polish communities in exile.

General Anders died in London on 12th May 1970. In accordance with his wishes, he was buried among his men at the Monte Cassino Polish Military Cemetery.

In 1958 my mother took employment with Maison Galin, thus entering the London world of *haute couture*. In 1964, at the age of 70, she returned to public duty by accepting Leon Colonna-Czosnowski's invitation to act as hostess and housekeeper to a succession of Polish academics visiting England. In January 1976 she was awarded the 50th Anniversary Medal of the Catholic University of Lublin in recognition of her 'many years of dedicated service' to the Polish academic community. She retired in February of the same year, and died three months later.

After the war my mother found Marteczka in People's Poland. They met in Toruń (where my mother's sisters lived) in 1960, and from then on Marteczka became one of the beneficiaries of my mother's personal aid programme. In death Marteczka preceded my mother by exactly one week. Before the war there was a custom in our household that on major expeditions Marteczka would go ahead of her mistress to get everything ready. This tradition was fulfilled on their final journey.

After we left Dereczyn in September 1939, the Polish community was depleted by the Germans; Janek, the seventeen-year-old eldest son of Kazimierz Dąbrowski, was executed alongside nine of his contemporaries. Some time in 1942 (or possibly in 1943) the Jews of Dereczyn were rounded up and marched in a single column to already prepared trenches, into which they fell, mowed down by German machine-guns. Only Mr Szelubski escaped this fate: during the march to the graveside he suffered a massive heart attack and died instantly. The news of this horror was brought to my mother in London in the 1960s by Józef Dąbrowski, himself a refugee in England.

In 1944 the Wehrmacht decided to take on the advancing Red Army at Łobzów. The decision was sound, because the manor stood on the site of an old defensive stronghold. During the engagement Soviet artillery obliterated the house, the park (what was left of it), and the outbuildings. It was an ending on the scale of *Götterdämmerung* – an ending, to this chronicler and heir *de jure* to Łobzów, far more acceptable than the other option facing the manors of the region: a slow and insulting decay through deliberate neglect under a regime that proclaimed itself progressive. In 1945 the Soviet authorities incorporated the denuded home farms of Łobzów and Kotczyn into a newly established *kolkhoz* called 'Shchara'.

In September 1990 my wife and I made a flying visit to my old childhood home. It was a traumatic experience. The once busy, indeed vibrant, Dereczyn was now a dilapidated ghost town. On the site where the manor of Łobzów once stood, we found semi-derelict sheds put up by the *kolkhoz*. There were no trees to be seen, the once carefully drained low pastures were waterlogged, and the fields – those generous providers of wheat and rye – were now stony, unkempt and deserted.

In the early 1920s the region of Nowogródek, and with it the vicinity of Dereczyn, remained devastated by the Russian mismanagement of the previous century, and by the First World War. The villages around Dereczyn had been reduced to subsistence or worse, and the manor was sinking towards bankruptcy. And yet the Łobzów home farms survived the crisis of the early 1930s, and towards the end of the decade began a cautious recovery. In the villages there appeared bicycles, and in the cottages sewing machines – according to my mother classic signs of progress. The era of motor transport arrived in Dereczyn with one private motor car (the Zięciaks'), at least two motor cycles, and a bus service to the railway station.

Economic historians incline to the view that in the 1930s the Polish Second Republic – and with it the region of Nowogródek – was on a par with Spain, and ahead of Portugal and Greece. All three have since made progress sufficient to qualify them for membership of the European Union. All three, in spite of their various political setbacks and deficiencies, had in common one advantage: they were spared the Soviet economic regime. One may venture a suggestion that the Nowogródek region, and more specifically the Dereczyn community – had it been given a chance of evolutionary growth, free of doctrinaire economics and social violence – could have matched, or even outpaced, its Iberian and Greek counterparts.

I still ask myself the question: would a lawful and civilised, as distinct from a violent, redistribution of Łobzów's home farms in favour of local villages have served the community better than the continued existence of a manorial agricultural enterprise? I confess that I cannot even attempt an answer. But solutions that emerged in Western Europe and elsewhere prompt me to say this: the Łobzów manorial residence with its grounds (as distinct from the home farms), so lovingly restored by my parents, could have become in the fullness of time an historic and cultural asset accepted as a common good by both its owners and the local community. It is certain that no one at all can benefit from its present desolation.

～

The passing of the Old Order is one of the themes of this book. Another is survival. For the majority of those rescued by Anders's army, survival had to be followed by a long and usually difficult process of renewal. Mine was one example of all those many returns to normal life.

'The rest of my life' – post-1947 – has turned out to be useful and interesting. Aircraft design and operations, and later consultancy in developing countries, took me across four continents. At the same time my researches in the medieval history of Central and Eastern Europe have escalated into serious study alongside scholars at Oxford Univesity.

Now in my 80th year, I rejoice in my wife and our hospitable home that rivals the salons of my youth. I watch with interest – and some trepidation – my children's high-risk pursuits; and, always hopeful, I make notes for a sequel to this book.

Acknowledgements

A great many people took an interest in this book, provided information, read early drafts, and offered comments. This is not the place to list them all. The tributes below single out only those standard-bearers who enabled me to turn corners. Let them represent all the others.

The early version of *Crater's Edge*, long and detailed, was read cover to cover by Hugo Brunner. He came back with a blueprint of a structure for the next draft. My daughter Coky provided a series of sharp suggestions for serious weeding. Hubert Zawadzki patiently helped with the historical canvas. To these three I am indebted for the transformation of an unwieldy MS into something useful – the '2004 version'.

This I gingerly presented to Peter Stanford. He suggested that my somewhat academic text should be made more accessible to those less familiar with manners, means, and events east of the River Oder. Norman Davies also read the '2004 version' and said that it was a useful glimpse of the Other Half of Europe, exotic yet a part of the One Europe. His intervention at the lowest point in the saga encouraged me to continue.

Four years on it was the late Maggie Evans who wisely and patiently explained how to move the book forward. To her go my special thanks.

Skilful surgery was required, and Sarah Sackville-West unveiled Alex Martin. He, an experienced editor, author and translator, applied a scalpel to the text. The result – sharpened and reshuffled – was deemed *sortable*. Anthony Weldon, otherwise 'Bene Factum', took the book on. It is now before you. Both Alex, the editor *extraordinaire*, and Anthony, the risk-taker, loom large over this debutant author.

The long enterprise, from gestation through adjustments to final honing, was driven by my wife Rosy. Throughout she remained a stern nurse to the author and a no-nonsense midwife to the project; in short, my muse and its *animatrice*. She is the invisible co-author.

Oxford 23rd April 2009

1. THE GIEDROYĆ FAMILY – A GENEALOGICAL OUTLINE

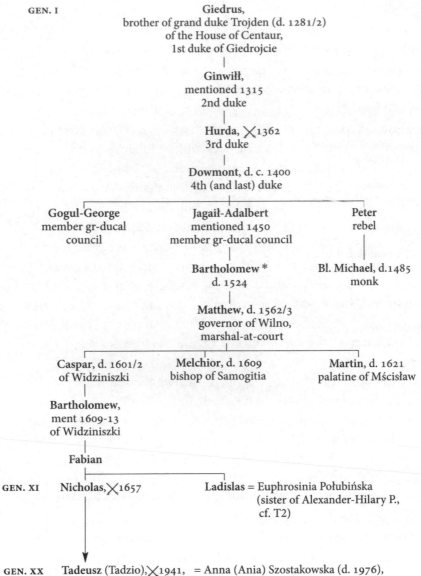

GEN. I

Giedrus,
brother of grand duke Trojden (d. 1281/2)
of the House of Centaur,
1st duke of Giedrojcie
|
Ginwiłł,
mentioned 1315
2nd duke
|
Hurda, ✕1362
3rd duke
|
Dowmont, d. c. 1400
4th (and last) duke

Gogul-George
member gr-ducal
council

Jagaił-Adalbert
mentioned 1450
member gr-ducal council

Peter
rebel

Bartholomew *
d. 1524

Bl. Michael, d.1485
monk

Matthew, d. 1562/3
governor of Wilno,
marshal-at-court

Caspar, d. 1601/2
of Widziniszki
|
Bartholomew,
ment 1609-13
of Widziniszki
|
Fabian

Melchior, d. 1609
bishop of Samogitia

Martin, d. 1621
palatine of Mścisław

GEN. XI   **Nicholas,** ✕1657

Ladislas = Euphrosinia Połubińska
(sister of Alexander-Hilary P.,
cf. T2)

GEN. XX   **Tadeusz** (Tadzio), ✕1941,   = **Anna** (Ania) Szostakowska (d. 1976),
of Owile, senator II Polish Rep.,   cf. T3

*: orignator of 'Branch B'; the other branch ('A') , prominent in 18th century, issues
from Alexander, mentioned in 1528, presumed first cousin of Bartholomew; 'Branch
A' had no connection with Łobzów and Kotczyn.

2. THE POŁUBIŃSKI FAMILY – A GENEALOGICAL OUTLINE

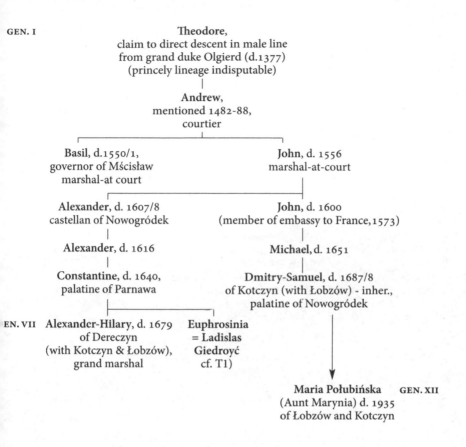

GEN. I

Theodore,
claim to direct descent in male line
from grand duke Olgierd (d.1377)
(princely lineage indisputable)

Andrew,
mentioned 1482-88,
courtier

Basil, d.1550/1,
governor of Mścisław
marshal-at court

John, d. 1556
marshal-at-court

Alexander, d. 1607/8
castellan of Nowogródek

John, d. 1600
(member of embassy to France, 1573)

Alexander, d. 1616

Michael, d. 1651

Constantine, d. 1640,
palatine of Parnawa

Dmitry-Samuel, d. 1687/8
of Kotczyn (with Łobzów) - inher.,
palatine of Nowogródek

GEN. VII
Alexander-Hilary, d. 1679
of Dereczyn
(with Kotczyn & Łobzów),
grand marshal

Euphrosinia
= Ladislas
Giedroyć
cf. T1)

Maria Połubińska GEN. XII
(Aunt Marynia) d. 1935
of Łobzów and Kotczyn

Sources Table 1
Oxford Slavonic Papers, XVII, 1-22.
J. Wolff, *Kniaziowie…*(Princes…), 1895, 65-76.
T. Lenczewski, *Genealogie Rodów Utytułowanych…* (Genealogies of Titled Families…),
  1995-6, 15-36.
Rody Rzeczypospolitej… (Families of the Commonwealth…), Inst. of Central-Eastern
  Europe, Lublin, 2008, 49-66.

Sources Table 2
Wolff, op. cit., 368-391.
The XVII cent. Geneal. Tree of the P. Fam. by A. Tarasewicz (1640-1727).
Dobra Dereczyńskie… (The Dereczyn Domain…), The Papers of the Univ. of Poznań, XI
  (1971), 45-69.
R. Aftanazy, *Dzieje Rezydencji…* (A History of Residences…), II (1992), 197-201(for
  Dereczyn).

3. THE GIEDROYĆ-POŁUBIŃSKI ALLIANCE THROUGH THE UMIASTOWSKIS AND THE SZOSTAKOWSKIS

Victor Połubiński, mentioned 1787–94,
direct descendant in the male line of Dmitry-Samuel P.
of Kotczyn, Łobzów, etc., cf. T2

N. P.

John P.

Henry P. = Pelagia P.
of Kotczyn | of Łobzów

Anthony Umiastowski = Emily P., d. 1863
d. 1852, of Kwiatkowce,
etc, jurist

Maria P., d. 1935,
(Aunt Marynia)
of Łobzów and Kotczyn

Emil U., d. 1892,
of Kwiatkowce, etc.,
dep. govr of Grodno Region

Leon Szostakowski, d. 1904, = Melanie U., d. 1922
of Sokółki in Pol. Livonia,
jurist

Tadeusz Giedroyć = Anna Sz. (Ania), d. 1976
(Tadzio) of Owile, ✕1941,
senator of II Polish Rep., joint
inher. of Łobzów and Kotczyn

Michał G., b. 1929,
heir *de jure* to Łobzów and Kotczyn

Sources Table 3
The Dereczyn Domain…, op. cit.
'Nałęcz' (Janina Marchioness Umiastowska), *Szmat Ziemi…* (A Stretch of Land…), 1928,
   passim.
A. Włodarski, *Ród Szostakowskich…*(The Szostakowski Family…), 1932, passim.
'Ród Szostakowskich…', a review in *Miesięcznik Heraldyczny* (The Heraldic Monthly,
   Warsaw), 12 (1933), 122-125.
Aftanazy, op. cit., 248-251 (for Łobzów).

Index

[198]